TROUT CAVIAR

*

Trout Caviar

RECIPES *from a*

NORTHERN FORAGER

Written and photographed by

* *Brett Laidlaw* *

Minnesota Historical Society Press

www.mhspress.org

The Minnesota Historical Society Press is a member of the Association of American University Presses.

Manufactured in Canada

10 9 8 7 6 5 4 3 2 1

⊗ The paper used in this publication meets the minimum requirements of the American National Standard for Information Sciences—Permanence for Printed Library Materials, ANSI Z39.48-1984.

International Standard Book Number
ISBN: 978-0-87351-819-2 (cloth)

LIBRARY OF CONGRESS CATALOGING-IN-PUBLICATION DATA

Laidlaw, Brett.
Trout caviar : recipes from a northern forager / Brett Laidlaw.
p. cm.
Includes index.
ISBN 978-0-87351-819-2 (cloth)
1. Cooking (Natural foods) 2. Cooking, American—Midwestern style.
3. Sustainable living. 4. Cookbooks. I. Title.
TX741.L337 2011
641.3'02—dc23

2011018551

For Mary

*

CONTENTS

A Forager's Way   1

A Stern Caution   8

Bide-A-Wee   9

Notes on Ingredients and Substitutions   16

Smoking Basics   22

---

1 STARTERS * 25

Trout Caviar   30

---

2 SALADS * 37

A Weed Is Not a Plant...   43

In the Garden   53

---

3 SOUPS * 59

Wild Mushroom Cookery Basics   75

---

4 VEGETABLE MAINS * 79

Marché Madness   91

---

5 PASTA *and* PIZZA * 97

Natural Appetites   112

---

6 MEAT * 117

The Importance of Bacon   135

---

7 POULTRY ✳ 139

Duck Confit   149

Cooking Game Birds   152

November Cover   158

8 FISH ✳ 161

From Northern Waters   169

Of the Stream and the Season   175

9 VEGETABLE SIDES ✳ 185

10 DESSERTS *and* DRINKS ✳ 201

The Cheeses of Our Climate   209

11 *And . . .* CONDIMENTS ✳ 215

A Wild Food Year   233

Where to Forage for Wild Food   237

Acknowledgments   241

Index   243

TROUT CAVIAR

*

A Forager's Way

I am the product of an idyllic childhood spent among the woods, fields, streams, and ponds of Eden Prairie, Minnesota. Anyone familiar with the southwestern suburbs of Minneapolis—of which Eden Prairie is one—in recent years will likely have to read that sentence over a couple of times in an effort to reconcile "idyllic," "woods," and "streams" with the sprawl of McMansions and strip malls that is Eden Prairie today. But I was there, I tell you, and it was idyllic.

Back then, in the 1960s and early '70s, Eden Prairie consisted of a mere handful of subdivisions on the northern edge of a rolling countryside of farms, woods, and fields. Three houses down from our modest rambler on North Eden Drive, The Woods commenced. I usually entered The Woods through a gap in the barbed-wire fence at the bottom of the steep hill in the Morins' backyard (we negotiated that gap, perilously, on sleds and toboggans in winter), and I would wander the hills along paths worn by cows and kids and deer and, earlier, tractors—and, much, much earlier, probably horse-drawn wagons. Oak and aspen and elm, groves of sumac, creek-side alders. At the bottom of that long, sweeping sledding run the trail gave out onto The Pond, just a little tadpole hatchery in summer, which we cleared of snow in winter to make a hockey rink. Most winter afternoons after school we raced from the bus stop home, grabbed skates and sticks and pucks, and flew down the hill to get in an hour of madcap shinny before the early winter sunset. We went home only when we literally could not see the puck—or had lost all of them in the snowbanks.

Summer adventures often took us away from The Woods, on our bikes down Townline Road and across the county road to Birch Island Lake, where we pursued perch and bass but mainly caught bullheads, which, to my retrospective shame, we sometimes placed on the railroad tracks that ran above the bank where we fished, to be pureed by a passing train.

In my introverted early teens I spent a lot of time in The Woods. I considered a hermit-like existence there, sheltered from the weather in an underground hide I had constructed by excavating along the edge of a group of large boulders, laying logs across the opening, and covering those with turf I painstakingly dug up and hauled from a distance, so as not to give away the location of my fort to The Mean Boys. I also took an interest in wild foods like sumac tea, cattail root flour, and gingerroot, though I never much acted on these observations. Perhaps I felt I was establishing a basis to build on, for when I one day would bid my human family and all civilization adieu, to go and live in harmony with Great Nature and all its creatures.

That was a sustaining fantasy for some years, and one which, I must admit, I may never have fully gotten over. More tangible encounters with the woods and the wild and nature's foods came each summer when our family traveled north to Winnipeg, Manitoba, my parents' birthplace, and from there east to our family's cottage on Lake Brereton in the Whiteshell, the lakes region of eastern Manitoba. We fished, of course; we fished every day, trolling in the old wooden Peterborough boat with its three-horsepower motor for walleye (*pickerel,* my Canadian relatives called them) and northern pike (*slimy jackfish,* my grandfather derided these, though we ate them). Sometimes we practiced "still fishing" for perch, anchoring near the mouth of a picturesque rocky stream, dropping minnows on weighted lines down to the cool depths that sweet-fleshed perch were thought to prefer.

The boat outings took place in the morning, and then through the day, sporadically, and as evening came on, my brother Bill and I would try our luck casting from the dock, tossing and retrieving red and white Dardevle spoons, Lazy Ikes, and Rapalas. Such tactics were generally futile, but true fishermen are rarely deterred by either logic or failure.

I can recall so clearly all the sensations of cleaning the fish we caught, an activity which took place in late morning in the cool shade of the pines beside the cabin, on a wooden table covered with newspapers in the yard of packed dirt with a patina of pine needles. I recall the smell of the fish, kept on a stringer in the lake until we were ready to clean them. They smelled . . . *lakey,* not fishy, not bad at all, but fresh and watery. When I'm lucky enough to find supremely fresh fish today, I'll take a good whiff and think, *Ah, it smells like Lake Brereton.*

I recall the sound of the filleting knife going up the belly of the fish from vent to gills, the sight—and somewhat less entrancing smell—of the guts coming out. Then the filleting, how my father's or grandfather's skillful hands held the fish in place, worked the thin blade down along the backbone, flipped over the fillet to show the pearlescent flesh, peachy pink. We always said *FILL-ett*, by the way, stressing the first syllable, pronouncing the final *t*, not *fill-AY*, how some fancy folks or, god forbid, the French, would say it (now I love all things French, but my English Canadian family—though German by heritage—would have none of it).

I don't recall that I particularly relished the taste of the fish, usually shallow-fried in a cast-iron skillet with a light coating of flour (of course, we would never have called that *à la meunière*). I don't recall *not* liking it, either. It was good fresh food, and we ate it happily. There was usually potato salad and coleslaw, maybe a tin of Vienna sausages for the fish-averse, or that peculiar Canadian concoction, a can of pork and beans and a can of spaghetti mixed together (Hemingway's hero Nick Adams delights in that dish in the story "Big Two-Hearted River").

We picked blueberries, a full-family affair. Everyone piled in the car, and we drove a short distance down the road past the water pump (stopping to fill jugs on the way back—and now I smell iron on my hands from grasping the pump handle, hear the *screech-screech-screech* of the rusty pump working, smell the fresh scent of the clean, cold water gushing out) to an area of rocky scarps where the only things that seemed to grow were lichens and blueberry bushes. We made our tenuous way over the steep, rough, gray rocks, working careful fingers into the bushes to extract the berries with a minimum of leaves and twigs. The air was cool and dry, but the sun of late northern summer was hot. Talking would cease as everyone from the littlest kids to parents and grandparents worked diligently to fill their collecting containers, and if the rhythm of one picker's *plink plink plinking* gathered speed, you could hear everyone else picking faster to match that pace.

I have almost painfully vivid memories of my grandmother's blueberry pie, a sugar-sprinkled crust of unearthly lightness and richness wrapped around the filling of those tiny, intense berries that opened in the baking to create a syrup dark as the darkest night and sweet-tart with a flavor I'll never taste again. Needless to say, I am utterly ruined for those cultivated blueberries the size of ping-pong balls and with flavor to match. I do not even think of them as fruit.

The Brereton cabin was sold when I was in my teens. I didn't fish for a couple of decades. When I did find my way back to the water, it was to Wisconsin trout streams with a fly rod in hand. Fly-fishing for trout became a consuming passion, changed the way I live and eat, and led me, though circuitously, to eventually purchase land in rural Wisconsin; and that, in its own roundabout way, led to this book.

Nor should I neglect to mention what was perhaps my deepest connection to the local food world, a curious endeavor that my wife, Mary Eckmeier, and I pursued for seven-plus years: Real Bread, "a journey of ten thousand loaves," a home-based farmers market bakery, discussed in more detail elsewhere.

* * *

That's where I'm coming from, then, in a few quick sketches. That's the backstory for my subsequent interest in natural food and foraging, whether from woods, stream, lake, garden, or market. I ate my share of TV dinners growing up, mac and cheese, Chef Boyardee; I developed an unnatural obsession with Jeno's Pizza Rolls at one point, and with greasy frozen tacos at another. But we also ate vegetables fresh from our garden and from the farm stands, meats simply broiled or grilled, fresh apples, melons, peaches, and plums. I came through the still-continuing, still-increasing onslaught of processed foods with my taste for the authentic intact.

A taste for the authentic is what informs every aspect of this book, every recipe in it. Whether it's a somewhat oddball preparation like Popcorn Salad (p. 43), a local twist on a French classic like Buckwheat Trout with Sorrel Sauce (p. 174), or my own "inventions," like a dish of pasta tossed with wild hen of the woods mushrooms and aged Gouda (p. 99), my interest is always with that kernel of authenticity.

It's that quest for the authentic that lies behind, explains, and I hope gives life to the somewhat unconventional take on foraging upon which this book is based. Mention foraged food and most people will think of wild foods: mushrooms, wild greens, nuts, and berries. That's only natural—it's a long-held and quite correct interpretation of foraging. (It's worth noting here that I do not consider myself an expert on wild foods in general. I know what I know, and I'm always learning; what I bring to the table—pun fully intended—is the background and imagination to present a few wild foods in what I hope is a fresh and appetizing light.)

What I'm proposing here is an expanded understanding of the idea of foraging, from strictly wild foods to a broader sense of gathering food with purpose and intent from many sources, whether mushrooms from the woods, a fish from a stream or a fish market, raw milk from a local farm, or seasonal produce from a farmers market. In my own cooking, I don't really think much about whether what I'm preparing comes from the woods, my garden, a farmers market, or a local butcher. I obtain raw materials from all those places, more or less through force of habit by now, and do the best by my ingredients that I can.

Another way to put it: 90 percent of good cooking is good shopping—taking *shopping* here in its broadest sense, as well. Chefs talk about "sourcing" their ingredients, and while I recoil a bit at the jargon, that's not a bad coinage as these things go. Over a couple of decades of increasing interest in local, seasonal foods, I've developed a network of sources, a sort of mental culinary Rolodex, if you will. So when I start to think about a dish I want to prepare, I may run through a shopping list that goes something like this: Au Bon Canard *duck breast* from *Clancey's,* and I've got that *blackberry jam from wild Bide-A-Wee fruit,* and that braid of *shallots from the Dallas market* is still holding out; the blackberry sauce is great on *potato (from the market) celery root (from the garden)* puree, need to check if I have enough *Hope Creamery butter,* and pick up *raw milk from Renee.* (Note: get some *cheese curds* when you stop for the milk, and don't forget the *Ritz crackers . . .*)

It's really not as exhausting as it sounds. It is, in fact, a genuine pleasure, and the way I shop-forage-source my food these days results in a lot of collateral benefits (to turn a well-worn euphemism to happier purpose). When I go for the duck I'll get to chat with Kristin for a minute or two, and the milk stop is a chance to catch up on doings at the dairy farm. It's rare that a visit to the co-op doesn't include running into a friend or neighbor, and the guys behind the butcher counter can seemingly tell from the hungry look in my eyes that I'm there for fresh pork belly to make a batch of bacon. I write elsewhere in this book at some length about the special bond that often develops between farmers market shoppers and vendors. On the wild side, an early spring trip to the woods for ramps and nettles gives me and the dogs a change of scenery, an opportunity to stop and smell the wildflowers and to check on water levels as opening day of trout season approaches.

Probably the most highly anticipated grocery errands of the year are the trips—pilgrimages, I'd almost say—to Halvorson Fisheries in Cornucopia, Wisconsin, on the south shore of Lake Superior. It's about a six-hour round-trip drive, but the journey is almost its own reward—except that the real reward is a walk on the beautiful Corny beach, lunch of broiled whitefish at the Village Inn, and filling a cooler with fresh and smoked lake trout, whitefish, and herring.

Another type of foraging I really enjoy is rummaging around in the closet of traditional food skills—smoking meat and fish, making confit, fermenting vegetables and fruits, pickling, and tapping trees for maple and birch syrup. In the last few years there's been a renaissance of these old-fashioned techniques, which once seemed to be on the road to extinction.

These are all parts of a life in which shopping, foraging, gathering, fishing, hunting, cooking, and eating are entirely intertwined; if you happen to write about these activities, it spills even wider. Ideally this life involves sharing all these things with people you care about. So in the long run, as pleasant as eating well-prepared food is, it's only fully enjoyable and, I dare say, meaningful taken in its larger context.

A few words about where the title came from: brown and brook trout are entering their spawning season in late September, and if you harvest the roe and mix it with a little sea salt, in a few hours it becomes a world-class delicacy—trout caviar.

It also becomes, at least to my way of thinking, emblematic of the very best aspects of local, seasonal eating. The French writer Claude Lévi-Strauss said that food is not only good to eat but good to think about as well, and I love to think about what trout caviar represents: the transformation of something utterly local but little known, usually disregarded or actually discarded—the transformation of that thing, through the *simple act of paying attention* (and, in this case, the addition of a little salt), into something wonderful, unique, and precious. In an early blog post I boiled down that notion to what I think of as the Trout Caviar Manifesto: *Our stuff is as good as anyone's stuff, and part of the reason that it's good is that it's ours.*

This is not intended to promote provincialism or a "homer" attitude; rather, it's a corrective to the tendency, long ingrained in modest midwesterners, to look elsewhere—to the coasts, across oceans—for the source of great food, while failing to realize how good we really have it here. That's why I sing paeans to Lake Superior herring, Wisconsin cheddar cheese, maple syrup, and other underappreciated glories of our regional cuisine. It's not an attempt to uphold some abstract principle of "locavorism" (a term I quite abhor); rather, it has to do with practicality and pleasure: I have these things, I like them—why would I look elsewhere?

Practicality and pleasure, along with the aforementioned authenticity, are what these recipes are built on. These dishes were developed in a home kitchen by a home cook; no special equipment or knowledge is required to execute them. Many were created in the very primitive kitchen at my off-grid Wisconsin cabin, Bide-A-Wee. While some are a bit elaborate, most are simple, and none are really difficult. At the same time, I think a good meal is worth a little effort. You'll find a few five-ingredient, fifteen-minute dishes, but that's not necessarily the focus of this cookbook.

The standard recipes in most cookbooks, it seems, serve from four to eight people. Most of mine serve two because, well, that's how many adult humans live in our household; the dogs eat separately. They are, for the most part, generous two-person servings. I think a lot more people these days are cooking for smaller households, but if you're serving a bigger party, the recipes are easily doubled or tripled—I always find it easier to multiply recipe quantities than to divide.

A few of the "flavor pillars" of my cooking are apples, cider, cider vinegar, maple syrup, bacon, cream, cheese, and all the alliums—onions, garlic, shallots, leeks, ramps. Some of these ingredients are undeniably high in fat, but in the context of these recipes they are generally used in fairly small quantities, and the payoff in flavor is great. I actually don't care for cream soups so rich you can stand up a spoon in them. I use cream judiciously for a silky finish to a sauce, to add richness to a salad dressing.

Likewise, a small handful of really flavorful cheese packs more punch than a gloopy coating of the bland industrial variety, with far less detriment to health or waistline. I'll eat cheese at any meal, any time of the day.

As for the bacon: I wouldn't go so far as to say that there's no dish that bacon can't improve, but I have gone so far as to pen (er, tap out) an ode to smoky, fatty pork, "The Importance of Bacon" (p. 135). As with the cream, it's something I generally use in small quantities, and where it is efficacious, it's worth its porcine weight in gold.

* * *

If I were forced to pick a side in that old "eat to live/live to eat" dilemma, I suppose I'd throw in with the latter camp. But it's really more complex—and more interesting—than that. We must eat to live, sure, and living to eat has its pleasures, but I'd rather stress, again, the context part, the joy and meaning, the plain fun and adventure that come from pursuing a wide-ranging forager's approach to cooking and eating. It will take you places, both literally and figuratively, that you might never have thought you'd go. People involved in the food world at all levels—cooks, fishermen and -women, foragers, cheesemakers, butchers, writers—are just a hell of a lot of fun to be around, I've found. Learning a bit about wild foods by taking a foraging class or joining a mycological (mushroomers) society will open up new worlds. Any meal, no matter how luxe or gourmet, is necessarily a fleeting pleasure; embracing the process as the goal extends the pleasure enormously.

Go forth and forage. Eat well and with joy. And remember: your stuff is as good as anyone's stuff, and part of the reason that it's good is that it's yours. ⌐

A Stern Caution
about Harvesting and Consuming Wild Foods

There's a great deal of fun, adventure, and good eating to be had from foraging for wild foods, but any discussion of the topic must begin and end with this emphatic admonition: **never, ever, under any circumstances, eat any wild food that you have not identified with absolute certainty.**

Please memorize the Forager's Poem: *When in doubt, throw it out.* And to you inherently trusting souls, disinclined to doubt: be more skeptical.

The best way to get started in gathering and preparing wild foods is with a trusted guide—a friend with experience in this area, or a foraging group like a mycological society. There are many excellent guidebooks to wild foods, several of which are listed at the end of this book. Familiarize yourself thoroughly with how to use the books before you head to the field; whenever possible, refer to more than one book. Never try to "make it fit": that is, don't assume that the mushroom you're holding is, say, a chanterelle and then go looking for evidence to confirm your hunch. Start from zero and build up your ID with all your best resources. And never attempt to identify wild foods—particularly mushrooms—with photographs or drawings alone.

In addition, when trying any wild food for the first time, eat only a small portion and see how it sits with you before consuming larger amounts. With wild foods as with the domesticated kind, different people may have different reactions to various kinds of foods.

And what else? Oh, yeah: *When in doubt, throw it out!* ⌒

Bide-A-Wee

I've been trying to move to the country for around fifteen years now, and currently I'm a little more than halfway there. In the fall of 2007 I turned forty-nine, and I vowed that before my fiftieth birthday I would own a piece of rural property, preferably near a trout stream and a grouse woods. In the course of the preceding decade, I'd been leaning more and more to the east side of the St. Croix/Mississippi watershed, drawn to Wisconsin woods and rivers on foraging, fishing, and hunting outings. Nothing against Minnesota, the state where I was born and have lived most of my life; my Badgerland inclinations were formed mostly by geography. It was fishing, first, and the fact that, while there are fine trout streams in southeastern Minnesota, my favorite waters there require a drive of an hour and a half to reach. Heading straight east from St. Paul, however, I can have my waders wet in a pristine Wisconsin stream in thirty minutes. When I started hunting grouse and woodcock in the late nineties, I found a welcoming abundance of public hunting grounds in western Wisconsin. The more time I spent there, the more I felt drawn to that landscape of mixed woodland and farmland, where dairy cows graze at the edge of a sugar bush, pastured horses cast curious glances at a fisherman casting a dry fly to a brook trout, and honor-system wagons full of squash and pumpkins brighten the roadsides in autumn. It came to seem like another country, as close as it is to the Twin Cities—a quieter, prettier country, where people concern themselves more with the things that matter and the pace of life truly is slower and more enjoyable, for all that making a living there is, for most people, more than a full-time job.

So, in October 2007 my wife, Mary, and I got straight to it, looking for land in western Wisconsin. Within a month we had made an offer on a twenty-acre parcel in northern Dunn County, an hour-and-a-half's drive from St. Paul. It took a few months to straighten out some zoning issues, and we signed the papers on February 29, 2008—a Leap Day plunge, indeed. We were so eager to claim the place as our own that we pitched a tent there, on top of the still-deep snow, two weeks after closing the deal, and nearly froze to death. We hauled both of our dogs onto the air mattress and shivered through the night. Note to any inexperienced winter campers: an air mattress *does not insulate* against the cold of frozen turf, let alone snowpack. Rather, it would appear to conduct the cold directly to those lying atop said mattress.

Subsequent camping trips as the weather warmed worked out better, but the tenting life quickly revealed its limitations. We wanted something a little more comfortable, and we considered and rejected many options, from yurts to kits to built-on-site actual cabins. Everything we looked at seemed either too little or too much, until one day as we drove the county road between the towns of Dallas and Chetek we found the answer: "Schrock's Hilly Acres, Custom Cabins," a hand-lettered sign said (it also advertised brown eggs and feeder pigs). We followed it and made the acquaintance of Ivan Schrock and family, proprietors of an Amish sawmill and carpentry business in Barron County. There was a showroom of sorts: charming wooden structures of many sizes and purposes, all built from local white pine milled on site, covered the grounds on both sides of the driveway—from dog houses and chicken coops to playhouses, sheds, and bunkhouses, on up to real log cabins constructed of thick timbers. We were drawn to a twelve-by-sixteen-foot shed with a deck on the front, Dutch doors, and window boxes for flowers. In no time we were sitting in Ivan's office talking about alterations to the design—add a loft, steepen the roof pitch, offset the wide access door to make room for a woodstove, double-plank the floor to keep out vermin and cold. Nix the window boxes: Ivan pointed out that when you opened the shutters, you would decapitate your flowers.

Ivan figured concertedly with pencil on paper. The final cost would be around $3,500, delivered. Then the question of the deposit, since this was a custom job. I was thinking he would ask for at least a third, maybe half down, and was wondering if we had enough in the checking account to cover it.

"On something like this," Ivan said, "I like to get at least seventy-five dollars."

We gave him a hundred, and a few weeks later, we had ourselves a cabin. They built it at the mill and then loaded it onto a flatbed tow truck, drove it the fifteen hilly, winding miles to our land, and deposited it on the parking pad at the bottom of our steep driveway. Ivan and the tow truck driver, Britt, leveled the building with car jacks and paver blocks—and we had ourselves a "house." The cabin came unfinished inside, and we insulated and paneled, made it cozy. After two years in the original cabin, we added a room in the fall of 2010, nearly doubling our usable space. I would never have thought that three hundred square feet could seem spacious.

A friend came up with the name, *Bide-A-Wee*, a Scottish phrase meaning "rest a while" or "stay a bit." It suits the rustic cabin perfectly. It's where I sit this January morning, snow deep all around, the temperature struggling toward the teens, while my dogs doze and the woodstove ticks. The Bide-A-Wee cabin is off the grid, as they say. No electricity, no proper kitchen, no modern amenities at all. We light the place mostly with candles, an oil lamp, and a propane camp lantern. We heat with wood using a very basic wood-stove designed for expedition tents. It earned its own name, Haggis. We cook on top of the Haggis or on a Coleman propane stove. When the fire pit isn't deep in snow, grilling is our preferred cooking mode.

Bide-A-Wee

The land is all hills, a half-dozen distinct hilltops, and scarcely a football-field's worth of flat land anywhere. It was once part of a larger farm, divided up over the years. It's about half wooded and half open meadows of goldenrod, milkweed, asters, evening primrose—beautiful from early summer through autumn, with hummingbirds, butterflies, and bees taking full advantage. As a rule (but one with exceptions), the valleys are open and the hilltops are wooded. There's a lot of birch and quaking aspen (locally known as *popple*) in the younger woods; the older stands of trees, mostly on the north end of the property, are composed mainly of mature birch, white and black oak, red maple, and black cherry. There are groves of wild plum; prickly ash forms dense thickets where catbirds and cuckoos nest. Though I've always thought myself quite the nature boy, I've learned the names of a lot of new plants and birds since we bought this land.

In older aerial photographs you can see that the flatter hilltop and valley sections were under cultivation. In those photos you can also see one of the key selling points for us: close to a hundred apple trees, scattered all over the land, in no particular arrangement. We sometimes refer to "the orchard," but this is no orchard in the conventional sense. There are a few clumps of six to ten trees in the flatter, more open parts of the property, but there are trees clinging to the steepest hillsides, too, and some solo ones completely subsumed by the woods—we only really notice these in the spring, when they bloom, and in the fall, when the fruit reddens. They are very difficult to harvest.

We don't know what varieties of apples are growing on the Bide-A-Wee land, and without a pomological DNA test, we probably never will. There are tiny, sour crabs and big beautiful, flavorful fruits miraculously untouched by insects and disease—and everything in between. Red ones and yellow ones and greeny red ones, soft fleshed and crisp, blandly sweet or bracingly tart, white fleshed and pink. Some ripen in August and drop by mid-September; some hang on the tree until after Thanksgiving. We don't know which ones were planted on purpose, which are wild. All commercially grown apples come from trees that are grafted—not grown from seed—which is the only way to make them produce true to type. Given the convoluted nature of apple genetics, any truly wild, seedling trees growing on our land might be unique in the whole long history of apples, a remarkable thing to consider.

All of our apple trees were in serious need of pruning, and we tackle a few each year in late winter. A lot of them are trees of many trunks, neglected for years, so the pruning provides us with lots of apple wood for the stove and for smoking and grilling.

The second year we owned the property, our trees produced an astounding crop of apples. Many of the trees were so laden that their limbs drooped to the ground; a few snapped off under the weight. We couldn't harvest more than a tiny percentage of the fruit. We bought a cider press that summer, invited friends out on an early October weekend, and made juice from the abundant harvest. We fermented a few gallons, and perhaps it was beginners' luck or the synergy of that great variety of apple types, but we managed to produce superb hard cider, which we bottled with a small dose of sugar per bottle to give a little fizz in the final fermentation. We also freeze gallons of sweet cider and thaw them as needed through the winter.

That fall we also began an ongoing and still fascinating exploration of the many uses of the apple: sauce, ketchup, syrup, relish, pickle, butter, dried, fermented. We put them in pancakes, bread, stews, salads, stuffings. Bake, sauté, roast, grill—I've yet to find a cooking operation that some kind of apple isn't suited for.

Blackberries grow wild from one end of our property to the other, and I have developed a complex appreciation and a great fondness for *Rubus fruticosus.* I appreciate the beauty of its blossoms in the spring and the brambly sweetness of its distinctive fruit, much more flavorful than the cultivated kind, in late summer through early fall (and year-round in preserves). I appreciate, as well, the tenacity of its canes, which form nearly impenetrable thickets on many of our hillsides, and the razor-like qualities of its thorns, which will punish any berry-picker who thinks he can get away without wearing long pants and a heavy, long-sleeved shirt. Blackberries combine wonderfully with apples in many preparations, and in fact they belong to the same botanical family, *rosacea,* which also includes roses and hawthorns. The layered flavors of wild blackberries—sweetness and tang, a smoky depth, an edgy vegetal quality, sort of tea-like—make them a perfect match for game birds, duck, and other rich meats.

* * *

In three years at Bide-A-Wee, we've discovered selling points that no realtor could have known about, like the woodcock dancing ground on the hill directly above the cabin. Male woodcock return early in the spring to their northern breeding grounds, and each stakes out his territory. As evening comes on, he begins a circling dance, uttering a distinctive note that ornithologists call a *peent*. (Before we knew the origin of this odd croak-like quack, we imagined its source was a mythical creature we called "the duck-frog.")

Round and round parades the peenting, amorous male, and then at a certain point he takes to the wing, rising in a wide, sweeping circle, making a new sound now, a whirring twitter. At the apex of his flight he stops in midair and flutters down, side to side, leaf-like, to land at the spot where he began. Our little deck at Bide-A-Wee happened to be directly under the woodcock's flight path last spring. I never got tired of watching him go streaking past, and I tried to track his path high into the darkening sky, waited to hear the odd chirping (yet a third kind of woodcock expression) that announced his fluttering descent.

Wild turkeys and ruffed grouse also inhabit the land; red-tailed hawks, turkey vultures, and bald eagles use the thermals off our hills to climb to impressive heights. Spring and fall we witness migrations of Canada geese, tundra swans, and sandhill cranes.

* * *

In the evenings at Bide-A-Wee, we listen to the radio, "The Ideas Network of Wisconsin Public Radio" or WOJB, "Woodland Community Radio," from the Lac Courte Oreilles Ojibwe reservation in Reserve, Wisconsin (the nearby town of Couderay shows how the band's name is locally pronounced). WOJB plays music to accompany the woodcutting season and maple sugar time and gives live, all-day coverage to the American Birkebeiner—cross-country skiing on the radio; it's sort of a Zen thing. There's a music request show on Saturday nights, and every week the same characters ask to hear the same songs: "He's in the Jailhouse Now," "Bar With No Beer," "Daddy's Girl," and more—oh, how could I forget Donna Fargo's masterpiece, "Happiest Girl in the Whole U.S.A." and "Yankin' on My Yohnson" (it's about trying to get an outboard motor started, doncha know)?

Before dinner we read by the light of candles and the oil lamp. After dinner we take a short walk to the top of the driveway. Sometimes we hear coyotes or barred owls. On clear nights we look up with undiminishing wonder at the proliferation of stars, compelling beauty reaching to every horizon and

Haggis with hot pot

to the crown of the heavens. We go to bed pretty early, and usually we wake up hungry. Corn and apple pancakes with a ladle of home-brewed maple syrup? Yes, please.

When it comes to cooking, the primitive conditions are absolutely inspiring. I've long been fascinated with cooking over fire—grilling and smoking and roasting in the coals. Along with the natural appetite boost you get from being outdoors, open-fire cooking adds the inimitable flavors of char and smoke to your food. At Bide-A-Wee we have a crude fire pit in our "gravel garden" terrace. If I'm going to grill our supper, I'll build a fire and we'll enjoy its ambience until it has burned down to a bed of coals and it's time to cook. In winter we often go for long-braised dishes that simmer on the woodstove. Oxtail stew, braised short ribs, home-cured ham simmered atop sauerkraut, or sausage-vegetable hot pots—these are the kinds of dinners we gravitate toward in fall and winter. Duck confit glazed with maple syrup and served with fried apples, or a warming chowder of Lake Superior fish and wild rice— these are reasonable compensations for short days and long, cold nights.

Procuring our raw ingredients is often as engaging as the cooking and the eating. From home-based forays to short jaunts to day trips, we find wonderful things to cook with on our land and at our fishing and hunting grounds, from area markets, local dairy farms, and cheese factories—from our neighbors, in brief. I really like living, if only part-time, in a place where our neighbors sell raw milk, great cheese, bison and lamb, wonderful vegetables and fruits, and even beer (Dave's BrewFarm, a wind-powered microbrewery, lies on a direct route from our St. Paul home to Bide-A-Wee).

This is Wisconsin, after all. ➥

Notes on Ingredients and Substitutions

Maple Syrup: Let's first be clear that real maple syrup has nothing to do with "pancake syrup," that quasi-criminal concoction of corn syrup, coloring, and chemicals that defiles the tables of pancake houses across the nation. Let's instead praise a truly wonderful northern food product, one that express *terroir* as fully as any Burgundy wine. Maple syrup is great on pancakes, of course, but it's also a wonderful addition to barbecue

Boiling sap

sauces and glazes, as part of the cure for smoked pork or fish, and in many desserts. I add it to salad dressings, soups, chutneys, even cocktails. Real maple syrup is expensive, no question, but a little goes a long way, and bottom line, it's worth it. It's less expensive if you buy in bulk from a co-op, where you may also find dark and flavorful grade-B syrup. You may also secure a bargain, and have a fine time, taking a drive in maple syrup country and buying directly from a local producer or small shop.

APPLE CIDER, SWEET AND HARD: For sweet cider, you want the cloudy stuff that comes straight from an orchard's pressing facility into bottles and directly to market. Given the choice, I prefer unpasteurized cider, but it can be difficult to find commercially. Either heat- or UV-pasteurized ciders are good choices if they come from a quality producer. Sweet cider can be preserved by freezing—be sure to leave adequate headspace in the container.

While fresh sweet cider is available seasonally, hard (alcoholic) cider is available year-round, and there are several brands on the market now. I've never found one of those commercial ciders that I really enjoy drinking, though they may be fine for use in cooking. There are some very nice ciders imported from France, but these are as expensive as good wine. That's not to say they're not worth the money, only that I wouldn't pour half a bottle of twenty-dollar cider over a piece of pork shoulder.

For cooking purposes, I've suggested a substitute for hard cider (Hard Cider Sub [and a drink called Shrub], p. 231) that combines sweet cider and cider vinegar.

APPLE CIDER VINEGAR: A pleasant by-product of our cider making has been homemade apple cider vinegar, produced once the sweet cider has fermented to dryness, then been exposed, either by chance or intent, to another kind of bacteria that turns the alcohol in the cider to acetic acid. What you get, especially when you start with flavorful apple juice, is a fragrant, mellow, complex vinegar, the kind of thing you could sip from a thimble glass, maybe sweetened with a bit of maple syrup. If you have access to unpasteurized apple cider, you can make your own by putting the cider in a container with an airlock (available at brewing supply stores) and leaving it in a cool, dark place for a couple of months. At this point you'll have hard cider, and maybe you'll want to save some for cooking or drinking. The rest you can inoculate with unpasteurized apple cider vinegar (available at co-ops and natural food stores), a quarter cup vinegar to a half gallon cider. Place that in a glass container, the mouth covered by cheesecloth to exclude fruit flies, and let sit for another couple of months.

In lieu of homemade vinegar, look for unpasteurized apple cider vinegar. Rice wine vinegar is similarly mellow. Good white wine vinegar would work fine in most of the recipes here, too.

DRIED APPLES: Dried apples have replaced almost all other dried fruit in my cooking. I love the tartness, the aroma, the chewy texture. In a baked dish like Cornmeal Maple Baked Pudding (p. 204), they soften in the cooking and almost dissolve, leaving behind an apple-y tang that balances the sweetness of the maple syrup. I like them in savory stuffings, too, where the tart sweetness gives counterpoint to salty richness. You can buy dried apples, of course, but you'll get a better product if you make your own. In late fall there are often bargains to be had in seconds apples at farmers markets. We picked up one of those nifty apple-peeling devices at our local hardware store and an inexpensive food dehydrator at a home store. The dehydrator isn't strictly necessary: you can dry apple slices on wire racks or string them with needle and thread to hang and dry in a cool, airy place out of direct sun. Then store them in plastic zip bags or covered containers.

ALLIUMS, THE ONION FAMILY, AKA "THE SOUL OF SAVOR": My larder almost always contains garlic, shallots, leeks, onions, scallions, and pickled ramps, and my garden grows chives and garlic chives. I use all these pungent, sweet and savory plants in almost everything I cook, frequently in combination: garlic and shallot in a salad dressing; leek and onion in a soup or braised dish.

While the flavor of each is distinct, they are, nonetheless, somewhat interchangeable. Okay, there's no substitute for garlic. But should you come across a recipe that calls for shallots and all you have are onions, try it with the onions. Then go get some shallots and try it again, the right way. And if a long-braised dish calls for leek and onion but leeks are absent from your pantry, add a little extra onion and get on with it. If the dish pleases you that way, try it next time with the leeks and onion and see if you can taste a difference. The main thing is, get the food on the table. Worry about the details later. These recipes are not so finely constructed that they will collapse if you pull out one straw, so to speak.

WILD FOOD SUBSTITUTIONS: A conundrum arises. On the one hand, I want you to make these recipes and taste in them what I tasted in them. On the other hand, I realize that wild foods like chanterelles, nettles, and ramps may be difficult to obtain. On yet a third, mutant sort of hand, I think that perhaps the pretty pictures of wild mushrooms and the appetizing recipe for

Ramps and Fiddleheads Tart (p. 107) might really encourage some people to take up foraging (be sure to read the Stern Caution [p. 8] before you start). I would love to inspire in that way. In the meantime, there are plenty of recipes here that don't call for any wild-foraged foods, and there are reasonable substitutions for many of those wild foods.

Reasonable substitutes for ramps are small leeks or spring onions (the bigger ones you see at farmers markets in spring, not little scallions); add an extra bit of garlic to the dish.

Asparagus and fiddlehead ferns don't really taste alike, but the texture is similar, and they appear at the same time of year.

Spinach or other tender greens can take the place of nettles; the cultivated greens generally require less cooking.

Wild "sheep" sorrel and garden sorrel are interchangeable; wood sorrel has a similar tangy flavor, too, but the leaves are so small, it is generally used as a garnish.

The greatest difficulty in substituting comes with the wild mushrooms. Nothing has the flavor of a morel, the aroma of a chanterelle, the texture of a hen of the woods. Fortunately, many of these fungi now appear at co-ops and

Shallot braid

specialty stores in season; on the down side, they are really expensive. For budget's sake, try going half and half with the pricey wild mushrooms and the cultivated kind. There are also interesting mushrooms to be had in the stores beyond the button and cremini, including oyster, shiitake, and dried porcini.

Eventually, if these recipes and this approach to food and cooking appeal to you, I imagine you'll find your way to the woods (if you're not already there) to forage your own.

QUATRE-ÉPICES: A classic French blend, it translates as "four spices," but this version contains six. I use this mix in Potted Pork Pâté (p. 31), Confit of Fresh Ham (p. 128), Duck Leg Confit (p. 149), and Apple Blackberry Galettes (p. 205). I also reach for it when making meatballs, meat loaf, or fresh pork sausage. Use sparingly: it is potent, and a little bit gives a really exotic, appetizing aroma.

> 2 teaspoons ground coriander
> 2 teaspoons ground allspice
> 1 teaspoon ground ginger
> 1 teaspoon ground cinnamon
> ½ teaspoon grated nutmeg
> ⅛ teaspoon ground cloves

Combine all spices and store in a tightly closed jar in a dark place.

SAMBAL OELEK, GROUND FRESH CHILI PASTE: I originally started buying this piquant paste of chilies, salt, and vinegar (as well as some preservatives I'm embarrassed to mention) to use in Sichuan cooking, but over the years I've found many other uses for it. It adds a sweet, bright heat to dishes from Steak Tartare (p. 119) to Sambal Carrot Slaw (p. 41). I find it especially welcome in winter cooking. Sambal oelek is available at Asian food shops, in the ethnic sections of some supermarkets, and online. Tabasco sauce or Sriracha chili sauce or fresh roasted medium-hot chilies are adequate substitutes. Indonesian in origin, the sambal oelek I buy comes from Huy Fong Foods in Rosemead, California; they also make the wildly popular Sriracha and appear to have cornered the market on these condiments.

ESPELETTE PEPPER (*piment d'espelette*): This mildly hot, wonderfully fragrant ground chile from the Basque region of southern France has become a standard seasoning in our house, right there beside the salt and black pepper. It's available in gourmet shops or online. Cayenne is hotter but, as it's used in quite small amounts, an adequate substitute. Or try a hot or smoked paprika, or Spanish pimentón—or just leave it out.

SALT: You might conclude from a scan of these recipes that I don't like salt. Not true. I like and value salt in cooking, but I generally add it by the pinch, at various stages in the preparation of a dish. If all goes well, the final product will be properly seasoned, but of course, tastes vary. If a dish tastes flat or dull, first ask yourself if it tastes salty, and then if you feel it's not *over*salted, try adding a pinch of salt and taste again. The thing about salt is that it doesn't just make things taste salty—it makes them taste good, and it brings flavors together. Sometimes a recipe that seems a total dud can be saved with a couple pinches of salt. (I'm sorry if this seems painfully obvious, but it's something of which I must remind my own dear wife time and again.)

CHICKEN STOCK: When chicken stock is called for in these recipes, as it often is, I usually specify unsalted stock. Making your own stock is the first choice, of course, but not always practical. Part 1 of the Chicken in a Pot recipe (p. 141) has instructions for making a light, fresh stock in about an hour. Unsalted chicken stock can be purchased, frozen, from better butcher shops or grocery stores. Some canned or boxed options are available, too, though perhaps not widely. In soup recipes, low-sodium stock can be substituted: adjust the added salt to compensate. In dishes where the stock is reduced to make a sauce, only unsalted will do.

Smoking Basics

Smoking was once a common means of preserving food—and still is in many parts of the world. In modern America we smoke for flavor more than preservation, and we've mostly turned the job over to large, industrial producers. It's worth relearning the basics of home smoking because

* it's fun and satisfying to smoke your own, and your friends will be impressed;
* you can produce smoked foods without the chemicals inherent in commercial smoking; and
* your results will be more delicious than anything you could buy.

I was intimidated by the idea of smoking food at home for a long time. It seemed, on the one hand, like one of those instinctual activities that we modern humans had just lost the knack for and, on the other, like a gourmet procedure of daunting difficulty. Then it occurred to me one day, just one of those light-bulb moments: "Hey, cavemen did this. Maybe I can, too."

A bit of a learning curve was involved. A few batches of what could charitably be called trout jerky came out of my smoker. Now I fire up the smoker several times a year, mainly for bacon and brown trout but occasionally for pork shoulder, chicken, or duck.

By "fire up the smoker," what I really mean is prepare my barbecue grill, along with a second, smaller grill. I do not use any special equipment beyond that. There are, of course, lots of home smokers on the market, and if you have one of those, follow the manufacturer's instructions for using it. If you're new to smoking food, here's a simple way to start.

You will need:
* A covered barbecue grill (mine is a Meco, clamshell type, though the ubiquitous Weber will work)
* A smaller grill, preferably also covered, to hold hot coals to replenish the smoker
* Natural chunk charcoal, available at most larger grocery or even hardware stores
* A chimney starter for the charcoal (no lighter fluid, please)

* Some fragrant wood, chips or chunks (I use oak and apple; in the past I've used maple and hickory bark)
* An instant-read meat thermometer, inserted in the top vent, handy for monitoring temperature

This technique is hot smoking, as opposed to the cold smoking that produces lox and certain other delicacies. It involves cooking the pre-cured (salted or brined) meat or fish rather slowly with indirect heat in the presence of smoke.

Light a chimney starter full of charcoal. When it's ready, dump half the charcoal in the main grill, half in the smaller. Move the coals in the main grill to one side. Add some fresh charcoal to the smaller grill, and put the lid on with the vents open just a tad, so those coals stay hot but don't burn up too quickly.

Place some smoking wood—apple, oak, etc., a handful of chips or a chunk or two—on top of the coals in the main grill. Place the items to be smoked on the side of the grill grate away from the coals: it's important that the food isn't directly over the coals. Put the lid on with the vent about halfway closed. Place the instant-read thermometer in the vent opening. Adjust vent and coals to keep the temperature around 200 degrees. Replenish with coals from the smaller grill as needed. Add more smoking wood chips or chunks as needed.

Fish of up to a pound will be done in one and a half to two hours; bacon in chunks of one to one and a half pounds will be done in two to three hours. Turn the meat or fish every 45 minutes or so. At temperatures this low (even though it's called *hot smoking*), it's hard to overcook the foods. If, after smoking for the times designated, you're not sure the food is fully cooked, just place it in a 200-degree oven for another thirty minutes.

It's as simple as that. Once you're comfortable with the basics, there's no end of resources—books, TV series, classes, etc.—to take you on myriad smoking adventures. (One book I really like is *Peace, Love, and Barbecue* by Mike Mills.)

Some notes:

* Many smoking recipes tell you to soak the smoking wood. I don't. The point of the smoking wood is to produce smoke, not steam.

* Remove the lid from the smaller grill about ten minutes before you want to add fresh coals to the larger grill. This step allows air in to perk up those coals, which are merely smoldering.

* While the salting and smoking provide a certain amount of preservative qualities, the finished products of these recipes are not intended for long-term storage. The bacon can be frozen, but the fish should be eaten promptly.

Grilled herring, onions, and tomatoes

STARTERS

*

✳ HAZELNUT-CRUSTED GOAT CHEESE

The hazelnuts can be wild foraged or store bought. Wild hazelnuts grow abundantly in Minnesota and Wisconsin. Look for the fascinating, frilly green husks on hazel shrubs in late summer. It's best to pick them when they're still a bit green; if you wait until they're fully ripe, the squirrels will likely beat you to them. Stash them away for a few weeks (like the squirrels do), and use them once the husks have browned and shrunk away from the nuts. Discard any that have tiny holes in the shell—there's nothing inside those.

Serve with Cranberry Maple Chutney (p. 216) or a relish of your choice or atop a salad of tender lettuces or frisée tossed with your favorite vinaigrette. To chop the hazelnuts, I find it easiest to crush them first—between two cutting boards or on a cutting board with the bottom of a skillet.

Per person
2 ounces soft fresh goat cheese (chèvre)
Canola oil
Freshly ground black pepper
1 tablespoon finely chopped hazelnuts

Hazelnut-Crusted Goat Cheese

Preheat broiler; place one rack near heat source and another rack in the lower third of the oven. Form the goat cheese into little disks, or pucks, about 1 inch thick and 2½ inches across. Grease aluminum foil with oil, place on a baking sheet, and add cheese disks. Grind coarse pepper on the cheese, and press the nuts all over the top. Place the baking sheet under the broiler for a minute or two, until the topping is well browned and fragrant, watching constantly to make sure the nuts do not burn. Move the baking sheet to the lower rack for 1 minute to allow the cheese to warm through. Remove from heat and serve immediately. ⁓

✳ PICKLED RAMP CREAM CHEESE

MAKES ½ CUP

A simple, tasty cracker spread. Serve as is, or top with a few flakes of smoked fish.

- 4 ounces cream cheese, regular (softened at room temperature for 30 minutes) or spreadable
- 2 tablespoons mayonnaise
- 2 tablespoons finely chopped pickled ramp bulbs (p. 224; 2–3 bulbs)
- Freshly ground black pepper to taste

Combine all ingredients, mixing and mashing with the back of a fork. The spread will keep for 3 or 4 days in the fridge, growing "rampier" all the while. ⁓

✳ SHALLOT-SCENTED CHÈVRE

MAKES ½ CUP

So much nicer than onion-soup-mix dip. Enjoy pre-dinner, on crackers or crostini with a glass of wine—or dollop atop a salad. It's best when prepared a few hours to a day ahead, to let the shallot flavor really permeate the spread.

- 1 tablespoon butter
- 1 shallot, minced
- 4 ounces soft fresh goat cheese (chèvre)
- Freshly ground black pepper

Melt the butter in a small saucepan over medium heat and add the shallot. Cook for a bare minute, just enough to take off the raw flavor; remove from heat. Mix the shallot into the goat cheese with coarse black pepper to taste. Pack into a ramekin for serving. ⌒

✳ CHILE CHEDDAR SPREAD

MAKES ABOUT 1½ CUPS

Southern pimento cheese (or puh-minna chayz) was the inspiration for this combination, but after I perused a few recipes that called for processed cheese product and canned pimento bits, I realized we could teach our southern cousins something about cheese spread. An aged sharp white cheddar from Wisconsin and a medium-hot roasted red chile make for an extremely appetizing cracker topping or sandwich spread.

  2 tablespoons minced onion
  5–6 ounces aged (at least two years) white Wisconsin cheddar, grated medium (about 2 cups)
  1 medium-hot red chile (jalapeño or Anaheim), roasted and chopped, or 1 teaspoon sambal oelek chili paste
  ¼ cup plus 2 tablespoons mayonnaise (or to taste)
  Paprika or cayenne

Mix the onion, cheese, chile or paste, and mayonnaise thoroughly with a fork or spatula; sprinkle with paprika or cayenne. Serve. ⌒

✳ LAKE TROUT MAPLE-SPICE GRAVLAX

SERVES AT LEAST 4

Lake trout is a member of the char family, related to brook trout and arctic char. While it doesn't have the fatty qualities of salmon, it still cures into a dense, translucent gravlax to serve as an appetizer or as part of a brunch buffet, with good bread and Honey Mustard (p. 218).

  1 (8–12 ounce) lake trout fillet, skin on
  2 tablespoons maple syrup

Lake Trout Maple-Spice Gravlax

3 tablespoons salt, divided
1 teaspoon freshly ground black pepper
½ teaspoon crushed fennel seeds
½ teaspoon crushed caraway seeds
Honey Mustard (p. 218)

Brush the fish with maple syrup, mostly on the flesh side, using all the syrup. Place a piece of plastic wrap on a platter or baking dish large enough to hold the fillet and sprinkle with one-third of the salt. Place the fish, skin-side down, atop the salt. Sprinkle the pepper and fennel and caraway seeds on the flesh side and then cover fish with the remaining salt. Wrap tightly and refrigerate for 24 hours, turning occasionally.

Rinse the fish to remove excess salt and spices. Slice it very thin, cutting at an angle from the flesh side toward the skin (discard skin). Serve with whole-wheat or rye sourdough bread, good butter, sliced red onions, and Honey Mustard.

Trout Caviar

AKA "The Titular Delicacy." Only after many years of regretfully discarding the jewel-like egg sacs of September-caught trout did I finally come up with one of the simplest and most delicious "recipes" I've ever concocted. It is literally nothing more than trout roe and salt. The first time I made it I was riven with conflicting emotions: delighted, and more, to have discovered such a magnificent taste; rueful, deeply, at all the trout eggs I had tossed into the trash or streamside bushes over the years.

I use the roe of brown and brook trout, but you can do the same thing with rainbow trout, steelhead (which are lake- or ocean-going rainbows), or salmon roe. The roe of arctic char and lake trout, both relatives of brook trout, would also likely work.

So let's say you've gone fishing in September, and you've caught and killed a couple of gravid trout. As you gut them you'll see that the egg sacs nearly fill the cavity—remarkable how many eggs are produced by even a small fish. Pull out those sacs and give them a quick rinse, and then set them on a cutting board and, using two kitchen knives, gently work the eggs free of that gray membrane, the skein. It doesn't matter if you get it all: once you rinse and salt the eggs, the remnants will contract into pieces you can quite easily see and remove, and some of it will simply dissolve.

Rinse the eggs and drain them in a sieve. Weigh the result on a kitchen scale, and to each 50 grams of roe (about a quarter cup) add 4 grams of salt (a scant quarter teaspoon). Put the roe in a small bowl or ramekin and gently mix in the salt. Cover with plastic wrap. In a couple of hours you'll have caviar: the salt penetrates that quickly. The caviar will keep for 3 or 4 days in the fridge.

We serve our trout caviar with dark bread or blini, good butter, sour cream or crème fraîche, and all due ceremony. Maybe some September I'll have such success on the trout stream that this little miracle will become old hat. It hasn't happened yet.

In the interest of equal-opportunity omnivorism, I should add that you can also eat trout milts—the sperm strips that the males develop in the fall. These I lightly flour and fry. They are sweet and nutty.

✳ POTTED SMOKED TROUT

MAKES ABOUT 1 CUP

This dish was inspired by the potted spiced shrimp popular in Britain. Here fresh seasonal herbs take the place of the spices. Spread on grilled baguette slices, or serve alongside a salad for a lunch dish or first course.

> 6 tablespoons (3 ounces) unsalted butter, divided
> 1 tablespoon finely chopped shallot
> 6 ounces smoked trout, skinned, boned, and flaked
> 2 sprigs fresh tarragon, finely chopped
> 1 tablespoon chopped chives
> Salt and freshly ground black pepper

Melt 4 tablespoons of the butter in a small saucepan and add the shallot. Remove the pan from the heat and set aside for 10 minutes.

In a mixing bowl combine the trout, tarragon, chives, and shallot-butter mix, stirring vigorously for about a minute to bring the mixture together. Season with pepper and salt to taste. Pack the mixture into 2 ramekins. Melt the remaining 2 tablespoons butter and pour it over the top to seal.

Refrigerate for a few hours or overnight. Let come to room temperature an hour or two before serving. ⌒

✳ POTTED PORK PÂTÉ (*Rillettes*)

MAKES ABOUT 3 CUPS

These days, it seems everyone is an expert in charcuterie, *the French art of cured sausages, hams, and such. But there's another French word I love even more:* cochonnailles. Le cochon, *that's the pig; thus* cochonnailles, *tasty things made from pork. The Loire region is famous for its cochonnailles, and little pots of rich, savory* rillettes, *potted pork pâté, are perhaps its most common expression, a perennial favorite as an aperitif snack. Stateside, the Upper Midwest is pork central, and small-scale producers are changing the way we think about this wonderful meat, too often taken for granted.*

With rillettes smeared on a slice of baguette, cornichons (p. 226) and a mustard pot nearby, and a glass of cold white wine or beer or cider at hand, there's no better way to start off a relaxing meal.

The pork should be about one-third fat, two-thirds lean; if you find a very fatty piece of pork shoulder, you may not need the pork belly.

2 pounds pork shoulder, cut into 2-inch cubes
1 pound pork belly, cut into 2-inch cubes
1 teaspoon salt
⅛ teaspoon quatre-épices (p. 20)
1 bay leaf
1 healthy sprig fresh thyme
Freshly ground black pepper
1 tablespoon minced shallot
Melted lard, clarified butter, or duck fat

Place the cubed pork in a large saucepan or Dutch oven, cover with water by an inch, bring to a boil, and then reduce the heat to maintain a brisk simmer. Scum will rise to the surface: skim, then skim again; after about an hour it will subside. Add the salt, quatre-épices, bay leaf, thyme, and a few grinds of black pepper. Cook for 4 to 5 hours, partly covered, at a brisk simmer. Add water to cover as needed, until the pork becomes very tender, falling apart at a mere stir. Add the shallot and continue simmering until most of the water has evaporated and the pork just begins to sizzle, cooking in its own fat. Remove the pot from the heat, cover, and let cool. Pull out the bay leaf and thyme stem. Refrigerate overnight.

The next day, with very clean fingers, get right into the unctuous mass to break up any remaining clumps of meat. Place the pan over low heat and slowly melt the mixture, working it with the back of a fork and further reducing it to a shreddy pulp.

Pack into ramekins or small crocks. Top with melted lard, clarified butter, or duck fat. Refrigerate for a day before eating, if you can resist. Protected by its layer of fat, this pâté will keep—and improve—in the refrigerator for at least a couple of weeks. It can also be frozen for up to 3 months.

* WILD MUSHROOM AND RAMP CREAM TOASTS

SERVES 4 TO 6

Any firm mushrooms will work in this preparation: hen of the woods, chicken of the woods, chanterelles, hedgehogs, oysters.

  10 ramp bulbs, fresh or pickled (p. 224)
  3 slices (about 3 ounces) thick-cut bacon, cut into ¼-inch cubes
  1½ cups chopped wild mushrooms
  Salt and freshly ground black pepper
  ¼ cup dry white wine or dry vermouth
  ½ cup heavy cream, divided
  1 cup unsalted chicken stock
  ¼ cup sour cream
  1 teaspoon fresh thyme or ¼ teaspoon dried
  ⅛ teaspoon cayenne or Espelette pepper
  Baguette slices
  Grated Gruyère or Gouda cheese, optional

Chop the ramp bulbs crosswise into ¼-inch pieces. With pickled ramps, rinse and drain. With fresh ramps, reserve some of the green tops to chop for garnish.

Place a skillet over medium heat and add the bacon. As the fat begins to render, add the ramps and cook for 2 minutes, until they begin to soften. Add the mushrooms and a pinch of salt and cook, stirring, for 4 to 5 minutes, until lightly browned. Add the wine and cook until most of the liquid has evaporated. Set aside 2 tablespoons of the heavy cream. Add the stock, remaining heavy cream, sour cream, thyme, cayenne, and a few grinds of black pepper. Simmer until the sauce is reduced by half. Transfer the mushrooms to a bowl, and stir in the reserved heavy cream. Taste and adjust for salt.

Serve immediately on toasted baguette slices, or place the mushroom-topped toasts under the broiler until nicely browned, some with a sprinkling of cheese, some without. Garnish with chopped ramp greens if you have them. ⌒

BLACK AND GOLD MUSHROOM "CAVIAR"

SERVES 4 TO 6 AS AN APPETIZER

The finer you chop the mushrooms, the more caviar-like the mixture will look, but it's just as delicious if the texture is coarser. For a very fine, tapenade-like texture, pulse the finished "caviar" in a food processor a few times. Serve on crackers or baguette slices, plain or toasted.

2 tablespoons unsalted butter, plus 2 teaspoons softened
butter, optional
¼ cup finely minced shallots
½ cup finely chopped black trumpet mushrooms
(about 1½ ounces)
½ cup finely chopped chanterelles (about 3 ounces)
1 clove garlic, minced
Salt and freshly ground black pepper
¼ cup dry white wine
½ cup unsalted chicken stock
2 teaspoons soy sauce
Pinch quatre-épices (p. 20)
Crackers or baguette slices
Finely chopped onion for garnish, optional

Black trumpet mushrooms

Melt the 2 tablespoons butter in a small saucepan and add the shallots; cook over medium-low heat for 2 minutes. Add the mushrooms and garlic and a pinch of salt, and cook, stirring occasionally, 4 to 5 minutes, until the mushrooms have started to shrink. Add the wine, stock, soy sauce, quatre-épices, and a few grinds of black pepper. Cook over very low heat until most of the liquid has evaporated.

Transfer the mixture to a serving bowl. For a richer texture, stir in 2 teaspoons softened butter. Serve warm or at room temperature, on crackers or baguette slices, with a sprinkling of chopped onion if you like. The "caviar" can be stored, refrigerated, up to 1 week, and warmed in a low oven or on the stovetop before serving: the butter may taste grainy if it's not reheated.

2

SALADS

*

APPLE TURNIP SLAW *with Buckwheat Honey Dressing*

SERVES 2

Turnips grow sharp and pungent as they age but are sweet and fresh tasting when young, like a mellow radish with a foreign accent. They take well to braising or sautéing but are also lovely raw in salads.

1 small (about 2-inch-diameter) turnip, peeled, sliced very thin, and cut into matchsticks
1 small apple, peeled, cored, and cut into matchsticks
1 small carrot, peeled and cut into matchsticks
¼ small red onion, slivered
Salt and freshly ground black pepper
2 teaspoons buckwheat honey
1 tablespoon cider vinegar
1½ tablespoons sunflower or grape seed oil
1 teaspoon Dijon-style or brown mustard

Toss the turnip, apple, carrot, and onion with 2 pinches of salt and set aside. Stir together the honey, vinegar, oil, mustard, and a pinch of salt. Pour the dressing over the vegetables, add pepper to taste, and mix well. Let sit for 20 minutes before serving.

BUTTERMILK CUCUMBERS *with Chervil and Garlic Chive Shoots*

SERVES 2 TO 4

If you have garlic chives in your garden, you probably have a lot of them. They spread both by dividing underground and by distributing their little black seeds, copiously. Their dark, flat, blade-like leaves have a nice, pungent, garlic-onion flavor and aroma—a bit like wild ramps—but the best part is the flower stalk before the flower has opened. By running your hand up the stalk and letting it break off where it wants to, you get just the tender sweet tips, which are delicious chopped into salad dressings or, if you have a quantity, stir-fried with some soft-scrambled eggs.

Buttermilk Cucumbers with Chervil and Garlic Chive Shoots

2 smallish, thin-skinned cucumbers, or 1 larger English
   or Asian cucumber
6 tablespoons buttermilk
2 teaspoons cider vinegar or white wine vinegar
1½ teaspoons sunflower or vegetable oil
Scant ¼ teaspoon salt
2 tablespoons finely chopped garlic chive shoots, tender top few
   inches only (or substitute regular chives)
Few sprigs fresh chervil (or substitute tarragon), chopped

Slice the cucumbers very thin, to about ⅛ inch, using a mandoline if you
have one. Whisk together the remaining ingredients and add cucumbers,
mixing well. Refrigerate and allow the flavors to meld for at least 1 hour or
up to 1 day before serving.

FRISÉE SALAD *with Smoked Trout and Horseradish Dressing*

SERVES 2

A variation on the bistro classic frisée aux lardons, *French bacon and egg salad. Smoked trout plays bacon here.*

1 head frisée (curly endive)

8 ounces smoked trout (or other smoked fish)

1 tablespoon sour cream

1 tablespoon heavy cream

1 teaspoon grated fresh horseradish, or 2 teaspoons prepared horseradish, or to taste

1 small clove garlic, finely minced

2 tablespoons canola or grape seed oil

1 tablespoon white wine vinegar

Salt and freshly ground black pepper to taste

2 large eggs, poached or soft-cooked

2 teaspoons milkweed "capers" (p. 225), optional

Remove the outer leaves of the frisée and discard; trim the darker green tops of the remaining leaves so that you are left with the blanched, light-green heart (save the trimmings to add to soups or stir-fries). Cut or tear the frisée into 2-inch pieces, rinse well, and spin dry. Break the trout into large flakes and set aside.

Mix together the sour cream, cream, horseradish, garlic, oil, and vinegar with a pinch of salt and pepper to taste. Toss this dressing with the frisée 10 to 15 minutes before serving. Divide the frisée between 2 plates; top with trout and poached eggs. Sprinkle milkweed "capers" over each plate if you have them. Serve.

✳ LACINATO KALE SALAD *with Poached Egg on Toast*

This salad really is a gardener's delight, best when you have access to the tender leaves of spring or those frost-nipped leaves of autumn. It's a salad for those who don't mind a chew and good strong flavors. Lacinato kale is also called Tuscan, dinosaur, or black kale. Young leaves of other types of kale (blue, red Russian) would work too.

> Per person
> About 12 small leaves lacinato kale, shredded very thin
> 1 small clove garlic, finely minced
> 1 tablespoon sunflower oil
> 2 teaspoons cider vinegar
> Good pinch coarse sea salt, plus more for garnish
> ¼ teaspoon sambal oelek chili paste
> Freshly ground black pepper
> 1 slice sourdough whole-grain toast, buttered (plus more
>   for mopping up, if you like)
> 1 large egg
> Chives or other fresh herb, optional

Toss the kale with the garlic, oil, vinegar, salt, sambal oelek, and a few grinds of pepper; let sit at least 15 minutes. Pile the salad atop buttered toast. Poach the egg; place it on top of the salad. Grind a bit of black pepper and snip some chives over the dish. Sprinkle on more coarse salt to taste just before serving. ✐

✳ SAMBAL CARROT SLAW
SERVES 4 AS A SIDE DISH

Versatile, colorful, vibrant—this simple slaw is a favorite at our house. We always store a good supply of carrots in our root cellar for the winter. Even in mid-February, the bright flavors of this salad seem summery. Adjust the sweet-hot ratio to your liking with sambal oelek and honey. I like it both sweet and hot. It's my go-to hot dog topping.

2　large carrots, peeled and coarsely grated

　1　shallot, thinly sliced into translucent rings

　2　good pinches salt

　2　tablespoons canola or grape seed oil

　1　tablespoon cider or red wine vinegar

½–1　teaspoon sambal oelek chili paste, to taste

1–2　teaspoons honey, to taste

⅛　teaspoon freshly ground black or Sichuan pepper

Toss everything together and let sit at room temperature for 15 or 20 minutes. Serve as a salad in a western meal, as part of a multicourse Chinese
meal, or as a condiment-slaw for hot dogs or pulled pork sandwiches.

Popcorn Salad

SERVES 4

Clem's Homegrown Popcorn, from a small producer in Castle Rock, Minnesota, has inspired my devotion for several years now. It's not widely available, so I stock up when I'm passing by Greg's Meats on U.S. Highway 52, the route to southeastern Minnesota trout waters—another kind of foraging. A recipe sent to me by Clem Becker's daughter-in-law, Cindy Plash, prompted me to develop my own version. For your next share-a-dish event, I bet you'll be the only one bringing popcorn salad. Made with nice sharp cheddar and sweet-tart apple, this is delicious, addictive.

   2 cups popped popcorn
   1 rib celery, chopped (about ¾ cup)
  ½ medium red onion, chopped (about ¾ cup)
   1 small apple, peeled, cored, and cut into ½-inch pieces
   3 ounces sharp cheddar cheese, grated (about 1 cup)
  ½ cup mayonnaise

Mix it all up. Let it set a bit. Enjoy.

A Weed Is Not a Plant . . .

. . . it is an idea about a plant.

I had a community garden plot in south Minneapolis a few years ago, and one day in May I received an e-mail from the garden's dreaded "Weed Police." As warnings from this feared group go, this one was quite pleasant. Presented in the form of a limerick, it began

There was a young fellow from Leeds,

Who lost sight of his flourishing weeds . . .

I wasn't sure what Leeds had to do with it. I think it was just there for the rhyme. At any rate, I was urged to take care of those weeds, which eight inches in height did exceed. I planned to plant tomatoes and squash in that plot, and the May weather had been chilly, so I'd been waiting for warmer days. After the warning I promptly stopped over to assess the weed situation for myself.

The garden was messy but not too much of an eyesore. I had most of the weeds out in an hour and a half. While I weeded, I realized that some of what I was tossing in the compost pile could be considered not weeds but salad. The young lamb's-quarters were delicious, more flavorful than most lettuce. With such a cool spring, there were also plenty of palatable dandelion greens. And the pansies that had migrated from a neighboring plot were very pretty, but in this context they were weeds—except that they could also be garnish for that wild salad.

In my home garden, the dill plants reseed reliably, providing welcome early flavor in salad dressings and sauces. But they come up so widely and indiscriminately that when I'm ready to plant those beds, they shift from herb to weed. As I put together the salad described below I threw in some dill, just to add to the ontological complexity.

As for the chives in the dressing, those are just chives. They stay where they're meant to be and don't cause anyone any trouble or epistemological worry. They are simply good citizens of the allium sort.

———————————

SPRING LAMB'S-QUARTERS AND DANDELION SALAD WITH CHIVE-DILL DRESSING (*a salad of plants both intentional and unintentional, occurring where they should and shouldn't, depending*)

If you have a garden, you have lamb's-quarters. If you have a yard, you have dandelions—unless you poison them with chemicals, in which case do not attempt to gather salad from your yard. Needless to say, only collect wild edibles from an area you know to be chemical free.

Gather sufficient young, tender lamb's-quarters and not-too-bitter young dandelion greens. Look for dandelions that have not yet sent up a flower stalk. Taste a leaf. You will know if it is too bitter.

Make this dressing, or another one you like:

> Glug, glug of grape seed oil or an oil of your choice
>   (flavorful walnut oil, perhaps?)
> Splash and a half red wine vinegar (or white; it doesn't
>   matter that much)
> Drizzle honey
> Pinch salt

Grind grind grind fresh pepper

Chopped chives and dill, as much as you please (or another
   herb that you like)

Make a salad. Decorate with a few pansy blossoms, if you have them and
you feel like it. Or use other edible flowers—violets, nasturtiums, marigold.
Not all flowers are edible, however. Consult a good guide to wild edibles.

WARM SALAD OF WAX BEANS *with Caramelized Shallots and Blackberry Vinaigrette*

SERVES 2

The sweetness of the blackberry jam is balanced by the tartness of the vinegar and the richness of the oil. Sometimes a little sweetness is nice, anyway. You could use green beans, but yellow wax beans lend a lovely hue.

   1 tablespoon butter
   2 tablespoons olive oil, divided
   2 shallots, cut into ¼-inch-thick slices (about ⅔ cup)
   Salt and freshly ground black pepper
   2 large cloves garlic, sliced thin
   2 good handfuls (about 24) yellow wax beans, rinsed
      and stem ends trimmed
   1 tablespoon blackberry jam (or Quick Wild Berry Sauce, p. 208)
   1 tablespoon blackberry or red wine vinegar
   1 teaspoon fresh thyme leaves, optional

In a medium sauté pan over medium heat, melt the butter and add 1 tablespoon of the olive oil, the shallots, and a good pinch of salt. Cook over medium heat until the shallots start to wilt; reduce the heat to medium-low and cook gently, stirring often, for 10 to 12 minutes, until the shallots are very soft and just starting to brown. Add the garlic and continue to cook for 2 minutes more.

Meanwhile, blanch the beans for 3 minutes in boiling water. Drain and set aside. Mix the jam, vinegar, remaining tablespoon oil, a good pinch of salt, and a few grinds of black pepper.

Warm Salad of Wax Beans with Caramelized Shallots and Blackberry Vinaigrette

Add the beans to the pan and cook, stirring, for 1 minute. Add the vinaigrette, mix thoroughly, and transfer everything to a serving dish. Taste and adjust for salt. If you like, sprinkle fresh thyme leaves over the salad. ◡

✳ WATERCRESS BACON SALAD

SERVES 2

Watercress is usually the first wild food to brighten our plates in late winter or early spring. I find it in springs that bubble up at the base of limestone cliffs along the streams where I fish for trout. It's important to gather it near the source and to take only the upper leaves and tender stems, not disturbing the roots. Cultivated watercress is available at co-ops year-round.

> 1 slice thick-cut bacon, cut crosswise into ¼-inch pieces
> Juice of ¼ lemon (about 2 teaspoons)
> Salt

1 small bunch watercress, leaves and tender stems
    (about 2 cups), rinsed
  ¼ small red onion, shaved
  1 clove garlic, sliced very thin
  ¼ cup grated aged Wisconsin white cheddar

In a small skillet, gently cook the bacon. When it is lightly browned, remove it from the pan and set aside. Squeeze the lemon juice into the pan drippings and add a pinch of salt. Divide the cress between 2 salad bowls and distribute the onion and garlic slices and bacon over top. Drizzle with the drippings-lemon dressing, top with cheese, and serve. ⌒

✳ ROASTED BEET SALAD *with Aioli and Walnuts*

SERVES 4

A pretty composed salad. The fun is in messing it up.

  4 medium beets (about 12 ounces), any color
  ½ cup walnuts, coarsely chopped
  ½ cup aioli (p. 221)
  ½ small red onion, sliced thin
  Freshly ground black pepper
  Coarse sea salt

Preheat oven to 425 degrees. Scrub the beets and roast them, covered, in a baking dish for 40 to 60 minutes, until tender when pierced with a paring knife. As soon as they are cool enough to handle, peel and quarter the beets and then cut them into ½-inch slices.

Heat a dry skillet over medium heat and add the walnuts. Toss them in the pan until brown in spots and quite fragrant.

Divide the beets among 4 plates. Dollop a generous tablespoon of aioli on the beets, and sprinkle with chopped walnuts and a few slivers of onion. Finish with a grind of black pepper and a sprinkle of coarse salt. ⌒

Roasted Beet Salad with Aioli and Walnuts

* THE WINE-DARK BEETS

SERVES AT LEAST 6

A dramatic presentation of toothsome roots, though perhaps not exactly Homeric. A good way to use up those not-quite-empty bottles of wine. It does not matter if the wine if not quite at its prime, and combining vintages is fine. Buckwheat honey's earthiness goes well with beets, but other flavorful honey will work, too.

1½ pounds beets—an assortment of red, golden, and chioggia
  makes a beautiful salad
¾ cup red wine
1 tablespoon buckwheat honey
1 clove garlic, minced
3 tablespoons canola, sunflower, or grape seed oil
1 teaspoon red wine vinegar
Salt and freshly ground black pepper

Fresh soft goat cheese (chèvre), optional
Fresh dill or tarragon, chopped, optional

Preheat oven to 400 degrees. Scrub the beets and roast them, covered, in a baking dish for 40 to 60 minutes, until tender when pierced with a paring knife. As soon as they are cool enough to handle, peel and cut them into bite-size pieces. I like a jumble of irregularly sized pieces, especially if I have a variety of beet colors.

In a small saucepan bring the wine to a boil and reduce to 3 tablespoons. Watch very carefully toward the end, or it will all boil away in a flash. Add the honey, garlic, oil, vinegar, a couple pinches of salt, and a few grinds of black pepper; mix well. Pour the dressing over the beets and allow the flavors to blend for at least 30 minutes, or make the salad a day ahead, refrigerate, and bring to room temperature before serving.

For a pretty first course salad, serve a portion of beets topped with a tablespoon of goat cheese and a sprinkle of chopped fresh dill or tarragon.

The dressing also produces a beautiful slaw when tossed with shredded green cabbage, carrots, and red onion.

* PICKLED RED CABBAGE WEDGES (RECONSTRUCTED COLESLAW) *with Blue Cheese Dressing*

SERVES 4

Chefs are all the time "deconstructing" dishes; I think it's about time some things got reconstructed. This winter salad brings a lot of crunch and interest to a dark day's plate.

¼ large head red cabbage
1½ cups warm water
1 tablespoon salt
2 tablespoons sugar
½ cup plus 1 tablespoon cider vinegar, divided
1 small clove garlic, minced
2 teaspoons minced shallot

1½ ounces blue cheese, crumbled (about ⅓ cup)

¼ cup heavy cream

2 tablespoons mayonnaise

2 teaspoons minced carrot

1 cornichon (p. 226), minced (about 1 tablespoon)

Freshly ground black pepper

Leaves stripped from 2 sprigs fresh thyme

Cut the cabbage into 4 wedges, taking care to keep the leaves connected at the root end. Combine the water, salt, sugar, and ½ cup of the vinegar in a pan large enough to hold the cabbage. Bring the brine to a boil, add the cabbage, and simmer for 3 minutes. Remove from heat and let the cabbage cool in the brine. Set aside 2 tablespoons brine. Combine the remaining ingredients (garlic through thyme), including reserved brine and the remaining tablespoon cider vinegar, and mix well. Divide the cabbage wedges among 4 plates and swipe a spoonful of dressing across the middle of each. Serve with bread to mop up extra dressing.

✳ CELERY ROOT WATERCRESS REMOULADE

SERVES 4 AS A FIRST COURSE OR SIDE DISH

Céleri rémoulade goes green with the addition of watercress to the dressing. For a light, elegant first course, serve an assiette de crudités—a dollop each of celery root remoulade, Sambal Carrot Slaw (p. 41), and Roasted Beet Salad with Aïoli and Walnuts (p. 47).

1 medium celery root (9–12 ounces untrimmed, 6–8 ounces trimmed), peeled (see tip, p. 197)

⅛ teaspoon salt

Juice of ¼ lemon (about 2 teaspoons)

2 tablespoons mayonnaise

2 tablespoons goat milk yogurt (or sour cream)

Handful watercress, stems and all, finely chopped (⅓–½ cup)

Freshly ground black pepper to taste

Grate the celery root medium to coarse, or shred it on a mandoline. Toss the shreds with salt and lemon juice, and let sit 20 minutes. Add the mayonnaise, yogurt, cress, and a few grinds of pepper. Mix well and let sit at least 30 minutes before serving. ⌒

* SNAP PEA SALSA

MAKES 1 GENEROUS CUP

Serve with tacos, maybe Walleye Tacos (p. 165), or use as a bed for grilled fish. You could add some herbs to the mixture: basil, parsley, mint, or cilantro.

- 1 cup sugar snap peas, strings removed, cut into ¼- to ⅓-inch pieces
- 2 green onions, the white and some of the green, cut into ¼- to ⅓-inch pieces
- Juice of ¼ lemon or lime (about 2 teaspoons)
- 2 tablespoons sunflower or olive oil
- 2 pinches salt
- ½ teaspoon sambal oelek chili paste, or 1 small hot chile, finely chopped

Combine all ingredients and mix well. Let stand for 20 minutes or, refrigerated, up to 1 day before serving. ⌒

* EASY CREAMY DRESSING

MAKES ½ CUP

Sort of a cheater's ranch dressing, this one is good on any salad of hearty greens—frisée or escarole or a mix of lettuces and young turnip, kale, or mustard leaves.

- 2 tablespoons mayonnaise
- 2 tablespoons half-and-half, heavy cream, buttermilk, or yogurt
- 2 tablespoons cider vinegar
- 2 tablespoons finely chopped red onion
- 1 small clove garlic, minced

Pinch salt

Freshly ground black pepper

Pinch cayenne, dash hot pepper sauce (Tabasco), or smidge
sambal oelek chili paste, optional

Combine all ingredients and mix well. The dressing will keep for several
days in the fridge.

Variations: Pickled Ramp Dressing: Substitute pickled ramps (p. 224) for
red onion and 1 tablespoon ramp brine for 1 tablespoon of the vinegar.

Creamy Herby: Mix in chopped dill, tarragon, chives, parsley, chervil, or basil, or any combination thereof, to taste. ⌒

✳ THE NATIVE BAY TOMATO CLOCK

*Native Bay was a wonderful restaurant on the shore of Lake Wissota in Chip-
pewa Falls, Wisconsin, where chef-owner Nathan Berg produced inspired
seasonal cooking in a rather out-of-the-way place. Alas, like many innovative
endeavors, this one truly was before its time and closed its doors after just a
couple of years.*

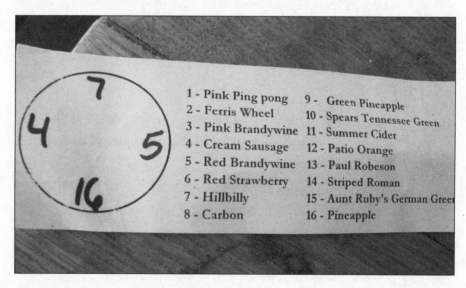

*The Native Bay
tomato clock*

1 - Pink Ping pong
2 - Ferris Wheel
3 - Pink Brandywine
4 - Cream Sausage
5 - Red Brandywine
6 - Red Strawberry
7 - Hillbilly
8 - Carbon

9 - Green Pineapple
10 - Spears Tennessee Green
11 - Summer Cider
12 - Patio Orange
13 - Paul Robeson
14 - Striped Roman
15 - Aunt Ruby's German Green
16 - Pineapple

This dish is a pure steal from a salad we were served at Native Bay. A plate of four slices of perfectly ripe heirloom tomatoes came to the table accompanied by the slip of paper pictured opposite. Each tomato had its distinctive flavor, and tasting them side by side was revelatory. "Cooking" doesn't get simpler than this, or more compelling. I don't know if anything else accompanied the tomatoes. You could add just a sprinkling of sea salt, perhaps a wee dash of olive oil; I wouldn't do more.

When the tomatoes are at their prime, get yourself to the garden or farmers market and select a variety of heirloom tomatoes, maybe seven or eight kinds in different shapes and colors. Then make up your own tomato clock. Serve a different selection to each of your dinner guests. Lively discussion and plate sharing will ensue. ⁓

In the Garden

Gardening is the alchemy of soil and sun, creating from dross not gold but green, a far better bargain. Sun and soil, just add water. It all starts here, starts and ends here: this is the engine that drives the planet, drives all life. So when you take up gardening, that's a lot of responsibility. Well, it is if you hold the cosmic view, which gardeners sometimes do, but mostly their eyes are on the ground, where their feet, likewise, are firmly planted. I think that one of the surest paths to contentment in life is to take up gardening. The gardeners I know tend to keep things in proper perspective, to understand how things work; it's not that they're Pollyannas, or even necessarily optimists, but they encounter nature on a personal, intimate level. They see its benefices and its terrors and learn to deal with both sides, and it settles them. They garden for the sake of that relationship with Our One Great Mother. And for the Brandywines.

A masseuse friend once told me—and I'm sure she was sincere, not just self-promoting—that the world would be a better place if everyone got a massage at least once a week. The world also would be a better place if everyone had a garden. When you tend a piece of earth, you are distracted from becoming consumed by life's petty demons, and so if someone should come around and try to embroil you in some scheme or grudge or other nonsense, you can say, "Excuse me and thank you very much. I have my own row to hoe."

It strikes me that a guy who lived for a while by a pond in Massachusetts a couple centuries ago said something quite like this. Well, he and a few others, I imagine. It might seem a repudiation that we have to keep saying it, while the world keeps hurtling hellward in handbasket, but I don't think so. Just because wisdom isn't heeded doesn't mean it isn't wise. There would be no literature if people always did what they ought to. Is this a reasonable exchange, endless strife for interesting reading? Discuss.

I've been gardening since I was a kid, though I've never actually considered myself "a gardener." Back in those simpler times of the last third of the previous century, gardening was something you did, not something you were. We were more humble about who we were then, I think, less insistent about our almighty Personal Identity. Anyway, every spring, Memorial Day weekend, my parents planted a vegetable garden, and my brother and I helped. We had compost piles, a couple of chicken-wire cylinders into which we put kitchen scraps and yard waste which gradually decomposed, feeding the tomatoes planted around the outside. We also grew green beans and wax beans, lettuce, radishes, and a kind of squash called vegetable marrow, which I gather is popular in England and Canada (where my parents were from). My father would take half-moon slices of marrow, dip them in egg and then in bread crumbs, and fry them in butter. It was about the only thing that got fried at our house—where food generally was baked, broiled, or boiled—and it was delicious.

We had a big rhubarb plant in the back corner of the garden, and on hot summer days we would sit in the shade on the stoop by the back door, bare feet on the cool concrete, and eat those crimson stalks raw, dipping them into a bowl of sugar. I can taste that sweet-tart-astringent explosion of flavors even now. Perhaps a sense of gourmandise was born there.

In my early teens, I took a small plot in the northwest corner of our backyard and planted a wildflower garden in the shade of a big blue spruce. From a nearby woods I transplanted (quite illegally, in some cases) nodding trilliums and wild ginger, Solomon's seal true and false, jack-in-the-pulpit, yellow bellwort, delicate wood anemones, and rue. From a nursery, with my mother's help, I purchased lady's slippers, one "showy"—the Minnesota state flower—and one yellow. The yellow one did well; the showy took years to bloom, was magnificent for a season, and perished the next. I marvel a bit, forty years down the road, at the seriousness and dedication that the younger me showed in establishing and tending that garden (but then, I was the kid who formed the North Eden Drive Nature Club and forced Becky Goetze and Timmy Morin to memorize facts from the *Audubon Nature Encyclopedia:* "Latin name for the beaver? *Castor canadensis!*").

Eventually, other interests prevailed, weeds crept in—poison ivy had entered my Eden with the Virginia bluebells—and buckthorn seedlings got a foothold. But even decades later there were still traces, some of that wild ginger with its felted leaves and shy coral flowers, a patch of lily of the valley fragrant in the springtime.

Now I garden for food. And to garden. I grow vegetables, and I take an extremely tempered approach, which to others might seem messy and lazy, but only because it is. To call my lazy-man's technique anything like Zen would be pushing it, but it does seem that in paying attention to process I've discovered that the less I do, the more I get. I try to work with nature. Attempting to impose one's will upon nature is clearly futile, though still popular—just look at all those shiny, green, weedless lawns across America, and our waterways becoming equally, alarmingly green. That will be my final curmudgeonly comment (for this essay, anyway).

I do many of the usual things that dedicated organic gardeners do: keep a compost pile, mulch a lot, plant heirloom vegetable varieties, start my own tomatoes and other long-season vegetables from seed. When the first couple of waves of weeds arrive, I pull them. And come midsummer, when all the plants have sorted themselves out, have decided which ones want to stick around, then I give them a good, deep watering, mulch heavily with half-finished compost, and deliver a garden valedictory: "Well, my leafy friends, we've come to a turning point. I won't be seeing you as often as I have in the past. But I've given you an excellent start, all the advantages in life; now you're on your own. Good luck. I'll check in from time to time to see how you're doing, and to eat you." My plants say little in response, struck dumb with emotion they must be.

So then I just happily harvest for the rest of the year. I may plant some late greens and radishes if I think of it, to carry my harvesting deep into the fall. I keep leeks, carrots, and beets in the ground as long as I can. The timing can become a kind of Russian roulette game with the weather—will that mid-November cold snap mellow to a late Indian summer or settle in to deep winter? I have, more than once, found myself knocking icy clumps of soil from frozen roots as I pry them out with a garden fork. With every frigid clunk I tell myself, *You are so dumb.*

But there are benefits to the lackadaisical approach, to letting nature have its way in my garden. Volunteer plants are the main one. Every year we benefit from offspring that have freely seeded from last year's plants. We harvest the product of intentional accidents, to coin an oxymoron. Fennel, lettuce, dill, and arugula are most common. Every year we gather lovely leaves of purple mustard, and I have not planted purple mustard in ages. The compost pile sometimes yields a small crop of potatoes, and one year, a bounty of squash.

When sweet dumpling and delicata squash sprouted in the compost bin, I was not surprised: I had tossed one of each that had come to no good in the

November turnips

root cellar. What did surprise me was the unknown squash that emerged on the opposite side of the yard, in packed earth in the shade of an arborvitae tree. I let it be, never thinking it would amount to anything; what would I gain from pulling it?

For weeks it hardly seemed to grow at all, until it crept out far enough to catch a little sun, and then it went crazy. What turned out to be buttercup squash grew with astounding speed from late July onward. The buttercup marched eastward from the west side of the yard while sweet dumpling and delicata vined to the west from their roothold by the eastern fence, and it was my very fond hope that before a hard frost they would meet in the middle, a volunteer vegetable version of the transcontinental railroad. But the sweet dumpling had trouble surmounting the garden fence and then succumbed to powdery mildew, which eventually shriveled the buttercup's leaves as well. Still, we filled a tote with squash free from nature, the genius of letting it be.

Now, to the down side: because I'm slothful about thinning and plant too densely to start with, a warm, wet summer turns my garden into a slug farm. Once a critical population of slugs is established, you're done. They are disgusting, incredibly destructive, and, at least in my mind, indicative of a moral flaw in the gardener; I'd really just rather not think about them.

The habit of gardening yields benefits in all seasons: in winter, when the seed catalogs start to arrive in the mailbox, a sense of hope (we must always have snail mail, if only to facilitate the arrival of seed catalogs); in spring, at plant sales or swaps, a sense of community, comradeship, and seasonal ceremony; in summer the table shows the sweet rewards of the spring's labor, and autumn's last efforts fill the pantry and root cellar, a satisfying denouement.

Though I still don't think of myself as "a gardener," in looking back I find that keeping a garden has been one of the most constant threads in my life. From those childhood gardens to community plots kept in my days as a young adult urbanite to more permanent ones tended as a homeowner, I've always tried to stay involved with raising food from seed. And now I have a sizable chunk of rural property that offers almost too many opportunities for growing things, without enough amenities, currently, to take advantage of them.

I didn't used to ponder concepts like the alchemy of sun and soil. It was enough to think about just getting some tomato seeds into potting mix and remembering to water. But if you do something long enough, many of the technical aspects become second nature, so that your mind is freed to consider larger implications. Baking bread has also yielded the same result for me. Beginning bakers are afraid of and confused by yeast. If their dough doesn't rise, they think they've done something wrong, and they probably have: they haven't waited long enough. The analogy is particularly apt, as both bread and gardens involve coming to understand living, growing things and processes that can be helped along but really must not be rushed.

So, the virtue of patience may be the key lesson that gardening teaches, patience and attention. An August tomato is worth the wait, and so is a November leek. Not having everything all the time makes each thing sweeter when you taste it. Veering toward platitude, but I think again of that brilliant taste of rhubarb dipped in sugar and note that one very important thing a gardener cultivates is memory.

3

SOUPS

* BIG BORSCHT

SERVES 6 GENEROUSLY

I put up a few jars of fermented vegetables each late summer and fall (see p. 222)—sauerkraut, beets, kale. I also like to do a gallon of mixed vegetables—green beans, cauliflower, carrots, onions—in a liquid brine. An assortment of these tangy vegetables gives unique character to this soup.

If you don't have home-fermented veggies, substitute good store-bought sauerkraut or pickled beets for the fermented component. The Russian classic takes on a bright, down-home accent with the addition of a bit of maple syrup and cider vinegar.

8 cups liquid, a combination of meat and/or vegetable stock, mushroom soaking liquid, and water

6 cups chopped fresh vegetables (beets, carrots, parsnips, potatoes, turnips, onion)

1 cup chopped fermented vegetables (or sauerkraut or pickled beets)

12 ounces cooked meat: pork shoulder, smoked sausage, ground beef, or chicken, optional

3 large cloves garlic, coarsely chopped

1 ounce dried mushrooms, soaked and chopped, optional

1 teaspoon salt, or to taste

1 small dried red chile, crumbled, optional

2 tablespoons maple syrup, or to taste

1 tablespoon cider vinegar, or to taste

Freshly ground black pepper to taste

Sour cream

Fresh herbs—dill, tarragon, parsley, or thyme

Combine everything but the sour cream and herbs in a large soup pot. Simmer for 30 to 45 minutes, until the vegetables are tender. It's best when it sits, refrigerated, for a day or two. Adjust the sweet/sour balance with additional syrup and vinegar before serving, and also taste and adjust for salt. Serve hot, topped with sour cream and garnished with fresh herbs. A good whole-grain sourdough wheat or rye bread is almost required. ◡

✳ CHESTNUT BUTTERNUT SOUP

SERVES 4 AS A FIRST COURSE, 2 AS A MAIN DISH

This might seem like kind of a nutty soup, but the butternut is actually squash. With three kinds of soft sweetness, from chestnuts, squash, and potatoes, it's a comforting study in close contrasts. The garnishes of goat milk yogurt, croutons, and crunchy sage leaves all create vivid interplay with the velvety soup.

1½ tablespoons unsalted butter

1 small leek, chopped

1 shallot, chopped

Salt and freshly ground black pepper

4 ounces shelled chestnuts, coarsely chopped (about ⅔ cup; see p. 143)

6 ounces butternut squash, peeled, cut into 1-inch cubes (about 1½ cups)

1 medium (5- to 6-ounce) potato, peeled, cut into 1-inch cubes

3 cups unsalted or low-sodium chicken stock

1 cup water

4 fresh sage leaves, plus more to fry for garnish, optional

Toasted croutons

Goat milk yogurt or sour cream

In a large saucepan over medium heat, melt the butter and add the leeks, shallots, and a pinch of salt. Cook gently, without browning, until very soft and fragrant, 6 to 8 minutes. Add the chestnuts, squash, potato, stock, water, 4 sage leaves, a few grinds of pepper, and ⅛ teaspoon salt. Bring to a boil and then simmer, partly covered, for 40 minutes. Remove the sage leaves. Crush the vegetables with a potato masher or slotted spoon.

Now a decision: serve it chunky, smooth, or semi-smooth? I prefer the third option: remove a cup of the soup, mostly solids, and puree it in an electric blender or food processor and then return it to the pan.

Serve with croutons of good sourdough bread crisped in a skillet with a bit of butter or olive oil. Fry a few fresh sage leaves along with the croutons if you like, for an extra garnish. Dollop on a tablespoon of goat yogurt or sour cream just before serving. ↲

CREAM OF CHANTERELLE AND SWEET CORN SOUP

SERVES 4

When the golden chanterelles start to pop up in our local woods in midsummer, good eating ensues. I often find black trumpet mushrooms when I'm gathering chanterelles; they make a striking garnish on the pale yellow soup.

12 ounces chanterelles, trimmings reserved

3 cups unsalted or low-sodium chicken stock

4 cups water

2 shallots, minced, divided

1 small leek, white and light green parts finely chopped, trimmings reserved

3 ears corn, shucked

2 tablespoons unsalted butter

¼ cup white wine or dry vermouth

Salt

1¼ cups heavy cream

Black trumpet mushrooms, optional

Chervil or parsley, optional

Cream of Chanterelle and Sweet Corn Soup

Take a little less than one-third of the chanterelles—the less nice-looking ones—and chop them fairly small. In a stockpot or large saucepan, add the chopped chanterelles to the combined stock and water, along with any trimmings from the other chanterelles. Add half the minced shallot and the chopped outer layers of the leek—the part you would otherwise throw away. With a mandoline or very sharp knife, strip the kernels from the cobs and set aside. Add the stripped cobs to the pot and simmer briskly, covered, for 30 minutes. Strain the stock, pushing on the mushroom pieces with the back of a spoon; discard solids. You should have about 6 cups stock; add water if you're short.

Slice the remaining chanterelles thin, to about ¼ inch. Melt the butter in a large saucepan or Dutch oven and add the remaining shallots, leeks, and chanterelles; cook gently until everything is wilted. Add the corn kernels, wine, stock, and a couple pinches of salt. Simmer, covered, for 20 minutes.

Add the cream and simmer for 5 minutes. Taste and adjust for salt. If you have some black trumpet mushrooms, cook them briefly in a bit of butter and use to garnish the soup. Make it pretty with a leaf of chervil or parsley, if you like, and serve hot. ⌒

✳ NETTLES AND WILD RICE SOUP
SERVES 4

Handle the nettles with care—or with gloves. Once they're exposed to heat, the sting is gone. Without the smoked fish or Gouda, it's a hearty, comforting soup; with those additions, it becomes a wholly satisfying meal.

⅓ cup wild-harvested, hand-parched wild rice

3 cups water, divided

Salt and freshly ground black pepper

3 packed cups young nettles (wood or stinging), leaves and tender stems

2 tablespoons unsalted butter

1 small carrot, chopped

1 rib celery, chopped

1 medium onion, chopped

2 cloves garlic, minced

3 cups unsalted or low-sodium chicken stock

1 medium (5- to 6-ounce) potato, peeled and cut into ½-inch cubes

½ cup heavy cream

6 ounces smoked trout or whitefish, flaked, optional

¾ cup grated smoked Gouda, optional

Combine the wild rice and 1 cup of the water in a small saucepan with a pinch of salt. Bring to a boil, cover, reduce the heat to very low, and cook for

15 minutes. Remove from heat and let sit for 10 minutes. Drain excess water. Set rice aside.

Rinse the nettles in several changes of water to remove all grit and then blanch them for 30 seconds in boiling water. Drain and chop; set aside. In a Dutch oven or large saucepan, melt the butter. Add the carrot, celery, onion, and a pinch of salt, and cook over low heat, without browning, for 4 to 5 minutes. Add the garlic and cook for 1 additional minute.

Add the stock, remaining 2 cups water, wild rice, potato, nettles, a few grinds of pepper, and ⅛ teaspoon salt. Bring to a boil and simmer, covered, for 30 minutes. Add the cream and simmer for 5 minutes. Taste and adjust for salt. If desired, add smoked fish to each bowl at the table, and sprinkle on grated cheese. ⌒

※ **CARROT APPLE SOUP**
SERVES 4 AS A FIRST COURSE, 2 AS A MAIN DISH

At first sight and first bite, this soup might remind you, strangely, of canned tomato soup reconstituted with milk. The sweet carrots and tart apples create a remarkable trompe-bouche *tomato effect. Subsequent spoonfuls, however, should dispel that comparison. Two fine garnishes are offered here: use one or the other or both—your choice.*

- 1 shallot, sliced
- 4 (⅛-inch) slices fresh ginger root, plus 1 teaspoon minced fresh ginger root
- 2 cloves garlic, crushed, plus 1 small clove garlic, minced
- 1½ teaspoons canola or grape seed oil
- 3½ cups unsalted or low-sodium chicken or vegetable stock
- 3 medium carrots, peeled and chopped (about 1½ cups)
- 2 tart apples, peeled, cored, and chopped (about 1½ cups)
- 3 sprigs thyme or 1 teaspoon dried
- Salt and freshly ground black pepper
- ¼ cup heavy cream

Garnish 1
2 tablespoons olive oil
½ small carrot, finely shredded or grated
1 small shallot, thinly sliced

Garnish 2
1 clove garlic, minced
½ cup grated Swiss or Gruyère cheese

In a large saucepan or Dutch oven, cook the shallot, sliced ginger, and crushed garlic in the oil over medium heat until they take on a good bit of color, 4 to 5 minutes, watching carefully so that the garlic does not burn. Add the stock and bring to a boil. Reduce heat and simmer, partly covered, for 30 to 40 minutes. Strain the stock and return it to the pan; discard the vegetables. You should have at least 2½ cups liquid; add stock or water if you're short.

Add the carrots, apples, thyme, minced ginger and garlic, ¼ teaspoon salt, and a few grinds of black pepper. Bring to a simmer and cook, covered, until the carrots are very tender, 40 to 45 minutes. Let the soup cool for 10 minutes and then puree it in an electric blender or food processor until it is very smooth. Run the mixture through a food mill or pass it through a sieve back into the saucepan. Add the cream and taste and adjust for salt. Reheat gently just before serving.

Garnish 1: Heat olive oil in a small saucepan. Add the carrots and cook until they become shrunken and a bit brown. Remove carrots from the oil and set aside. Add the shallot to the oil and cook until lightly browned. Remove shallot from the oil and set aside, reserving the oil. Place a spoonful of the carrots on top of each bowl of soup and a spoonful of shallots on top of that. Drizzle some of the olive oil around the edges.

Garnish 2: Place ½ teaspoon minced garlic and 2 tablespoons grated cheese in the bottom of each bowl. Carefully ladle hot soup into the bowls. The aromas of garlic and cheese released by the soup will make your guests swoon.

Sorrel Shallot
Potato Soup

✳ SORREL SHALLOT POTATO SOUP

SERVES 2

Sorrel is a hardy perennial plant that survives even our harsh northern winters. It's best in the spring—and so welcome, too, as one of the first green sprouts—or in fall after a couple of frosts. Its tart, lemony bite may be an acquired taste, but once you have it, you'll never lose it.

  2 tablespoons unsalted butter
  2 large shallots, finely chopped
Salt
  2 large cloves garlic, sliced thin
  2 cups unsalted or low-sodium chicken stock
  2 medium (5- to 6-ounce) waxy potatoes, peeled, quartered,
     and cut into ½-inch slices
  1 whole clove
  1 allspice berry
  1 bay leaf

6 whole black peppercorns

1 small bunch sorrel leaves, thick stems removed, chopped
(about 2 cups), plus more for garnish

In a medium saucepan, melt the butter over low heat and add the shallots and a pinch of salt. Cook gently, without browning, until the shallots shrink and become translucent, about 5 minutes. Add the garlic and cook for 3 minutes. Add the stock, potatoes, clove, allspice, bay leaf, peppercorns, and ⅛ teaspoon salt. Bring to a boil over medium heat and simmer gently for 30 minutes, until the potatoes are very tender. Add the sorrel and simmer for 10 minutes. Remove and discard whole spices. Taste and adjust for salt. Serve garnished with a chiffonade—fine ribbons—of sorrel leaves. ◡

✳ FALL COLORS SOUP

Not all the appealing colors of autumn are found in the turning trees. The soup pot can take on its own sort of autumn splendor.

A big heavy soup pot, with a nice pool of olive oil. Sweat down a leek, an onion, perhaps some shallot if it's handy. Add a chopped Anaheim chile, a rib of celery or some fennel stalk, a diced carrot. A couple of large cloves of garlic, chopped, are next. Now cabbage (choose red for color, green if that's all you have) and some kale or turnip or mustard greens (or, surprise: radish tops or carrot greens)—use a lot, they really cook down. Some biggish chunks of butternut or another squash can go in now.

Add water and/or stock to fill about two-thirds of the pot. Salt now, by the pinch, tasting as you go. You'll be surprised by the sort of savor you can get out of a mess of vegetables. Once you're getting your simmer on, toss in diced pattypan squash or zucchini, green beans, snap peas, a potato.

Now you can hardly stir it, but there's always room for more: some shell beans, oh, a beet and its greens, a tomato or two, even a green one—these are all welcome. Thyme is required in a soup like this; I'm pretty much addicted to that herb, I think. Sage is a fine flavor for fall, too. Simmer until you're ready to eat. A drizzle of olive oil, a piece of grilled bread, a scatter of grated cheese. It got quiet in here—no sound but the slurping. ◡

SMOKED TROUT AND WILD RICE CHOWDER
(*Homage to Mel's*)

SERVES 4 AS A FIRST COURSE, 2 AS A MAIN DISH

A trip to the North Shore of Lake Superior requires a stop for smoked fish along the way. Mel's smokehouse in Knife River was always my favorite spot. "We Smoke Our Own" was Mel's motto, and they smoked the best brown-sugar lake trout around.

Twenty-plus years I'd been stopping at Mel's. Then in the summer of 2007—a beautiful day, the lake brilliant blue, an air of vacation giddiness prevailing—we pulled into Mel's small gravel parking lot just across the Scenic Drive from the rocky beach. Getting out of the car, I noticed . . . something wrong. Just a weird feeling, until I glanced up at the sign to see that Mel's was no longer Mel's. "North Woods Candy Kitchen," the new sign read. I entered the shop in a daze. All the same fixtures were there, but where once the cases had held smoked trout, whitefish, herring, and ciscoes, now there were truffles, turtles, chocolates, and pralines. One of the women behind the counter was someone I recognized from Mel's. I asked her what had happened, and she said they just closed down, decided to call it quits. The work was hard, the season short, the winters long. She looked like she was going to cry—maybe because I looked the same way.

So it was the end of an era. Things change, sure, but they never had seemed to on the North Shore. I concocted this chowder in homage to Mel's. You can use whatever kind of smoked fish you like. Nowadays when I make it, I like to "smoke my own." You'll find a recipe for Maple-Basted Smoked Lake Trout Fillets on p. 184. Also: look for wild-harvested, hand-parched wild rice. It's pricier than the farmed stuff but worth the cost.

⅓ cup wild rice (see headnote), rinsed

2 slices (about 3 ounces) thick-cut bacon, cut crosswise into ¼-inch pieces

1 medium onion, chopped

1 small carrot, finely chopped

1 rib celery, finely chopped

1 tablespoon flour

2 cups unsalted or low-sodium chicken or fish stock, divided

1½ cups milk

¼ cup heavy cream

1 medium (5- to 6-ounce) potato, cut into ½-inch cubes, rinsed

1 bay leaf

2 sprigs fresh thyme or pinch dried

Salt and freshly ground black pepper

5 ounces smoked trout (lake, brown, or rainbow), in large flakes
(a generous cup)

Dash hot pepper sauce (Tabasco), or to taste

Combine the wild rice and 1 cup water in a small saucepan. Bring to a boil and then simmer, covered, for 20 minutes. Remove from the heat and let sit 5 minutes. Drain excess water and set rice aside.

In a Dutch oven or large saucepan, gently cook the bacon until it has rendered most of its fat. Remove the bacon from the pan and set aside. Add the onion, carrot, and celery and cook gently until the onion is translucent, about 5 minutes. Sprinkle in the flour. Cook for 1 minute, stirring. Add 1 cup of the stock and stir until smooth. Add the remaining cup stock, mixing well.

Combine the milk and cream in a bowl and ladle in some of the hot stock to temper it—keep it from curdling—and then add to the pot.

Add the potato, bay leaf, thyme, ⅛ teaspoon salt, and a few grinds of pepper, and simmer for 15 minutes. Add the wild rice, bacon, trout, and a dash or two of hot pepper sauce, and simmer for 15 minutes. Remove and discard bay leaf and thyme stem. Taste and adjust for salt. Serve.

✳ SUMMER LAKE TROUT CHOWDER

SERVES 4 AS A FIRST COURSE, 2 AS A MAIN DISH

I love chowder, but in the summer a thick, creamy soup isn't usually what I want to eat. This lighter version uses fresh and smoked lake trout, but fresh and smoked whitefish, often easier to find, would also be delicious. There are two wild-foraged ingredients here—wood sorrel and wood nettles. Garden sorrel can stand in for the wood sorrel, and spinach for the nettles.

If you like, save the skin from the lake trout and crisp it in a little oil in a skillet or directly over the coals of a grill. Use the crisp skin as a garnish.

4 cups water

4 new potatoes, cut into ¼-inch slices

2 medium carrots, sliced on a long diagonal

1 medium onion, sliced thin

Salt

Good handful very young green beans, stems trimmed

1 small zucchini or yellow squash, cut into small cubes

6 ounces fresh lake trout or whitefish, skinned (see headnote),
   cut into 2 chunks

3–4 ounces smoked lake trout or whitefish, flaked (about ⅔ cup)

40 leaves wood nettle, rinsed, blanched, chopped, or a good cup
   spinach leaves, chopped

½ cup wood sorrel leaves, or a few small garden sorrel leaves,
   plus more for garnish

3 tablespoons heavy cream

2 teaspoons butter

12 cherry tomatoes, halved

In a large saucepan, combine the water, potatoes, carrots, and onion with 2 good pinches of salt. Bring to a simmer and cook briskly for 15 minutes. Add the green beans and zucchini and simmer for 5 minutes. Add the fresh and smoked fish and simmer for 5 minutes. Add the nettles (or spinach) and sorrel and simmer for 3 minutes.

Divide the fish and vegetables between 2 shallow soup bowls, leaving the broth in the pan. Add the cream and butter to the broth, taste and adjust for salt, and then bathe the fish and vegetables in this lightly rich broth. Garnish with cherry tomatoes and additional wood sorrel leaves. Serve.

BUTTERMILK, APPLE, AND CUCUMBER GAZPACHO

SERVES 4 TO 6 AS A FIRST COURSE, 2 AS A MAIN DISH

Soup and salad in one bowl: perfect on hot summer evenings.

  1 apple, peeled and cored
  Lemon juice
  Salt
  1 large Asian or English cucumber, or 2 small, thin-skinned
     slicing cucumbers
  1 shallot, chopped
  1 large clove garlic, chopped
  2 yellow roma tomatoes, or 1 larger yellow or ripe green tomato,
     like Green Zebra, chopped
  ½ cup water
  1 cup buttermilk
  ¼ cup heavy cream
  2 teaspoons each chopped fresh chervil (or tarragon) and mint,
     plus additional leaves for garnish

*Buttermilk,
Apple, and
Cucumber
Gazpacho*

1 flavorful red tomato, peeled, seeded, and chopped

Croutons of sourdough bread, toasted in a skillet with
a little butter or olive oil

½ cup watermelon, cut into small cubes, optional

Cut half the apple into ¼-inch cubes and mix with a bit of lemon juice and a pinch of salt in a small bowl; set aside. Coarsely chop the other half and set aside. Peel and seed half the cucumber and cut it into ¼-inch cubes. Toss with a pinch of salt in a small bowl and set aside. Coarsely chop the remaining cucumber—no need to peel or seed—and place it along with the coarsely chopped apple in the bowl of a food processor or in an electric blender. Add the shallot, garlic, and yellow or green tomatoes. Add water and ⅛ teaspoon salt. Process for about 1 minute, until liquefied. Run the mixture through a food mill or pass through a sieve; discard any solids. Stir in the buttermilk. Refrigerate for at least 1 hour or up to 2 days.

Just before serving, add the cream, chervil, and mint. Taste and adjust for salt—but don't overdo it; I like this soup a little undersalted, to let the fruit and vegetable flavors really shine.

Ladle the soup into individual bowls and serve with the garnishes: apple, cucumber, red tomato, croutons, optional watermelon, and chervil or mint leaves.

* WINTER TOMATO SOUP *with Fried Bread*

SERVES 2

One good thing about the dry indoor air of a northern home in winter: bread does not tend to mold. One bad thing: it dries out faster than you can say pain au levain. *One good thing about quality dried bread: it can be saved in a number of ways. Even a loaf well past its prime can be turned into something delicious.*

6 ounces stale bread, preferably a whole-grain sourdough type—
something with character

¼ cup olive oil

2 cloves garlic, crushed

1 small onion, sliced

12 ounces (1½ cups) Oven Tomatoes (p. 229, or substitute
   excellent canned tomatoes)

1½ cups unsalted or low-sodium chicken or vegetable stock

Salt and freshly ground black pepper to taste

Grated Gruyère cheese or similar

If your bread is merely stale, cut or tear it into chunks roughly 2 inches square. If the bread is very, very dry, break it into large pieces and toss it in a bowl with ¾ cup water. Cover with a plate and let stand for 2 hours, mixing occasionally. If the bread soaks up all the water before softening, add a bit more. If it gets waterlogged, squeeze it like a sponge to extract excess water. When you have something workable, cut or tear it into 2-inch pieces.

Heat the olive oil in a heavy skillet and add the bread and garlic. Fry until the bread is nicely golden and a bit crisp. Remove and discard garlic. Add the onion, cooking until it wilts a bit. Remove the bread from the pan, dividing it between 2 soup bowls.

Add the tomatoes, stock, salt, and pepper to the skillet. Simmer for 10 minutes. Taste and adjust for salt. Spoon the tomatoes over the bread and top with cheese. Serve. ⌒

✳ LAST LEG DUCK CONFIT AND CHICKPEA SOUP
SERVES 2

There once was a soup, Portuguese Kale Soup from Provincetown, from a very good cookbook, The Country Gourmet, *that I made a lot and really loved, but I never seemed to have all the specified ingredients on hand, so it came to be known in our house as Portuguese Substitution Soup, always a different variation. One night, planning a typical substitution soup adventure, I went in the fridge for some pork shoulder to make into sausage. There on the middle shelf was the last leg of duck confit from a batch I had made a couple weeks earlier. Light bulb, done deal: Last Leg Duck Confit and Chickpea Soup. Excellent on a cold winter night. Substitutions encouraged.*

1 piece Duck Leg Confit (p. 149), drumstick and thigh

4 cups unsalted or low-sodium chicken stock

1 small onion, halved and sliced

½ carrot, finely chopped

4 large leaves kale, any kind, stems removed, leaves chopped

3 cloves garlic, chopped

1 potato, peeled and cut into ½-inch cubes

1 cup cooked chickpeas

½ small dried red chile, seeds removed

2 whole cloves, or pinch ground cloves

2 allspice berries, crushed

⅛ teaspoon salt

Stale baguette slices, optional

Grated cheese, Swiss or Gruyère or as you please

Freshly ground black pepper to taste

Remove the skin from the duck and set aside. Pull the meat from the bones and shred with your fingers or chop coarsely; set aside. Place the duck bones in a large saucepan and add the next 11 ingredients (stock through salt). Bring to a boil and simmer for 20 minutes, until the potatoes are tender.

Optional tasty garnish: while the soup is simmering, crisp the duck skin in a small sauté pan over medium heat, turning a couple of times. Coarsely chop the crisp skin and set aside. In the fat rendered from the skin, brown the baguette slices.

Add the confit meat to the soup and simmer for 10 minutes. Remove and discard bones and whole spices. Spoon the soup into wide bowls, float a baguette slice in the soup, and sprinkle grated cheese and freshly ground black pepper over top. Garnish with chopped crispy skin if desired.

Wild Mushroom Cookery Basics

I'll first dispense with the question of whether one should wash mushrooms by quoting one of my food heroes, Jacques Pépin: "It's not that you don't *wash* mushrooms," Jacques said on one of his *Today's Gourmet* shows, "If they are *dirty*, then you *wash* them." Wild mushrooms frequently are dirty and must be washed. I can't think of anything that will dampen my enthusiasm for eating more than the grating of sand between my teeth. Brush off loose dirt or leaf matter and trim any really dirty bits, and then quickly rinse, drain, and pat the mushrooms dry. Any water they do absorb will boil off in the cooking.

Which leads to another main point: most edible wild mushrooms must be thoroughly cooked to avoid gastric upset. Oyster mushrooms and giant puffballs are the two exceptions I can think of, but to my taste they're better cooked, anyway.

Wild mushrooms are sought after because they have strong and distinctive flavors, and the simplest preparations are often the best way to showcase them. With morels and chanterelles, two singular and frequently abundant mushrooms of our region, my favorite preparation is a simple sauté in good unsalted butter or olive oil. Garlic is a near constant in mushroom recipes, but with morels and chanterelles, I generally leave it out, adding instead a bit of chopped shallot or sweet onion. Once the mushrooms are wilted and barely browned, I serve them beside fresh, soft-scrambled eggs or a plain French-style omelet. Gilding the lily just a bit, I may finish off the cooking with a splash of white wine, sherry, or brandy, a moistening ladle of chicken stock, and/or a slosh of heavy cream. This can be napped on the eggs or served on toast.

Thyme accompanies the gutsy flavor of wild mushrooms very well; rosemary and sage are other good choices.

Late summer often brings ample harvests of chanterelles, hen of the woods, sulfur shelf, hedgehog, and others. As the evenings cool, we don't mind turning on the oven to roast a chicken, like so:

ROAST CHICKEN WITH WILD MUSHROOMS

SERVES 4

Separate a whole chicken into leg quarters, wings, and breast on the bone (save the back for stock), or use an already cut-up chicken. Brush the chicken with olive oil, season it with salt and pepper, and squeeze on some lemon juice. Place it in a roasting pan atop a bed of fresh thyme. Lay more thyme sprigs over the chicken. Roast at 450 degrees for 25 minutes. Remove the breast from the pan and set aside. Lower the heat to 375 degrees and roast for 15 minutes more. Now to the roasting pan add 2 cups roughly chopped or shredded wild mushrooms (it's usually hen of the woods and chanterelles at my house), a quartered onion or a chopped-up leek, a sliced carrot, a few whole cloves of garlic in their jackets (I don't mind garlic here, as it becomes so sweet in the roasting). Return the breast meat to the pan and roast for 30 minutes, or until the chicken is done and quite brown and all the mushrooms have cooked down into crazy-umami-schmaltz-and-pan-juices wonderfulness. Serve out the chicken and vegetables, remove and discard the thyme, and deglaze the pan with a splash of wine and a half cup water or stock. Reduce by half and finish with a spoonful of butter. Serve.

* * *

Hen of the woods is one wild mushroom that serves workhorse duty in my kitchen. These large, firm-fleshed fungi can grow to great size: I've brought home twenty pounds or more in a day, in just five or six specimens. A happy trait of hens is that they are easily preserved in a couple of ways. One: freeze them, raw, in manageable pieces. Take out and thaw as needed—and if you forget to take them out in advance, you can generally cut or shred them partly frozen. They'll give off some liquid as they thaw; just blot with paper towels and carry on. Two: oven hens. Pull the mushrooms into bite-size shreds, toss with olive oil, salt and pepper, and some thyme, and roast in a 375-degree oven until they've reduced in volume and become a bit brown. Freeze in half-cup portions in plastic sandwich bags to use in pastas, to top a pizza, or to chop into an egg dish or a pan sauce for steak, chops, or fish.

Morels dry well if you have more than you know what to do with; this has never been a problem for me.

With chanterelles, the only satisfactory way I've found to preserve them is to briefly sauté them and then freeze them—I imagine the oven method, as for hen of the woods, would work, too. Drying is often recommended for chanterelles, and it's true that they dry well; however, in my experience, they don't un-dry very well. The texture of rehydrated chanterelles is extremely chewy, and the flavor can be bitter. The best thing to do is enjoy them while they're fresh, in season, at the height of flavor.

That goes for just about everything else, too.

4

VEGETABLE
MAINS

✳

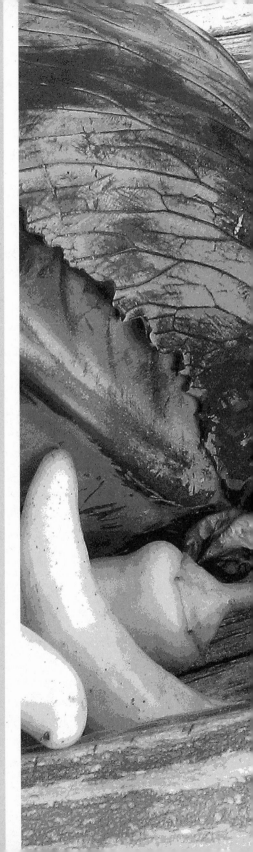

FRITTATA TIMES TWO

What a versatile dish is the frittata (or is this more of a Spanish tortilla? I'm not really sure). It can be served hot, cold, or at room temperature, at dinner, brunch, lunch, or cocktail time. It travels well, for a forager's lunch. Make it ahead up to the point of adding the cheese and then finish it under the broiler just before serving. As a final touch, perhaps a drizzle of olive oil and a sprinkling of chopped fresh herbs.

You will need a 10- or 11-inch nonstick ovenproof skillet with a lid for both frittatas.

HEN OF THE WOODS AND POTATO FRITTATA

SERVES 4 AS A FIRST COURSE OR BRUNCH DISH, 2 AS A MAIN COURSE

- 5 tablespoons olive oil, divided
- 2 slices stale sourdough bread, crusts removed, cut into ½-inch cubes (about 1½ cups)
- 1 medium (6-ounce) potato, peeled, cut into ⅓-inch cubes, rinsed, drained, and patted dry
- Salt and freshly ground black pepper
- 5–6 ounces hen of the woods mushrooms, coarsely chopped (a generous cup)
- 1 small onion, chopped
- 3 cloves garlic, chopped
- 5 eggs
- ¼ cup milk
- 1 teaspoon fresh thyme leaves or ¼ teaspoon dried
- ½ cup grated Asiago cheese

Heat 1 tablespoon of the olive oil in a nonstick, ovenproof skillet and add the bread cubes. Cook, stirring, over medium heat until they are brown and crisp. Remove them from the pan to a large bowl. Add 1 tablespoon of the olive oil to the skillet and then add the potatoes and cook over fairly high heat, tossing frequently, until they are lightly browned and tender firm, 5 to 6 minutes. Season with a good pinch of salt; add the potatoes to the bread cubes. Add 1 tablespoon of the olive oil to the pan and then add the mushrooms and onion and a pinch of salt. Cook, stirring, for 5 to 6 minutes, until the onions are translucent and the mushrooms lightly browned. Add the garlic and cook for 1 minute. Add the mushroom mixture to the bread and potatoes. Wash and dry the skillet.

Combine the eggs and milk in a mixing bowl with a couple pinches of salt and a few grinds of pepper. Add the bread-potato-mushroom mixture and thyme to the eggs and mix well.

Place the skillet over medium heat, and add the remaining 2 tablespoons olive oil. When the oil is shimmering, pour in the egg-vegetable mixture. Reduce the heat, cover, and cook for 10 minutes or until the eggs are set. Meanwhile, preheat the broiler. Sprinkle the cheese over the frittata and place it under the broiler for a minute or two, until the top is browned and the cheese is melted. Serve.

CHICKPEA, PICKLED RAMP, AND CARROT FRITTATA

SERVES 4 AS A FIRST COURSE OR BRUNCH DISH, 2 AS A MAIN COURSE

With their Middle Eastern associations, I don't tend to think of chickpeas as a midwestern product, but in fact they're grown in southwestern Minnesota by Whole Grain Milling Co., my favorite flour producer. They lend a wonderfully distinctive texture to this frittata. If you don't have pickled ramps, substitute a shallot or three or four green onions.

    4 pickled ramps (p. 224), sliced thin
    ½ cup cooked chickpeas
    3 tablespoons olive oil, divided
    1 small carrot, peeled and grated
    1 small potato, peeled and grated
    5 large eggs
    ¼ cup milk
       Pinch ground cloves
       Pinch ground allspice
    ¼ teaspoon crushed dried red chile
       Salt and freshly ground black pepper

½ cup grated Swiss, Gruyère, or Gouda cheese
Chopped fresh herbs, optional

Rinse the pickled ramps in two changes of water. Drain well and pat dry with a paper towel. Place the chickpeas in the bowl of a food processor and pulse a few times to roughly chop them (or crush them by pressing them between two cutting boards).

Heat a nonstick, ovenproof skillet and add 1 tablespoon of the olive oil. Add the ramps, carrot, and potato, and cook over medium-high heat for 6 to 8 minutes, until the carrots and potatoes are a bit soft. Remove from heat.

In a large bowl, beat the eggs together with the milk. Add the chickpeas, cloves, allspice, chile, 2 pinches of salt, and a few grinds of black pepper. Add the sautéed vegetables and mix well.

Place the skillet over medium heat, and add the remaining 2 tablespoons olive oil. When the oil is shimmering, pour in the egg-vegetable mixture. Reduce the heat, cover, and cook for 10 minutes or until the eggs are set. Meanwhile, preheat the broiler. Sprinkle the cheese over the frittata and place it under the broiler for a minute or two, until the top is browned and the cheese is melted. Serve garnished with chopped fresh herbs if desired.

✳ TARTIFLETTE
SERVES 2 AS A MAIN COURSE, 4 AS A SIDE DISH

This elementally satisfying combination of potatoes, cream, bacon, and cheese tastes as if it must have been served for generations in shepherds' huts and alpine chalets. But in fact, tartiflette is a dish of relatively recent origin, an invention of the people who make Reblochon, a washed-rind cow's-milk cheese from the Savoy region of France. You can't exactly make this dish in the United States because Reblochon is a young raw milk cheese, banned from these shores. A pasteurized "Reblochon" is sold as "Fleur des Alpes," or you may find something similar from a local cheesemaker. I like a Wisconsin cheese from the Crave Brothers called Les Frères (or, in a smaller format, Petit Frère). A combination of brick and Swiss would be good, too.

This is a great simple supper after an autumn hike or winter afternoon ski. A green salad and some crusty bread make it a meal.

- 4 medium russet or Yukon gold potatoes (about 1½ pounds), peeled and quartered
- 3 slices (about 3 ounces) thick-cut bacon, cut crosswise into ½-inch pieces
- 1 small onion, chopped
- ¼ cup dry white wine
- 1 clove garlic, crushed
- Salt and freshly ground black pepper
- ½ cup heavy cream
- 8 ounces "Reblochon," or a combination of Swiss and brick or other flavorful, melty cheese, cut into ½-inch slices

Cook the potatoes in boiling water until tender but not falling apart, 15 to 20 minutes. Drain and let cool and then cut into ½-inch slices. Set aside.

Heat oven to 375 degrees. In a small skillet over medium heat, cook the bacon until most of the fat has rendered. Remove the bacon and set aside. In a couple tablespoons of bacon fat, cook the onion until tender and translucent, about 5 minutes. Add the wine to the onions, and immediately remove the skillet from the heat.

Rub the inside of a 6-cup gratin (oval baking) dish or 9-inch pie plate with crushed garlic; discard the garlic. Add the potatoes, bacon, and onion-wine mixture to the dish. Season with a couple good pinches of salt and a few grinds of pepper, and pour the cream over top. Lay cheese slices atop potatoes. Bake for 20 minutes or until the cheese is nicely melted and the top is brown. Serve hot.

BUCKWHEAT CRÊPES *with Creamed Leeks and Gruyère*

SERVES 4

I like to serve this dish with Fresh Tomato Sauce (p. 230).

½ cup all-purpose flour
½ cup buckwheat flour
¼ cup whole wheat flour
  Salt
½ cup milk
1¼ cups water, divided
4 large eggs
3 tablespoons unsalted butter, plus more for crêpe pan
6 medium leeks (about 2 pounds), rinsed well, white and light
  green parts cut crosswise into ¼-inch slices (5–6 cups)
1½ cups heavy cream
  Freshly grated nutmeg
6 ounces grated Gruyère cheese (about 1½ cups)

Stir together the flours and a pinch of salt in a mixing bowl. Whisk in the milk and ½ cup of the water, and then whisk in the eggs one at a time. Cover and set aside for 1 to 2 hours. The batter should be quite thin, pouring easily off a spoon. If it seems thick, add a little more water.

Heat an 8-inch crêpe pan (or nonstick skillet) over medium-high heat. Add a little butter and then wipe the pan with a paper towel. Add ¼ cup batter and turn the pan to coat the bottom. Cook for 30 seconds, flip the crêpe, and cook for 30 seconds. Transfer the crêpe to a plate and set aside. Repeat; this will make a dozen crêpes.

Melt 3 tablespoons butter in a large skillet; add the leeks, ½ teaspoon salt, and the remaining ¾ cup water. Cover and cook gently until the leeks are very soft, about 40 minutes, adding water as needed. When the leeks are soft and most of the water is gone, stir in the cream and a few gratings of nutmeg and cook for 5 minutes. Remove from the heat.

Preheat oven to 300 degrees. Divide the leeks among the crêpes and add a small handful of cheese to each. Roll up the crêpes, enchilada style, and place in a baking dish. Bake for 15 minutes, until the cheese is melted. Serve hot.

✱ SUGAR BUSH BEAN POT

SERVES 4 AS A SIDE DISH, 2 AS A MAIN COURSE

This dish gets its name from the bit of maple syrup that flavors it; our home-smoked bacon is also cured with maple syrup, reinforcing the theme. You can garnish this dish with savory meats to make it more cassoulet-like: nestle duck confit or browned sausages into the beans for the final hour of cooking.

- 1½ cups (10 ounces) dried cannellini beans
- 1 medium onion, chopped
- 2 cloves garlic, chopped
- 1 small carrot, chopped
- 4 ounces slab bacon, cut into ½-inch cubes (save the rind if you have it)
- 2 teaspoons grainy or Dijon-style mustard
- 3 tablespoons maple syrup
- 1 bay leaf
- 1 small dried red chile, halved
- 1 teaspoon fresh thyme leaves or ¼ teaspoon dried
- Freshly ground black pepper
- ½ teaspoon salt
- Duck confit or browned sausages, optional
- 1 cup bread crumbs tossed with a bit of fat (soft butter, duck fat, bacon fat, or oil), divided

Place the beans in a saucepan with water to cover by an inch or so. Bring to a boil and cook at a fast simmer for 10 minutes. Remove from the heat, cover, and let sit 15 minutes or more. Drain the beans, discarding the cooking water. (This step improves the digestive qualities of the beans.) Return the beans to the pot, cover with water, bring to a boil, and simmer for 20 to 30 minutes, until al dente. Drain the beans, retaining 2 cups cooking liquid (add water to make 2 cups if necessary). Preheat oven to 275 degrees.

Stir together the beans and cooking liquid with next 11 ingredients (onion through salt) in a lidded baking dish or Dutch oven. If you have the bacon rind, place it on top of the mixture. Bake, covered, for 1½ hours. Increase the oven temperature to 325 degrees and remove the lid. Add a little more water if the beans are becoming dry. Add browned sausages or duck confit if you like.

Top the beans with half the bread crumbs. Bake, uncovered, for 30 minutes, and then push the bread crumb topping into the beans and sprinkle the remaining bread crumbs over top. Bake until crumbs are golden and the beans are tender, about 20 minutes more. Remove bay leaf. Serve piping hot, with a little extra drizzle of maple syrup, if you like. ⌒

✳ GRILLED RATATOUILLE
SERVES 4

This grilled version of the Provençal classic adds the appeal of smoke and char—and keeps you out of a hot kitchen. Serve as a side dish with grilled meat or chicken or over grilled country bread with grated cheese as a vegetarian main course.

Onions,
peppers, and
tomatoes on
the grill

2 medium eggplants (about 2 pounds), cut into ¾-inch slices

1 onion, quartered through root end to hold pieces together

2 zucchini, quartered lengthwise

1 leek, halved lengthwise

Olive oil

Salt and freshly ground black pepper

1 large red bell pepper

3 cloves garlic, thinly sliced

4 ripe tomatoes, seeded and chopped

Handful fresh basil leaves

Brush the eggplant, onion, zucchini, and leek with olive oil and season with salt and pepper. Prepare a fire of natural wood charcoal, and grill the vegetables until lightly charred and tender. Grill the bell pepper until the skin is black and blistered. Place it in a covered bowl or paper bag for a few minutes and then scrape off the skin, remove the seeds, and cut the pepper into strips.

Roughly chop all the grilled vegetables. In a large saucepan or sauté pan, heat ¼ cup olive oil. Add the garlic and swirl until it just barely starts to color. Add the grilled vegetables, tomatoes, a couple good pinches salt, and a grind of black pepper. Mix well; remove from heat. Tear the basil leaves and drop them in. Serve. ⁀

＊ STUFFED DELICATA SQUASH

SERVES 4

I like to serve this dish with Fresh Tomato Sauce (p. 230).

2 delicata squash, halved lengthwise, seeds removed

Olive oil

10 ounces lean ground lamb

Salt and freshly ground black pepper

1 medium onion, chopped

1 medium (1-inch diameter) leek, chopped

1 small carrot, finely chopped

1 rib celery, chopped

1 small hot chile, like a Serrano, or ½ jalapeño, finely chopped, or ½ teaspoon sambal oelek chili paste

1 small apple, peeled, cored, and finely chopped

1 medium tart tomato, like a Green Zebra, or 1 underripe red tomato, seeded and chopped

2 cups coarse bread crumbs, divided

1 cup unsalted chicken stock

4–5 large leaves sage, chopped

3 ounces grated Gruyère or Swiss cheese (about ¾ cup)

Preheat oven to 425 degrees. Place the squash halves, cut-side down, in a lightly oiled baking dish. Add ¼ inch water, cover with aluminum foil, and bake for 20 minutes. Remove the foil and bake 10 minutes longer. The water should be gone and the squash soft. Reduce heat to 400 degrees.

Carefully turn over the squash while it's still warm or it may stick. Tent foil over the pan and let the squash cool. Then, being careful not to tear the skin,

Ingredients for Stuffed Delicata Squash

scoop out most of the flesh with a spoon—leave a thin layer of flesh next to the skin. Coarsely chop the squash flesh and set both skin and flesh aside.

While the squash is baking, heat 1 tablespoon olive oil in a large skillet. Add the ground lamb and a good pinch of salt. Cook, stirring, over medium-high heat until the meat is lightly browned and excess moisture has cooked away. With a slotted spoon transfer the lamb to a large mixing bowl. Add 1 tablespoon olive oil to the pan. Add the onion, leek, carrot, celery, chile or sambal oelek, and a pinch of salt. Cook, stirring, over medium-high heat until the vegetables are wilted, about 5 minutes. Add the apple and tomato and cook for 1 minute. Remove from heat.

Add the sautéed vegetables, squash flesh, and 1½ cups bread crumbs to the lamb. Deglaze the pan with chicken stock and then pour the stock into the mixing bowl. Add the sage to the mixture, along with a few grinds of black pepper. Mix well. Taste and adjust for salt. Stir together the remaining bread crumbs with the cheese and 1 teaspoon olive oil.

Lightly oil a baking dish. Lay the squash shells in the dish and divide the filling between them. Sprinkle the cheese-crumb mixture on top, and bake for 25 to 30 minutes, until the top is brown and crusty. Serve.

The whole dish can be prepared a day or more ahead of time, up to sprinkling with the cheese-crumb mixture, refrigerated, and then baked as above.

STUFFED RED KALE LEAVES *with Herb-Wine-Butter Sauce*

SERVES 4

By early fall, the leaves of red kale in my garden are often enormous, like huge reddish green mittens. They stuff very nicely, creating a dish somewhere between stuffed cabbage and grape leaves. Other large leaves, like mustard or collard greens, could be used this way, too. Hen of the woods mushrooms combine wonderfully with the autumnal flavors of lamb, squash, and kale, but you can substitute button or cremini mushrooms if you don't have the wild ones.

Another distinctive ingredient here is sprouted wheat berries, which have a wonderful chewy texture and sweet flavor. They must be started two days ahead; if you haven't built in that lead time, substitute cooked barley.

4 ounces slab or 4 slices thick-cut bacon, cut into ½-inch cubes

1 medium onion, chopped

6 ounces hen of the woods mushrooms, chopped (a generous cup; see headnote)

8 medium red kale leaves, stems removed, leaves rinsed and chopped, plus 8 large red kale leaves—the largest you can find

Salt and freshly ground black pepper

3 cups unsalted chicken stock, divided

1½ cups wheat berries, sprouted for 2 days (or substitute cooked barley)

3 cloves garlic, chopped, divided

1 cup cooked winter squash (butternut or acorn), chopped

3 tablespoons unsalted butter, divided

⅔ cup white wine or dry vermouth, divided

½ cup chopped fresh herbs: a combination of thyme, parsley, basil, chervil, chives, sage

1 medium tomato, peeled, seeded, and chopped

Juice of ¼ lemon (about 2 teaspoons)

In a large skillet, gently render the bacon; as fat accumulates, add the onion and mushrooms. Cook over medium heat until the mushrooms are lightly browned. Add the chopped kale and a good pinch of salt and cook until the kale wilts considerably. Add 1½ cups of the chicken stock, scraping to deglaze the pan. Add the wheat berries or barley, 2 cloves of the chopped garlic, and a grind of pepper; cover and simmer for 15 minutes, checking halfway through to make sure there's still some liquid. Add a bit of water if the stock boils away.

Remove the lid and cook until most of the liquid is gone. Taste the wheat berries: they should be al dente—not soft but not unpleasantly hard. If they're not done, add a bit more water and cook 5 to 10 minutes more. Add the squash and a few grinds of pepper, and mix well. This mixture can be refrigerated for several days.

Preheat oven to 375 degrees. Blanch the larger kale leaves in boiling water for 2 minutes, refresh in cold water, and drain. Cut out the thickest stem at the base of the leaves. Fill each leaf with ⅓ cup vegetable mixture, and roll up like a burrito. Lay the kale rolls in a buttered baking dish. Dot 1 tablespoon butter around the top. Bake for 15 minutes.

Combine ¾ cup of the chicken stock and ⅓ cup of the white wine and pour over the kale. Bake an additional 30 minutes, basting every 10 minutes, and then remove from the oven. In a saucepan or small skillet, melt the remaining 2 tablespoons butter. Stir in the remaining clove chopped garlic, ¾ cup chicken stock, and ⅓ cup wine. Reduce by half. Stir in the herbs, tomato, and lemon juice. Taste and adjust for salt. Serve 2 kale rolls person, napped with sauce. ⌒

Marché Madness

I'm not sure how unusual it is to plan an entire three-week French vacation around a few hours shopping at one particular farmers market on one particular Saturday in October, but I've done it, and I recommend it.

My wife Mary and I first happened upon the Marché des Lices, in Rennes, the capital of Brittany in northwestern France, in October 2003. We'd spent a week touring the Breton countryside and then driven into Rennes to drop off our rental car and catch the train back to Paris. We had some time to kill, so we walked from the rental agency across the river, followed the helpful signs, and wandered into a farmers market–lover's paradise.

It was impressive for its size (third largest in France, we later learned) but even more so for its astounding variety of products. It comprised both indoor and outdoor spaces, including a hall of cheese, a hall of charcuterie, and one for fresh meat products as well as aisle after aisle of pastries, breads, honeys and jams, and cider. At the height of the growing season in this temperate climate, the produce stalls were almost a parody of abundance: piles of leeks, mounds of artichokes, mountains of squash, table after table of apples, pears, and quince. Most amazing of all, especially for a couple of midwesterners, was the seafood plaza, a square city block in size, row upon row of thrillingly fresh seafood, much of it still alive: langoustines, crabs, and lobsters, oysters galore—you could get a half-dozen on the half shell, too, and a glass of Muscadet. There were bins of shrimp still snapping and hopping: choose brown, rosy, or gray. The season's first coquilles St. Jacques, the famed Breton scallops, drew lines of eager shoppers.

It was an inspiring and utterly appetizing spectacle, but we only had time to grab a few things for a picnic on the train and then sprint to the station. We started plotting our return that very day; on our next visit we would have time enough, and a kitchen.

Over the following year we located a *gite,* a rental house on a farm a couple hours' drive from Rennes. We planned day trips in the surrounding area (some of those to other markets) and read up on Breton history. When we reached Rennes after driving out from Paris the next fall, it was a splendid day and the market was bustling. We made the whole circuit once before buying anything so we wouldn't miss some great find. We talked to a baker who was making bread in a wood-fired oven using recipes from the fifteenth century; we stood in line at a goat cheese counter with opinionated fellow shoppers who debated heartily over which cheeses we ought to try. We lunched on the market's fast-food specialty, *galette-saucisse,* a sausage wrapped in a buckwheat crêpe, and a glass of local cider.

Just after noon, we were on our way to the gite with far too much food. It was my first and only time to cook with live langoustines—so good, they alone might have been worth the trip. As much fun as the market experience was, however, the highlight turned out to be meeting our hosts, Chantal and Yves and their young son Maël, sharing a crêpes dinner with them, and pressing apples from their orchard in a hundred-year-old oak cider press. It all started with the market.

Maybe it's not a typical thing to plan a European vacation around grocery shopping, but I know Mary and I aren't alone in our obsession with farmers markets. I've been able to observe the habits of other market-smitten souls up close and at length, in large part because of an odd twist in my career path. By 2003, Mary and I had become so intrigued by farmers markets that we decided to start a small baking business just so we could spend more time at one. This endeavor, which we dubbed Real Bread, a journey of ten thousand loaves all baked in our home kitchen, could itself fill a book. What it showed me—beyond how to make a really good baguette and sourdough loaf—was the passion, the dedication, the outright love that many, many people, on both sides of the market table, feel for their farmers markets.

Our first season as bakers ended with a chilly but jovial Thanksgiving market. There was a break after Christmas, and then the winter market started. "Winter market" as in farmers market in Minnesota, outdoors, in winter. In fact, it was shopping at this very winter market, getting to know some of the vendors there, that had provided the final push to start Real Bread. So I knew it well, but still somehow I thought, "When it's twenty below, are people really going to come out to a windswept frozen parking lot to buy cheese, bread, and frozen meat?" Well, they came. It seemed that a sort of a pact became established between shoppers and vendors—or was it a dare? "You going to be here next week?" asks the shopper. "Oh, I'll be here. You?" "If you're going to be here, I will, too."

After seven-plus years of turning out around a hundred loaves of bread a week from our home kitchen, we turned off the Real Bread ovens. We burned out on the market grind, frankly, but it was all worth it. Most of the people we now call friends we met through the market.

It's difficult to explain the peculiar pull that farmers markets have on some people. Beyond the wonderfully fresh, local food you find there, I think a lot of people go to markets looking for connections—to their neighbors and fellow shoppers, to the vendors. In urban markets, city dwellers find a connection to the countryside. Some people find a taste of a distant home—we earned the devotion of several German transplants through a whole wheat sourdough loaf that reminded them of the bread they loved back in Germany. Connections and ritual: the visit to the Saturday market that we fanatics look forward to all week. And then, from a simple level of practicality, since you have to buy groceries anyway, why not buy them at a fun and festive place, where you get the freshest possible food and a chore is transformed into celebration?

In my market-going life before the bread business, I was a pretty faithful, one-market loyalist, but now I've embraced the dissolute life of a promiscuous market-hopper, and I don't think I'll go back. I love big city markets for their variety and energy, but more and more I've come to appreciate smaller country markets. Since I garden and forage for wild foods, there's not really a lot that I need from the market these days, but we still go for the entertainment and the discoveries. Even the smallest setups might hold treasures you'd never find in a market of a hundred stalls. At the tiny Dallas, Wisconsin, farmers market last summer, its first year in existence, I came upon—and devoured—the best doughnuts and root beer floats I've ever had. Beautiful braids of shallots and red onions also came our way from the Dallas market, providing charming kitchen decor and extra savor in our food all winter. This from a market that might have topped out at eight vendors, and two of them, Amish women, barefoot children in tow, arrived in horse-drawn buggies.

At other markets around the western Wisconsin countryside, I've been introduced to the wonderful meat of young goat and locally, organically grown rye flour, Mennonite noodles and pickled eggs, splendid lamb sausage and bison chops. The Menomonie, Wisconsin, market has become a regular Saturday breakfast spot for spicy Hmong sausage, chicken curry soup, pad Thai, and egg rolls (kind of greasy and never quite hot enough, but good just the same). This market sets up on the grass in a small park under spreading oaks. The crystalline notes from a hammered dulcimer sift through the September air. You can travel to Europe to engage in "gastro-tourism," but you can do the same thing in your own backyard and have a wonderful time, no airfare required.

The farmers market devotee might not have quite the connection to the passing of the seasons that the gardener has, but what's missing in intimacy can be made up for by delightful surprise. The gardener's not likely to be astonished, walking out to her plot in the morning—she just knows her rows too well, and familiarity works against surprise. But with each passing week the market-goer picks up his basket with renewed anticipation. Maybe today he'll discover a new kind of heirloom tomato, a crisp and fragrant bulb of fennel, a bouquet-bright basket of chilies, a celery root. There comes a day, after the summer's first full heat, when the market erupts with the scent of basil, and everyone wants to make pesto. The components of summer's best vegetable medley debut a week at a time—first zucchini, then garlic, eggplant, tomatoes, ripe peppers: ratatouille time. The first farmers to arrive with July's sweet corn are hailed as heroes, and in late August the early winter squashes overlap with sweet corn and the tomato glut to remind us that this fresh bounty isn't going to last forever.

There comes a morning in September when everyone arrives at the mar-

Market vegetables

ket in sweaters. The vendors shuffle their feet and chafe their hands—they've been here since before dawn (at less highly regulated markets, I've seen vendors huddled around open fires in metal buckets). The progression of the season reaches its peak and may then gradually decline into mellow Indian summer or drop off a cliff with a sudden hard frost. More than once I saw a grower open the back of his truck, loaded the night before, assess the produce, and then close the door and drive away without ever setting up, headed home with a load of frozen compost.

More often, though, we are graced with a gentler close to the season, a chance to stock up on some root vegetables for the winter, to grab a bargain in tomatoes for canning, cucumbers for pickling. A sunny October farmers market is one of my favorite places to be. The crowds are down, and it's pleasant to chat with other shoppers or vendors who've been too busy for a word all summer. There's satisfaction in another season passed, another notch of familiarity. The turn of the seasons in a northern clime is never without a hint of melancholy: time goes one way, and we anticipate the news it brings, but we can't help noticing what it has left behind. A sunny October market is a place to experience that sweet melancholy in all its tinged emotions and find a salve for it—lots of good things to eat, so many signs of Great Nature's beneficence, a warm circle of like-minded souls. Nobody knows what winter portends, but it doesn't matter. The sun will soon be slipping south, farther day by day, until a morning like this will seem a dream. One week the last of the corn sells out early, and the next there are only green tomatoes. Brussels sprouts occupy the space fragrant basil once held; apples, not watermelons, are the fruit of choice.

If there's a cabbage or a bunch of mustard greens or kale when the Thanksgiving market rolls around, you'll count yourself fortunate; the best you can really expect is onions, carrots, winter squash, beets. Some market shoppers will keep up the quest through the winter—for meat, cheese, baked goods, preserves—but most are ready to call it a season now. The last farewells are made with gratitude and best wishes, more than regret. Market lovers have in common with baseball fans the sustaining conviction that there's always next year.

* * *

Farmers market aficionados in the Gopher and Badger states should be aware of these: the Minnesota Grown guide, www.minnesotagrown.com, and the Farm Fresh Atlases of Wisconsin, www.farmfreshatlas.org.

5

PASTA
and
PIZZA

*

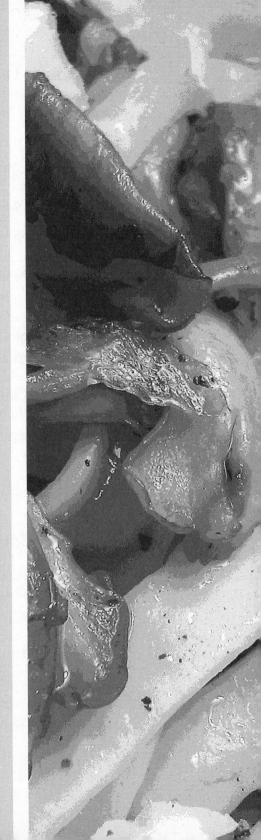

FARMERS MARKET CONFETTI VEGETABLE SAUCE
for Pasta

SERVES 4

This colorful medley, rich-tasting but light, showcases the freshest of market vegetables. Vary the ingredients depending on what's in season. Use snap peas in place of the beans, a small red bell pepper or a bit of hot chile pepper in place of the banana peppers. Go for a nice variety of colors and textures.

- 1 tablespoon olive oil
- 1 tablespoon unsalted butter
- 1 small onion, sliced thin
- 2 sweet banana peppers, halved, seeded, and cut crosswise into ¼-inch strips
- ¼ small head red cabbage, sliced into ¼-inch shreds
- Salt and freshly ground black pepper
- 3 cloves garlic, chopped
- 1 small zucchini, cut lengthwise into ½-inch slices, then ¼-inch strips, then 2-inch pieces
- Handful beans—green, wax, or purple—sliced on the diagonal into 1-inch pieces
- Kernels from 1 ear corn
- ¾ cup unsalted chicken or vegetable stock or water
- ¼ cup heavy cream
- ¾ cup cherry tomatoes, halved
- Handful basil leaves
- 10–12 ounces dried linguine or other pasta, cooked to taste and drained
- ½ cup grated Wisconsin Asiago or other cheese

In a large skillet or saucepan, heat the oil and butter over medium-high heat. Add the onion and cook for 2 minutes. Add the banana peppers, cabbage, and a good pinch of salt; cook for 3 minutes, stirring frequently. Add the garlic, zucchini, beans, and corn and cook for 2 minutes. Add stock or water, and simmer, partly covered, for 5 minutes. Add the cream. Taste and adjust for salt. Cook, uncovered, until the sauce thickens a bit, about 1 minute. Stir in most of the tomatoes, saving a few pieces for garnish. Tear the basil leaves into rough pieces and stir them in.

Serve over linguine or pasta of your choice. Sprinkle with cheese and a grind of black pepper to taste. Leftovers can be chilled and served as a salad. ⌒

✳ FETTUCCINE *with Hen of the Woods, Gouda, and Red Onion*
SERVES 2

A forager's reward; a seasonal delight in all simplicity.

5–6 ounces dried fettuccine or other pasta

1½ tablespoons unsalted butter

1½ tablespoons olive oil

6 ounces hen of the woods mushrooms, shredded
   into ½-by-2-inch pieces (about 2 cups)

Salt and freshly ground black pepper

½ medium red onion, sliced against the rings to ¼ inch

3 ounces aged or smoked Gouda, grated (about a cup), divided

Fettuccine with Hen of the Woods, Gouda, and Red Onion

Prepare the pasta according to package instructions. Meanwhile, heat a 10-inch skillet and add the butter and oil. Add the mushrooms and a pinch of salt. The mushrooms will start to give off liquid; in a couple of minutes, when some of the liquid has evaporated, add the onion to the pan. Cook and stir over medium-low heat for 8 to 10 minutes, until lightly browned.

Add the cooked pasta, ⅔ of the cheese, a good pinch of salt, and a grind of pepper to the mushrooms and onions; mix well with tongs. Serve, garnishing with the remaining cheese.

* LINGUINE *with Guanciale, Potatoes, Kale, and Cheddar*
SERVES 2

Guanciale, cured pork jowl, lends a deeply porky flavor to this pasta dish, which also includes cubes of potato and hearty greens—humble ingredients that create synergy on the plate. Guanciale is available at specialty or Italian butchers: if you can't find it, use pancetta (Italian unsmoked bacon) or good smoked bacon that you've blanched in boiling water for 30 seconds.

The potatoes must be in very small dice: ⅓-inch cubes are perfect. Big chunks will not look nice, will not cook in time, and will taste too starchy, especially as they're combined with pasta.

4–5 ounces dried linguine (or make your own fresh pasta)

2 ounces guanciale, cut into ⅓-inch cubes (see headnote)

1 medium (5- to 6-ounce) potato, peeled, cut into ⅓-inch cubes, rinsed, and patted dry (see headnote)

Olive oil

About 10 leaves kale, stems removed, leaves cut into 1-inch pieces

1 small onion, sliced

2 cloves garlic, chopped

Salt and freshly ground black pepper

2 ounces aged white cheddar, grated (about ½ cup)

Prepare the pasta according to package instructions, reserving ½ cup of the cooking water. In a large skillet with a lid, sweat the guanciale over medium heat until it has rendered most of its fat and is just beginning to brown. Remove it from the pan and set aside.

Turn the heat to medium-high and add the potato, tossing immediately to coat all pieces in fat. Cook, stirring, until lightly browned, 5 to 7 minutes. Remove from the pan and set aside. If the potatoes have absorbed all the fat, add 2 teaspoons olive oil. Add the kale and cook, stirring, until wilted; then add ¼ cup water, turn the heat to medium-low, cover, and steam for 5 minutes.

Remove the lid and increase the heat to boil off any remaining water. Add the onion and cook until it is wilted, 3 or 4 minutes. Stir in the garlic, guanciale, potatoes, and a pinch of salt. Reduce heat to low and allow everything to mellow together.

Add the pasta and reserved cooking liquid to the pan, plus a pinch of salt and a few grinds of pepper and mix well. Serve on warm plates, and sprinkle with grated cheddar at the table.

✳ WILD MUSHROOM LASAGNA

SERVES 8

A splendid, festive dish for when the wild mushrooms are abundant. Serve with Fresh Tomato Sauce (p. 230).

12 ounces dried lasagna noodles

3 tablespoons unsalted butter or olive oil, divided

1 pound wild mushrooms (hen of the woods, chanterelles, oyster, sulfur shelf, puffball, etc.), cut into ½-inch pieces

1 medium onion, chopped

2 large cloves garlic, finely chopped

Salt and freshly ground black pepper

2 tablespoons dry white wine or dry vermouth

2 tablespoons flour

1½ cups unsalted chicken stock

2 cups whole milk

⅛ teaspoon Espelette or cayenne pepper

1 teaspoon fresh thyme leaves or ¼ teaspoon dried

½ cup chopped fresh parsley

8 ounces Gruyère or other melting cheese, grated (about 2 cups)

4 ounces Asiago or other hard cheese, grated (about 1 cup)

Prepare pasta according to package instructions; drain and set aside. In a large saucepan or Dutch oven, heat 2 tablespoons of the butter or olive oil. Add the mushrooms and onion and cook over medium heat until the mushrooms begin to give off liquid. Reduce heat, cover, and cook for 5 minutes. Remove the lid, add garlic and a good pinch of salt, and continue cooking until the mushrooms are lightly browned and tender. (Some wild mushrooms, notably hen of the woods, will remain al dente even after quite a bit of cooking.)

Add the wine and scrape the pan with a wooden spatula to deglaze. Add the remaining tablespoon butter or oil to the pan and sprinkle in the flour. Cook, stirring with a wooden spatula, for 1 minute. Begin adding stock, just a little at first, stirring constantly. As the liquid thickens, add remaining stock and then slowly add the milk, stirring constantly. Add a few grinds of black pepper, the Espelette or cayenne, and the thyme. Gently simmer until the sauce reaches a gravy-like consistency, about 10 minutes. Remove from heat and stir in parsley. This is your mushroom béchamel.

Preheat oven to 375 degrees. In a 9-by-13-inch pan, spread a little béchamel on the bottom. Place a layer of noodles over that. Cover the noodles with one-third of the remaining béchamel and one-third each of the cheeses. Lay down more noodles, half the remaining béchamel, half the remaining cheeses. Add the last of the noodles, béchamel, and cheese.

Bake for 40 minutes, until the top is brown and bubbling. Serve.

* PIZZA

Pizza night is a regular event at our house, and we never let ourselves be constrained by preconceived ideas about toppings. In fact, it's rare that a tomato or a shred of mozzarella finds its way onto one of our 'zas—we tend to follow the lead of the garden, the market, or the foraging basket. The same basic dough goes from pizza to Bacon Onion Tart (p. 108) to Fougasse (p. 109). First the dough and method, and then some topping ideas.

PIZZA DOUGH
MAKES 2 (12-INCH) PIZZAS

This dough uses a poolish, *a yeast sponge that somewhat approximates a sourdough. It requires that you start the dough several hours before making the pizza. If time is short you can skip that stage: double the yeast and proceed to mix, knead, proof, and shape the dough as directed.*

- 1 teaspoon active dry yeast
- 1 cup warm water
- 3 tablespoons whole wheat flour
- ¾ cup unbleached all-purpose flour, plus 1–1½ additional cups
- ½ teaspoon salt
- 1½ tablespoons olive oil, plus extra to brush the crust

In a large mixing bowl, stir the yeast into the water and let stand for 5 minutes. Add the whole wheat flour and ¾ cup of the all-purpose flour and mix well. Cover with plastic wrap and let stand several hours or overnight. This is the poolish.

Stir the salt and 1½ tablespoons olive oil into the poolish. Mix in additional all-purpose flour a bit at a time to make a soft but workable dough. Turn the dough onto a floured surface and knead for a couple of minutes. Let it rest for 10 to 15 minutes; knead again for a couple of minutes, adding flour as needed, until the dough is smooth and elastic. Let rise 1½ to 2 hours at room temperature, or refrigerate and then allow to warm to room temperature an hour before you plan to shape it.

When you're ready to make the pizzas, divide the dough in half, make each half into a ball, and flatten each ball into a disk. With your hands or a rolling pin, gradually extend the dough into a 12-inch round. Don't rush it: when the dough resists, leave it alone for a few minutes—go prep your topping, say, or pour yourself a glass of wine. When you're done shaping, move the dough to a cornmeal-dusted peel (if you're baking on a stone; place the stone in the cold oven before preheating) or cornmeal-dusted baking sheet. Brush the dough lightly all over with olive oil and let it rise for 15 to 20 minutes.

Add the toppings of your choice (suggestions follow) and bake the pizzas in a 525-degree oven for 5 to 7 minutes, until the cheese is melted and the crust well browned. Remove to a wire rack. Let cool for a couple of minutes before slicing.

KALE, APPLE, BLUE TOPPING

You can substitute another dried fruit, like currants or chopped dried figs, for the dried apple–reduction mix.

For each 12-inch pizza:
- 8 medium leaves kale, stems removed, leaves rinsed and spun dry, sliced into ½-inch pieces
- 1 tablespoon olive oil
- ¼ cup chopped dried apples, roughly ⅓-inch pieces (see headnote)
- 1½ tablespoons Maple Syrup–Cider Vinegar Reduction (p. 217)
- 3 cloves garlic, sliced very thin
- 3 ounces blue cheese, crumbled

Toss the kale with the olive oil and let sit for 30 minutes. In a separate bowl, mix the apples with the maple-vinegar reduction and let sit for 30 minutes.

Distribute the garlic slices evenly over the dough. Add the apples and glaze to the kale, and then pile it on top of the dough: it will look like too much, but the kale will reduce dramatically. Dot blue cheese over the top. Bake as instructed above.

*Squash, Leek,
Goat Cheese
Pizza*

SQUASH, LEEK, GOAT CHEESE TOPPING

For each 12-inch pizza:

6 ounces butternut squash, peeled, sliced very thin
   (less than ⅛ inch), slices cut into ½-inch strips
1 small leek, white and light green parts, rinsed and sliced thin
   on the diagonal
1 small dried red chile, seeds removed, crushed
1 tablespoon sunflower, olive, or grape seed oil
Salt and freshly ground black pepper
3 ounces soft fresh goat cheese (chèvre)

In a large bowl, toss the squash with the leeks, chile, oil, a couple good pinches of salt, and a few grinds of pepper.

When you're ready to bake, spread the vegetables on the dough and dot with goat cheese. Bake as instructed on p. 104.

GRUYÈRE, GARLIC, ROSEMARY TOPPING

For each 12-inch pizza:
3 cloves garlic, sliced very thin
Freshly ground black pepper
Fresh rosemary, chopped
4 ounces Gruyère cheese, grated

Distribute the garlic slices evenly over the dough. Grind on some fresh pepper; then sprinkle chopped fresh rosemary to taste. Top with cheese. Bake as instructed on p. 104.

MINNE'SCONSIN MARGHERITA

Rescued from deep-fried ignominy, the cheese curd achieves its rightful destiny—midwestern mozzarella!

For each 12-inch pizza:
1 cup Fresh Tomato Sauce (p. 230)
Handful basil leaves
1 shallot or ½ small red onion, sliced thin
¾ cup white cheese curds, sliced ¼-inch thick

Spread the sauce over the dough. Tear the basil leaves and press them lightly into the sauce. Spread the shallot or onion and cheese curds over top. Bake as instructed on p. 104.

WILD MUSHROOM PIZZA

Most wild mushrooms must be thoroughly cooked: sauté the mushrooms before topping the pizza.

For each 12-inch pizza:
2 tablespoons olive oil
1½ cups (about 6 ounces) chopped wild mushrooms (hen of the woods, chanterelles, hedgehog, or a combination)
½ small onion, chopped
Salt and freshly ground black pepper

2 cloves garlic, chopped

Herbs to taste: thyme, rosemary, or basil, optional

¾ cup grated cheese (Swiss, Gruyère, Gouda, or mozzarella)

Heat the oil in a medium skillet and add the mushrooms, onion, and a pinch of salt. Cook over medium heat for 4 to 5 minutes, until the mushrooms are lightly browned. Add the garlic and remove the pan from the heat. Add pepper and herbs to taste. Spread the mushroom mixture over the dough and top with the cheese. Bake as instructed on p. 104.

RAMPS AND FIDDLEHEADS TART

SERVES 4 AS A MAIN COURSE

A wild springtime pizza. Fiddleheads are the immature fronds of ostrich ferns. I find them in the same damp woods where the ramps grow, along some of my favorite trout streams. Ramps and fiddleheads can be found in co-ops and gourmet shops in the early spring.

6 ounces ramps (10 to 20 depending on size)

2 tablespoons unsalted butter

Salt

½ cup heavy cream

3 ounces fiddlehead ferns (about 1 generous cup; or substitute asparagus blanched and sliced into 1½-inch pieces)

1 recipe Pizza Dough (p. 103)

2 ounces Gruyère, aged Gouda, Parmesan, or other cheese, coarsely grated

Slice the white bulbs and red stems of the ramps on the diagonal into ¼-inch pieces; slice the greens into ½-inch strips. Melt the butter in a sauté pan; add the white and red parts of the ramps and a good pinch of salt; cook over medium heat for a couple of minutes, until wilted. Add the greens and cook 1 minute more. Stir in the cream. Remove from the heat and let cool.

Rinse the fiddleheads well in several changes of water. Blanch the fiddleheads in boiling water for 3 minutes, and then drain and refresh them under cold running water. Drain and set aside.

Preheat oven to 475 degrees. Shape the dough into a roughly 12-by-14-inch rectangle, and transfer to a cornmeal-dusted peel (if you have a baking stone) or cornmeal-dusted baking sheet. Spread the ramps and cream mixture over the dough, covering to within ½ inch of the edge. Distribute the fiddleheads over the top, just like pepperoni. Sprinkle the cheese over top. Let rise 20 minutes.

Slide the tart onto the stone, or place the baking sheet on a middle rack. Bake for 8 to 10 minutes, until the cheese is melted and the crust is brown. Serve.

✳ BACON ONION TART (*Tarte Flambée or Flammekueche*)
SERVES 4

Bacon and cream on a pizza—what's not to like? Alsace, in northeastern France, is the first place I look for inspiration for delicious cold-weather dishes. Adding a couple handfuls Gruyère cheese before baking makes it absurdly rich and very, very good.

    2 teaspoons butter
    2 teaspoons grape seed or canola oil
    3 medium onions, chopped
    ½ cup heavy cream mixed with ½ cup sour cream
    1 large egg
       Salt and freshly ground black pepper
       Freshly grated nutmeg
    1 recipe Pizza Dough (p. 103)
    4 ounces slab bacon, cut into ¼-inch slices and then crosswise
       into ¼-inch pieces
    ¾ cup grated Gruyère cheese, optional

In a large skillet heat the butter and oil. Add the onions and cook gently for 6 to 8 minutes, until softened but not browned. Remove from heat. Mix the cream and sour cream with the egg and a good pinch of salt, a few grinds of black pepper, and a few scrapings of nutmeg. Add the cooked onions to this mixture and mix well.

Preheat oven to 500 degrees. Divide the dough in half, and roll or stretch each half into a rectangle roughly 10 by 12 inches. If you're using a baking stone, place the dough on cornmeal-dusted peels. If you don't have a stone, place the dough on cornmeal-dusted baking sheets.

Spread the cream-onion mixture on the dough, and then sprinkle bacon evenly over the top. Sprinkle the grated cheese over one of the tarts, if you like. Bake for 8 to 10 minutes, until the crust is brown and the cream is bubbling. Serve.

✳ FOUGASSE: PROVENÇAL HEARTH BREAD
MAKES 2 SMALL FOUGASSES

These garnished fougasses are sort of pizzas turned outside-in, the tasty stuff disguised (mostly) within the golden crust. Fougasses are similar to the Italian focaccia, with the distinctive difference that fougasses are usually cut to resemble something like very large pretzels: two traditional shapes are a ladder and a leaf. This dough can also be treated just like focaccia—patted into an oiled baking pan, dimpled, and oiled just before baking.

Prepare a batch of pizza dough using the poolish method described on p. 103, omitting the olive oil and increasing the salt to 1 teaspoon. Add cooled garnishes—wild mushrooms, ramps, or bacon and fat (recipes follow)—before adding the flour to finish the dough during the kneading. Let the dough rise for 2 to 3 hours, and then shape.

For fougasse, prepare a cornmeal-dusted peel (for baking stone users) or cornmeal-dusted baking sheet. Divide the dough in half and pat or roll each half into an oval shape roughly 10 by 6 inches.

For the ladder shape: With a very sharp paring knife or a razor blade, cut four incisions across the width of the dough, starting ½ inch from one side and ending ½ inch from the other. Carefully stretch the dough to open up

Fougasse ladder and leaf

the holes—if you don't, they'll close back up as the dough rises—and place the dough on the peel or baking sheet.

For the leaf shape: Holding one end of the dough oval with one hand, pull out and flatten the other end so that the dough resembles a teardrop. With knife or razor, make a cut starting ½ inch from the narrow end down toward the wider end, stopping about halfway down. Make another, shorter cut just below the first one, to within ½ inch of the bottom. Now make two short, angled cuts on either side of the dough—a crude approximation of a leaf's veins. Stretch open all the cuts and move the dough to the peel or baking sheet.

Allow shaped dough to rise for 45 minutes; preheat oven to 450 degrees. Bake for 18 to 20 minutes, rotating the pan after 12 minutes if the dough is browning unevenly. Remove to a wire rack to cool.

For focaccia: Small focaccia can be baked in a 9-inch square cake pan or a 10-inch ovenproof skillet; large ones in a 9-by-13-inch cake pan or a half sheet pan with a rim. Lightly oil the pan and pat in the dough to nearly fill. Brush the top generously with olive oil. Ten minutes before baking, vigorously dimple the dough all over with your fingertips. Bake small focaccia for 20 to 25 minutes, large ones for 25 to 30 minutes, until browned top and bottom.

WILD MUSHROOM FOUGASSE

2 tablespoons olive oil

4–5 ounces chopped wild mushrooms (hen of the woods, oyster, sulfur shelf, or hedgehog; 1 generous cup)

¼ cup chopped onion

Salt and freshly ground black pepper

2 cloves garlic, chopped

1 teaspoon fresh thyme leaves or ¼ teaspoon dried

Heat the oil in a medium skillet, add the mushrooms, onion, and a pinch of salt, and cook for 3 to 4 minutes, until the mushrooms have shrunken considerably and started to brown. Add the garlic, pepper to taste, thyme, and another good pinch of salt. Transfer to a bowl and let cool. Mix into fougasse as instructed on p. 109.

RAMP FOUGASSE

5 or 6 ramps, bulbs and greens

2 tablespoons olive oil

Salt

Slice the ramp bulbs thin—you should have about ½ cup. Chop the greens. Heat the oil in a medium skillet, add the sliced bulbs and a pinch of salt, and cook for 3 to 4 minutes, until the ramps just begin to brown. Add the greens, stir to wilt them, and then transfer mixture to a bowl and let cool. Mix into fougasse as instructed on p. 109.

BACON FOUGASSE

    4 ounces excellent slab bacon, cut into ½-inch cubes
    1 teaspoon olive oil

In a small skillet, combine the bacon and oil, and cook over low heat until the bacon has rendered much of its fat and started to brown. Remove the bacon from the skillet and drain on a paper towel; reserve 1 tablespoon of the rendered fat. Mix bacon and fat into fougasse as instructed on p. 109.

Natural Appetites

What leaf-fringed legend haunts about thy shape . . . ?
JOHN KEATS

Wild foods have been a part of my diet for enough years now that I don't really make a distinction between wild and cultivated foods anymore. It's not that I can't tell the difference between my vegetable garden and wild nature—well, in truth, that distinction does become a bit blurred at times, when weeds run rampant. But I do know the difference between a ramp and a scallion, nettles and spinach. Once they reach my kitchen, though, they're all the same to me: food, good food, local food. When I look in my refrigerator and see jars of cornichons, pickled ramps, bread and butters, and milkweed "capers," I don't think, "grown food, wild food, bought food, wild food"; no, I think, "pickles." And when I grill a trout or roast a grouse, I'm not doing it to channel my inner hunter-gatherer but rather because these are wonderful, natural meats (but you can't say they're free, or even inexpensive, when you know the price of a good fly rod or shotgun, licenses, and gas; they make the proverbial ten-dollar tomato look cheap).

What I think one gains from the foraging experience, beyond some interesting things to eat (and, of course, the bug bites), is an awareness that all food really comes from nature, even those products of big industrial farms. The sun above and the soil below, that alchemy I mention elsewhere, pertains in every case, though the sterilized soil that grows industrial crops is a perversion, to be sure. But if you were to leave those dead zones alone for even a little while, Great Nature would make things better. At Chernobyl, fungi are purifying radioactive soils and the forests flourish in the absence of humans; this wildlife refuge is now being marketed as a tourist destination.

Seeing how a ramp grows, or a blackberry, I know how things ought to grow and how they ought not. Sam Thayer writes compellingly of looking at a section of woods and seeing not a waste of farmland or suburban real estate, not even an idyllic tableau, but rather a great engine churning out food with unfathomable energy: maple trees and berry patches, burdock roots going down, milkweed shooting up, strawberries hiding near glades of un-shy nettles.

Looking out my window here at Bide-A-Wee this morning, I see a hill covered with box elder trees—those are maples; they'll give syrup. Just over there, under the snow, is my little garden plot; in one part of it last year, I planted lamb's lettuce (mâche), but wild sheep sorrel came up instead. Curious. There's a hawthorn, a plum tree, a raspberry patch, serviceberry. We tend to think there are only a few wild edible plants in forests full of deadly look-alikes, but when you start to examine it up close, something more like the opposite case prevails. What you see depends a lot on how you look at things.

Still, wild foods, especially mushrooms, frankly freak out a lot of people. This need not be so. You're not going to harm yourself or anyone else with wild food if you follow the simple rule of not putting something in your

Chanterelles

mouth unless you're sure what it is. An edible wild mushroom is an edible wild mushroom, period. A lot of people seem to think that when you go mushroom hunting you encounter a forest floor covered with fungi, some deadly and some delicious, and it requires magical intuition to know the difference. This is simply not the case. Nothing else really looks like a morel, a black trumpet, or a hen of the woods. There are dangerous wild mushrooms, sure, but there are dangerous fast food hamburgers and grocery store salad mixes, too. One big difference is that you can easily tell which mushrooms to avoid, while the salmonella salad will knock you out without warning.

Seeing how the ostrich ferns give us fiddleheads each spring, and the staghorn sumacs loads of tart, vitamin-packed berries, I'm drawn more and more to ideas of permaculture: gardening with nature; making nature my garden. Observe more, do less, grow what the soil wants to grow. This notion runs through the concept of local and seasonal eating, too: my habits and appetite have evolved to the point where what I want to eat is what I have to eat. Making something good from what's available is for me far more satisfying than filling my plate with exotic delicacies from afar.

Harvesting wild foods impresses one deeply with the fact that natural foods are in season, and then they're not. Ramps will appear as soon as the ground is barely thawed, and their leaves will wither with summer's first heat. Fiddleheads are even more fleeting, edible as long as the emerging leaves are tightly coiled; with just a little warmth, they unfurl rapidly. At best, you can harvest them for three or four weeks. "The titular delicacy," trout caviar, is available to me for a couple of weeks in September, while the fish are heavy with roe and the season is still open. Quite a difference from the eternal grocery store pink tomato. It's odd that we've come to think of that sort of thing as natural food at all.

When I look back over my life, I see that one constant has been the joy I take in being in the outdoors. Nowadays I fish with a fine bamboo fly rod strung with a French silk line, hunt over two pedigreed pointing dogs, and know the Latin names of more mayflies and fungi than I'd care to admit—but really I'm just a kid running around in the woods, like when I was eight years old in Eden Prairie. The impulse is the same—the joy in the freedom, the beauty, the sense of discovery in every trip afield. Which means that I am either admirably constant in my passions and devotion or a case of arrested development; truly, it's a toss-up.

We hear about children suffering symptoms of "nature deficit disorder"; I've noted the opinion of catch-and-release fishing advocates—fishermen themselves—that we shouldn't kill wild trout because "food comes from grocery stores." These things point to bewildering and perilous tendencies, a way of thinking that takes us out of nature, makes it ever more other. But we are part of nature; we are in nature, always. Maybe eating from nature is a way to realize that again.

6

MEAT

*

Chanterelle and Steak Stroganoff

* CHANTERELLE AND STEAK STROGANOFF

SERVES 2

The aroma of the chanterelles permeates the tangy cream sauce. You can make this with fresh chanterelles or with ones that have been briefly sautéed and then frozen.

> 2 teaspoons canola oil
> 4 teaspoons butter, divided
> 8 ounces steak (strip, rib eye, sirloin), cut
>   into 2-by-1-by-½-inch strips
> Salt and freshly ground black pepper
> 1½ cups sliced chanterelles (5 to 6 ounces)

1 shallot, sliced
2 cloves garlic, chopped
1 cup unsalted chicken or beef stock
½ cup heavy cream
¼ cup sour cream
Rice or buttered noodles
Sweet Buttered Cabbage (p. 190)

Heat a heavy skillet until it is very hot and add 2 teaspoons each of oil and butter. Add the steak and cook, stirring, until browned on all sides, about 4 minutes. Season with salt and pepper. Remove from the pan and set aside.

Add the remaining 2 teaspoons butter to the pan, and then add the chanterelles and shallot. Cook over medium-high heat for 4 to 5 minutes, until the shallots are wilted and the chanterelles lightly browned. Add the garlic and cook 30 seconds. Add the stock, heavy cream, and sour cream; cook until the sauce is reduced by about one-third and coats the back of a spoon. Return the beef and any accumulated juices to the pan and heat through. Add salt to taste.

Serve over rice or buttered noodles with Sweet Buttered Cabbage.

＊ STEAK TARTARE MAISON
SERVES 2

Steak Tartare is seasoned raw beef; buy your beef from a source you trust. My idiosyncratic additions to this classic are Hellmann's mayonnaise instead of the traditional raw egg and sambal oelek chili paste for a nice hot bite. Serve with buttered toast, oven-fried potatoes (see method on p. 192), cornichons (p. 226), a green salad, and red wine.

10 ounces beef (sirloin or top round), sliced ¼-inch thick
1 generous tablespoon finely chopped shallot
1½ tablespoons extra-virgin olive oil
2–3 shakes Worcestershire sauce, or to taste
¼ teaspoon sambal oelek chili paste, or a few shakes hot pepper sauce (Tabasco), or to taste

1 heaping tablespoon Hellmann's mayonnaise
Juice of ¼ lemon (about 2 teaspoons), or to taste
1 teaspoon finely chopped capers (milkweed "capers," p. 225, if available)
2 teaspoons Dijon-style mustard
Salt and freshly ground black pepper to taste

Freeze the beef slices for 15 to 20 minutes to make chopping easier. Working with a couple slices at a time, chop the beef very fine: your best, sharpest knife and all your knife skills come out for this. Mix the beef with the other ingredients and refrigerate for at least 30 minutes.

Divide the tartare between 2 plates and drizzle a little extra virgin olive oil over the meat. Bring Worcestershire, lemon, sambal oelek, salt, and pepper to the table for individual adjustments. ⌒

✳ THE BURGER AND THE BUN

A meat grinder and a piece of flavorful beef chuck are your best friends in the quest for a great homemade burger. And it's a sandwich, after all, so don't neglect the bread: the Cornmeal Honey Butter Bun is an ideal burger pedestal. It makes a tasty sandwich loaf, too.

THE CORNMEAL HONEY BUTTER BUN

MAKES 30 HAMBURGER BUNS

These instructions make a pretty big batch: halve it, or shape as many buns as you want and bake the rest of the dough in loaf form. The hamburger buns are a great base for tuna or chicken salad; we use the hot dog buns for lobster rolls and shrimp burgers, too.

1 cup cornmeal
1 cup boiling water
2 tablespoons active dry yeast
1 cup warm water
1 cup milk
1 cup water

½ cup honey

2 tablespoons salt

8 tablespoons (4 ounces) unsalted butter, melted and cooled

7–8 cups unbleached all-purpose flour

In a small bowl, mix the cornmeal and boiling water and let stand for 15 minutes. In a large bowl, mix the yeast and warm water and let stand for 5 minutes. Stir a bit of the milk into the cornmeal mixture to loosen it, and then add it to the yeast along with the remaining milk, 1 cup water, honey, salt, and butter.

Mix in 4 cups of the flour all at once. Stir in 1 more cup, and then 1 more. The dough should be very sticky at this point. Gradually add 1 more cup flour. You can start kneading in the bowl, or dump the dough onto a floured countertop and knead there. Knead for just a couple minutes, adding flour as required to keep the dough from sticking. Add a little flour at a time, but don't worry about adding too much: the honey and butter make this a sticky dough, but you need to be able to work it.

When you've kneaded it for a couple minutes and it's coming together, leave it alone for at least 10 minutes. It will seem lumpy and awkward at this point, but everything will get smoothed out in time.

After this resting period, knead the dough gently for 3 or 4 minutes, until smooth and firm. Return the dough to the mixing bowl, cover with plastic wrap, and let rise for 2 to 3 hours. It will rise rapidly, dramatically even, especially in warm weather. You can punch it down and let it rise again if you like, or refrigerate it for a while to retard fermentation and then take it out and carry on.

When you're ready to bake, measure out 3 ½-ounce portions for burger buns, 2½ ounces for hot dog buns. A kitchen scale is extremely useful here, but you can wing it knowing that a full batch makes 30 hamburger buns.

For burger buns, shape balls and then flatten them with your palm. Let these little disks rest for a few minutes and then flatten again to circles 3½ to 4 inches in diameter. For hot dog buns, form little baguettes about 5 inches long.

Preheat oven to 400 degrees. Place the dough on parchment-lined baking sheets. You can set the buns pretty close to each other—it's fine and actually quite attractive if they grow together during the final proofing and baking. Let rise 30 minutes.

Bake for 18 minutes, rotating the pans halfway through. Add steam to the oven if you like; I keep a small cast-iron skillet in the bottom of my electric oven, and I toss in a couple of ice cubes at the beginning of baking.

If the buns are browning too fast, reduce the heat to 375 degrees. When the buns are brown top and bottom, slide them off the baking sheet to cool on a wire rack. These freeze well in a plastic zippered bag. Use within 2 months.

THE BURGER

SERVES 2

To grind the beef, I use my KitchenAid's grinder attachment fitted with the coarse blade. The result is definitely coarser than a supermarket grind, and that makes an important difference in the texture: it's loose, almost fluffy, if you can use that word for ground meat. If you don't have a meat grinder or just don't want to bother grinding your own, you may do all right getting freshly ground beef from a butcher you trust.

I always used to favor the grill, and in the balmy months we definitely enjoy a char-grilled burger from time to time, but more often now we do them in a heavy skillet on the stove. The direct contact between meat and metal assures an excellent char, we have control over the heat, and juices remain in the pan to nap over the burgers as we serve.

> 11–12 ounces beef chuck (see headnote)
> Salt and freshly ground black pepper
> Worcestershire sauce
> Soy sauce
> Canola oil

Trim the chuck of gristle or sinews, but leave on a decent amount of fat. Grind it twice through the coarse blade of a meat grinder. To the ground meat add a couple good pinches of salt, a few grinds of pepper, 3 or 4 shakes

Worcestershire sauce, and ½ teaspoon soy sauce. The soy and Worcestershire give extra umami to the flavor and help the patties brown up beautifully in the pan. Mix in the seasonings with your hands quickly and lightly. Form two patties with a quick, deft touch—too much handling will compact the meat and wreck the texture. Refrigerate the patties until you are ready to cook.

Heat a heavy skillet until very hot—cast iron is ideal. Add a thin coat of oil and then the burger patties. Cook for 3 minutes per side for medium rare, 4 for medium. Start out with the heat very high but reduce it slightly after you add the patties. There may be smoke.

Remove the burgers from the pan when cooked to desired doneness, and let them rest while you do up your bun with whatever toppings you enjoy.

GRILLED VENISON *with Red Wine–Blue Cheese Butter*
SERVES 4

Venison is a rare treat in our house. When we're lucky enough to receive a gift of this marvelous meat, I prepare it quite simply. Grilling venison steaks to medium rare highlights the natural qualities of the meat, and the autumnal flavors of blue cheese and sage in the butter complete a seasonal tableau. The wine-cheese butter will improve most any grilled meat or poultry.

> 4 (6-ounce) pieces venison loin or sirloin, about 1 inch thick
> Olive oil
> Salt and freshly ground black pepper

Prepare a hot fire of natural charcoal. Pat the meat dry with paper towels. Brush both sides with olive oil, and season with salt and pepper to taste. Grill to medium rare, no more than 3 minutes per side. Transfer to a warm plate and let rest for 5 minutes before serving. Top with blue cheese butter to taste.

RED WINE–BLUE CHEESE BUTTER

This batch will amply anoint four steaks.

¼ cup dry red wine
1 tablespoon minced shallot
4 leaves fresh sage, chopped fine
Freshly ground black pepper
¼ cup crumbled blue cheese, at room temperature
2 tablespoons unsalted butter, at room temperature

In a small saucepan, combine the wine, shallot, sage, and a few grinds of pepper. Bring to a boil and reduce to 2 tablespoons. Allow to cool. Place the cheese in a small mixing bowl and gradually add the reduced wine and shallots, mashing with a fork to blend. Add the butter a bit at a time, stirring to incorporate. The final mixture will not be completely smooth and will have an interesting marbled pink and white appearance. Pack it into a ramekin and refrigerate until ready to use. ⌒

WINE-BRAISED OXTAILS *with Shallots and Carrots, Cumin and Cocoa*

SERVES 4

The main thing with oxtails is that they must be cooked to absolute tenderness. There's little better on a cold winter night, after a good brisk walk, snowshoe, or ski, than well-cooked oxtails—and little as disappointing as underdone ones that make you fight to get the meat off the bones. Make them a day or two ahead to avoid that unhappy fate and because, like many long-braised meat dishes, these improve greatly upon reheating. By the end of the long cooking, you'll hardly be able to pick out the separate flavors of cumin and cocoa, but they give added savor and depth. Serve over polenta or buttered noodles.

3 pounds oxtails
Salt and freshly ground black pepper
2 teaspoons canola or peanut oil
2 teaspoons butter
1 medium onion

2 cups red wine, divided

Pinch cumin seeds

1 bay leaf

2 large cloves garlic, crushed

½ small dried red chile, seeds removed

1½ teaspoons unsweetened cocoa powder

2 whole cloves

1½ cups water

2 large carrots, sliced on the diagonal to ¾ inch

4 shallots, quartered through root end to hold pieces together

½ cup tomato puree, or ¼ cup tomato paste mixed
with ¼ cup water

Preheat oven to 275 degrees. Lightly season the oxtails with salt. In a large Dutch oven over high heat, heat the oil and add the oxtails. Brown them on all sides, 12 to 15 minutes total. Remove the oxtails from the pan and pour off the fat. Add the butter and onion and cook over medium heat until barely wilted, a couple of minutes. Add 1½ cups of the wine, scraping to deglaze the pan.

Add the oxtails, cumin, bay, garlic, chile, cocoa, cloves, water, ¼ teaspoon salt, and a few grinds of pepper. Bring to a boil; transfer the pot to the oven and bake, covered, for 1½ hours, turning the oxtails after 45 minutes.

Stir in the carrots, shallots, and tomato puree and bake an additional 45 minutes. Add the remaining ½ cup wine and taste and adjust for salt. Add a bit of water if the braising liquid is getting low. Continue cooking until the meat is very tender: at minimum 3 hours total; 4 to 5 hours is better. Remove bay leaf and cloves before serving.

PAN-FRIED LAMB LEG CUTLETS

SERVES 2

The quality of the lamb is all important: get it from a local, trusted source. Depending on the age of the lamb, you may wind up with one larger leg steak to slice and share. Lamb shoulder chops would also be good prepared this way. So would pork chops or steaks. Excellent served with Mixed Mash (p. 196) or Celery Root–Potato Puree (p. 197).

2 (6-ounce) lamb leg cutlets, ¾ inch thick (see headnote)
Salt and freshly ground black pepper
2 tablespoons olive oil
6 cloves unpeeled garlic
3 sprigs fresh thyme
¼ cup dry white wine
¼ cup water
1 tablespoon butter

Season the lamb with salt and pepper. In a small saucepan, heat the oil and add the garlic. Cook over very low heat until softened but not browned, 8 to 10 minutes. Do not let the garlic get too brown, or it will be bitter. Remove from heat and set aside both garlic and oil. Discard the garlic skins.

Heat a skillet over medium-high heat and spoon in 2 teaspoons of the garlic oil. Add the lamb and cook for 3 to 4 minutes per side for medium rare. Toss in the thyme halfway through the cooking. Set the lamb to rest on a warm plate while you make the sauce.

Add the reserved garlic to the skillet; pour in the wine and scrape with a wooden spatula to deglaze. Add water and cook gently to reduce by half. Stir in any juices that have seeped from the resting lamb. Swirl in the butter and remove from heat. Slice the lamb ½ inch thick and serve it napped with the sauce. ⌒

* "IRON ON THE FIRE" GRILL-ROASTED LAMB AND VEGETABLES

The great thing about grilling, of course, is the smoke, the char, the glowing coals and all that they imply. The wonderful thing about roasting is that you can nestle meat and vegetables, mushrooms and starches all in the same pan, where their flavors mingle and the meat juices aren't lost to the coals. This method captures the best of both worlds.

You'll need a fire of natural wood coals (chunk charcoal or campfire) and a big cast-iron skillet. Let's take the example of these ingredients:

Grilling lamb

Leg of lamb steak, crosscut, or a butterflied piece of lamb leg
Olive oil
Thyme
Salt and pepper
Baby turnips
Small new potatoes
Spring onions
Green garlic, chopped
Young kale, mustard, and turnip greens
Red wine
Butter

An hour or two before grilling, marinate the lamb in a little olive oil, thyme, green garlic, salt, and pepper. Halve and blanch the turnips and potatoes for 5 minutes in boiling water, until barely tender. Put the skillet on the grill and add some olive oil, then the spring onions and garlic, the turnips and potatoes, then the greens. When the greens are wilted and the roots are starting to brown, set the skillet aside and turn to the meat.

Grill lamb for 4 or 5 minutes per side, to brown well but not cook through. Nestle the lamb into the pan with the vegetables and return it to the grill, letting it all cook together, turning the meat and stirring the vegetables a couple of times, for another 10 minutes. Remove the meat and vegetables to plates, deglaze the pan with a slosh of red wine, and swirl in a little butter for a very simple pan sauce.

Chicken works well in this method: you can crisp the skin nicely, brown it all around, and then, before the fat starts hitting the coals, move it to the skillet. I like to do chicken and wild mushrooms this way.

Softer vegetables, like summer squash and eggplant, can be tossed in olive oil and then given some color on the grill before joining the pan.

✳ CONFIT OF FRESH HAM *on Sauerkraut*
SERVES 4 TO 6

This festive, somewhat elaborate dish requires forethought and several steps, but none of the steps is difficult. It's best made with home-fermented sauerkraut, or seek out the best your co-op has to offer. Naturally fermented, small-batch krauts are showing up in stores more and more now as fermented foods gain notice for their healthfulness and deliciousness.

If you can't find a fresh ham roast, a pork shoulder roast of the same size can stand in.

- 1 (2½–3 pound) fresh ham roast
- 1 teaspoon salt
- 1 teaspoon crushed black peppercorns
- ½ teaspoon quatre-épices (p. 20)
- Handful fresh thyme sprigs
- 8 cloves unpeeled garlic
- 1 small shallot, minced (about 2 tablespoons)
- 2½–3 ounces good slab bacon, cut into ½-inch cubes (about ½ cup)
- 1 recipe Braised Sauerkraut (p. 189), prepared as described below
- 3 cooked fingerling potatoes per person

*Preparing
Confit of
Fresh Ham*

Using a razor or sharp knife, score the fat on the ham lightly in a crisscross pattern. Sprinkle the salt, peppercorns, and quatre-épices over all sides of the ham. Place a few sprigs of thyme in the bottom of an ovenproof, lidded dish a bit larger than the roast. Set the ham atop the thyme, and add more thyme on top. Refrigerate overnight.

Preheat oven to 275 degrees. To the baking dish add the garlic, shallots, and bacon. Add ½ inch of water to the pan, cover, and bake for 3 hours. Remove the lid and cook an additional 45 minutes. Remove from oven and let cool 30 minutes. Remove the ham and strain the juices into a glass or ceramic container. Refrigerate; as it cools, the fat will rise and solidify, and the highly flavorful stock will gel. Once this happens, separate the fat from the gelled stock and set both aside. Add the strained-out solids to the ham, discarding the thyme, and refrigerate.

Prepare the braised sauerkraut as directed, EXCEPT leave out the bacon and instead begin by heating 1 tablespoon reserved ham fat in a large skillet. Add the leek, carrot, etc., and proceed. Replace 1 cup chicken stock with ½ cup chicken stock and ½ cup reserved ham stock. Cook the sauerkraut for 30 minutes.

Brown the ham in a separate skillet in 1 tablespoon ham fat, and then place it on top of the sauerkraut. Simmer for at least 20 minutes. Add water or stock as needed so the pot does not cook dry. Add the potatoes during the final 10 minutes of cooking.

Serve potatoes and slices or chunks of ham (it will really be falling apart now) atop a bed of sauerkraut. Accompany with crusty bread and mustard and cornichons (p. 226), if you like.

✳ BRAISED PORK BELLY *with Fennel*
SERVES 4

This dish is best when prepared a day or two ahead of serving so that you can defat the sauce by straining it into a bowl and refrigerating it for a few hours. The fat will float to the top and solidify, making it easy to remove.

1½ pounds fresh pork belly, skin removed, in 2 chunks
Salt and freshly ground black pepper
1 teaspoon canola or grape seed oil
1 medium onion, chopped
1 small leek, white and light green parts, chopped
1 carrot, chopped
3 large cloves garlic, chopped
1 serrano chile, seeds removed, optional
1 cup hard dry apple cider or Hard Cider Sub (p. 231)
1 cup unsalted chicken stock
Few sprigs fresh thyme
1 cup water
2 small fennel bulbs, halved lengthwise, cut crosswise
   into ½-inch slices
Polenta or buttered noodles

Preheat oven to 350 degrees. Season the pork belly well on all sides with salt and pepper. Heat a Dutch oven or an ovenproof high-sided sauté pan over medium heat and add the oil. Brown the pork well on all sides, 4 to 5 minutes per side. Don't rush this stage, as a lot of the flavor in the finished dish is developed here.

Remove the pork from the pan and pour off all but a couple teaspoons of fat. Add the onion, leek, and carrot to the pan and cook, stirring, until lightly browned, 5 or 6 minutes. Add the garlic and chile and continue cooking for 1 minute. Add the cider, scraping the pan with a wooden spatula to deglaze. Return the pork to the pan and add the stock, thyme, and water.

Bring to a boil and then move the pan into the oven and cook, covered, for 45 minutes. Turn the pork and continue cooking, covered, 30 minutes more. Add the fennel, turn the pork again, and cook, uncovered, for 30 to 45 minutes, until the pork is very brown and tender. Add a bit of water if the braising liquid is getting low.

Remove the pork from the pan and strain the braising liquid into a bowl. Set aside the vegetables; discard thyme stems. A great deal of fat will have accumulated during the cooking, and it's best to remove most of it: use a fat separator cup or chill the liquid so the fat solidifies on top (see headnote).

Just before serving, slice the pork and reheat it along with the braising liquid and vegetables. Or, taking a tip from restaurant chefs, crisp the pork's exterior by putting it under the broiler for a few minutes, fat side up. Then slice it and reheat the sauce and vegetables. Serve over polenta or buttered noodles.

✳ HENS AND EGGS AND BACON

SERVES 4 AS A FIRST COURSE, 2 AS A MAIN DISH

Oeufs en meurette, a Burgundian classic, is poached eggs in a savory red wine sauce, its flavor made profound by bacon, mushrooms, and aromatic vegetables. This version gets an air of the sauvage from wild hen of the woods mushrooms. Regular button mushrooms are the usual choice. Use what you have or like. This recipe is a good one for practicing your knife skills: all the vegetables should be cut into very small, but distinct, uniform pieces.

Hens and Eggs and Bacon

3 ounces bacon, cut into ½-inch cubes (about ½ cup)

4 ounces hen of the woods mushrooms, chopped (about ¾ cup)

Salt and freshly ground black pepper

1 small leek, cut into ¼-inch pieces

1 carrot, peeled and cut into ¼-inch cubes

1 onion, cut into ¼-inch pieces

2 large cloves garlic, minced

2 tablespoons unsalted butter

1 tablespoon flour

1½ cups dry red wine

1 cup unsalted chicken stock

Fresh thyme

Parsley

4 large eggs

1 tablespoon white vinegar

Baguette slices

In a sturdy saucepan, gently render the bacon, and as it begins to brown, add the mushrooms and a pinch of salt. As the mushrooms begin to brown and smell mushroomy, add the leek, carrot, and onion. As these start to brown, add the garlic and butter. Sprinkle in the flour and cook, stirring constantly over low heat, until the flour starts to color and you achieve a blond roux. Gradually stir in the wine, scraping with a wooden spatula to deglaze. Add the stock, a couple sprigs of thyme, and a couple of stems parsley, along with a few grinds of black pepper and two good pinches of salt. Cover and simmer very gently for 45 minutes. Remove thyme and parsley stems. The sauce can be made a day or two ahead and reheated at serving time.

To poach the eggs, bring a saucepan of water to a boil and add the vinegar (which helps the eggs set up). Crack an egg into a ramekin or small bowl. Stir the water to create a vortex in the center and pour an egg into the vortex. Reduce heat and poach for 3 minutes with the water at a bare simmer. Remove with a slotted spoon and drain on a paper towel. Repeat with remaining eggs. Trim any ungainly egg-white appendages, place eggs in a ramekin (1 egg) or gratin dish (2), and nap liberally with warm sauce.

Sprinkle a little chopped parsley over the top and add a grind or two of black pepper. Serve with warm crusty baguette slices.

✳ KNIFE AND FORK BOT (BACON, ONION, AND TOMATO)

A BLT is a venerable sandwich—and one we hardly ever make. We're always subbing in something else for the lettuce, which is, after all, the blandest component. Our BLTs often become BBTs, basil taking the leafy part. Later in the season, when the basil's shot, there are still late tomatoes ripening on counters and plenty of onions. We'll sometimes put together a meal-size, open-face bacon sandwich. Top-shelf bacon is a must here.

> *Per person*
> 3–4 slices thick-cut bacon
> ½ small onion, sliced not too thin
> 1 thick slice bread with character—a country loaf or a grainy
>   sourdough
> Tomatoes, preferably mixed colors (Green Zebra and
>   Brandywine, for example), sliced
> Salt and freshly ground black pepper

In a heavy skillet, gently cook the bacon. Quality bacon should not be cooked to total crispness, I feel; it should be left a little translucent, so it will be chewy and yield some fat when you bite into it. When the bacon is done to your liking, remove and drain on paper towels. To the bacon fat add the onion and cook until slightly brown but still crisp, 4 to 5 minutes. For the final 2 minutes, place the bread on top of the onions, turning a couple times so it warms and absorbs some of the fat.

Transfer the bread to a plate, lay the bacon on the bread, scatter onions on the bacon, and top with slices of tomato, a sprinkle of coarse salt, and a grind of pepper. Serve with good grainy mustard, cornichons (p. 226) or Sweet and Spicy Apple Slices (p. 226), and maybe a cup of something like Carrot Apple Soup (p. 64).

GRILLED PORK STEAKS AND GREENS *with Easy Creamy Dressing*

SERVES 2

It's a bit odd: the nose-to-tail eating trend seems to have skipped right from the loin to the trotter, bypassing some very delicious and accessible cuts in between. You'll see pulled pork from a long-cooked shoulder on menus occasionally, but the pork steak, from the shoulder, rarely shows up on restaurant menus. That's a shame, for this cheap and flavorful cut of meat, properly cooked, is as tender as a chop. This preparation—inspired by David Chang's Momofuku Ssäm Bar in New York City—embraces simplicity and a few good, bold flavors. It's steak and salad on one plate.

   2 (6- to 8-ounce) pork steaks
      Salt and freshly ground black pepper
      Hearty salad greens—a head of frisée, trimmed, or romaine,
         or garden thinnings of young kale, mustard, or turnip greens
   1 recipe Easy Creamy Dressing (p. 51) or
        Blue Cheese Dressing (p. 49)
      Maple Syrup–Cider Vinegar Reduction (p. 217), optional

Prepare a hot fire of natural charcoal. Season the pork steaks liberally with salt and pepper. Toss together the greens and dressing and set aside.

Cook the pork steaks over hot coals, 3 to 4 minutes per side; they should have a nice sear and be cooked to medium in that time. Cook longer if you like: these are not delicate things that will be ruined if a bit overcooked. In the last minute of cooking, glaze with Maple Syrup–Cider Vinegar Reduction if you like.

Pile the greens on 2 plates. Top with hot pork steaks. A piece of grilled bread makes it a perfect summer meal.

The Importance of Bacon

There's not much middle ground in how people think of bacon. While the thought of a pan of bacon sizzling in its own clear, fragrant fat sends some scurrying for an egg-white omelet or a carton of yogurt, others behold those pliant strips of porcine exquisiteness and say, "Hey, why don't we wrap these around a hunk of sausage, roast it for a while, and serve it on buttered toast, maybe with cheese, and more bacon on the side?"

There is, indeed, something of a cult of bacon these days, and I understand why. When I was a vegetarian, many years ago, I had little trouble resisting the allure of hamburgers or steaks or pork chops. Poultry did not tempt me at all. But on weekends, when the college cafeteria set up the brunch line and the scent of cooking bacon and sausages wafted through the dormitory hallways, I had to jump on my bike and head for the hills, literally, in order to remain true to my principles. Though there was a chunk of lovely zucchini cheese puff awaiting me in the vegetarian line, I couldn't risk it.

The bacon cultists, they've taken to using bacon in every conceivable manner—candied, chocolate dipped, chicken fried, sprinkled over ice cream. Me, I think that's a little much. Though I'm definitely a pork fat fancier, I think the trend to inject bacon into every course of a meal is, well, trendy. Bacon deserves better than that. Bacon is important.

Its importance goes way back, to subsistence living and the need to preserve the foods of harvest and slaughter time for periods of the year when there were no fresh options. In some parts of the world, this is still the case. When I taught English in southwestern China in the late 1980s, I traveled into the countryside as often as I could, and on one trip to rural Guizhou Province, my companion and I were invited into the home of a Miao (Hmong, as we know them) family for a meal. Supper was a delicious but extremely humble hot pot of mustard greens and slices of their home-smoked bacon. I knew it was home-smoked meat because more of it was hanging over our heads, strung in the rafters to catch the smoke from the fire of twigs that kept the hot pot bubbling. We dipped the simmered greens and meat in fiery chili sauce, dabbed it on our rice. The highly flavored foods helped the bland rice go down. At the end we drank the salty, chili-laced broth.

The importance of bacon lies also in its versatility. As long as I have bacon in the house, I know that a great dish is never far away. First, when you've got really good bacon (and for me that now means home smoked), it can stand on its own. I don't generally make a meal out of nothing but bacon, though if you add a bit of bread, you've got a bacon sandwich, and I'd never turn up my nose at that. But it's in the dishes where bacon is a supporting player that you really see its versatility.

Bacon is essential to many classic French dishes—*frisée aux lardons, tarte flambée, cassoulet, choucroute garnie*—and pancetta, unsmoked bacon, is a staple in the Italian larder. Boston baked beans, the BLT, never mind the bacon double-cheeseburger. I use bacon in many, many ways, usually in small amounts: to add depth to a chowder or a pot of white beans; to flavor a red wine sauce that is napped over poached eggs; to add a salty surprise at the bottom of a ramekin in which an egg is baked, *en cocotte*. The lean meat of game birds benefits from the fat and smoke of companionable bacon.

Making your own home-smoked bacon requires no specialized equipment. From little effort and expense you get chemical-free bacon and the satisfaction of making your own version of something almost everyone loves and which most people think is difficult to make.

Finding the fresh pork belly is the first and perhaps the hardest step. Many Asian and Mexican markets carry it, as do custom butcher shops and grocery stores with excellent meat departments. The ethnic markets usually have the skin-on kind, which I prefer. My co-op carries skinless, but they buy it from the small local farms I like to support; I go back and forth. Once you

Fresh pork belly

have the meat, making bacon is a simple matter of curing the pork with salt and something sweet for a day and then giving it a couple of hours in the smoke. No, really: that's it. Twenty-four hours from now you could have a slab of fabulously delicious home-smoked bacon cooling on your kitchen counter. You're surprised, aren't you? I was.

Bacon is a common ingredient in this book's recipes, though it's rarely the main one. While I don't really expect everyone who reads this book to jump right up and get on to makin' bacon, I must put forth the point that not all bacons are created equal. A top-quality, dry-cured smoked bacon bears as much resemblance to the chemical-soaked, waterlogged bargain bacons as prosciutto di Parma does to those spongy pink canned hams. A butcher or grocery store with a good meat counter may make its own. Your farmers market may have locally produced, good-quality bacon, too.

I portion my bacon into roughly half-pound chunks and freeze all but the one in use. Once you've decided that home-smoked bacon is something you want to have on hand, you can do larger batches than the one described below. I usually smoke five or six pounds at a time, limited mainly by my primitive smoking setup. But I have no plans to expand: as with many food-processing tasks—canning, fermenting, jam making—I favor the small-batch approach. That way I always feel like the happy amateur, with no pressure at all. *Amateur* comes from the Latin word for love, after all. You should love what you do, and do what you love. Oh, yeah—and eat what you love, too.

HOME-SMOKED BACON
See Smoking Basics, p. 22.

> 2 pounds pork belly
> ¼ cup maple syrup or brown sugar
> 3 tablespoons salt

Rub the pork belly with the maple syrup, sprinkle salt on all sides, and let cure, covered, in the refrigerator for 24 hours, turning occasionally. For a brown sugar cure, mix the sugar and salt and pat it evenly on all sides of the meat.

The next day, rinse off excess salt, pat dry, and smoke at 200–220 degrees for 2 to 3 hours. The bacon will be both smoked and fully cooked. If you are unsure about whether the bacon is cooked at this point, set your mind at ease by placing it in a 200-degree oven for 30 minutes. A meat thermometer inserted into the bacon should read 160 degrees.

Be sure to sample a small slice of the still-warm bacon straight from the smoker and sweating fragrant fat. You'll see that it's more than worth the small trouble of smoking your own.

7

POULTRY

*

AUTUMN VEGETABLE, CHICKEN, AND SAUSAGE HOT POT

SERVES 4 TO 6

This is the sort of dinner we often simmer on the woodstove at Bide-A-Wee. Using great ingredients, time, and gentle heat, we feel like genius cooks for doing basically nothing. Vary the vegetables according to what you have— squash, rutabaga, kohlrabi, chard, kale, other cooking greens—adding them to the pot according to their respective cooking times.

Serve with Dijon-style mustard, crusty bread or croutons, some corni- chons (p. 226), or a freshly made vinaigrette—or all of the above, as you prefer.

Couple pieces good bacon rind or 1 slice bacon, optional
   but highly recommended
4 chicken thighs
Salt
4 sausages, like knockwurst or bratwurst, fresh or smoked
   or both
8 cups water
1 large parsnip, peeled, cut into 2-inch pieces
2 medium carrots, peeled or scrubbed, cut into 2-inch pieces
1 leek, white and light green parts, rinsed well, cut
   into 2-inch pieces
2 small onions, halved through root end to hold pieces together
2 large cloves garlic
Couple sprigs fresh thyme or pinch dried
1 small dried or fresh chile, seeds removed, optional
8 small new potatoes, scrubbed
3 small turnips, peeled, halved
½ head green cabbage, quartered

In a large Dutch oven, slowly cook the bacon over low heat until most of the fat has rendered and the bacon is brown. If you're not using bacon, put a little oil or butter in the pot. Season the chicken with salt on both sides and brown it alongside the bacon, starting skin-side down. Brown the sausages, too; they shouldn't take quite as long as the chicken.

Add the water and ¼ teaspoon salt along with the parsnip, carrots, leek, onions, garlic, thyme, and chile, if desired. Bring to a boil and simmer very gently for 30 minutes. Add the potatoes, turnips, and cabbage and simmer for 30 minutes more.

As long as you keep it at a bare simmer, it's pretty hard to overcook. Before serving, taste and adjust for salt and remove thyme stem.

You will probably have leftovers, and these are great simply reheated. Or turn them into a salad: chop meat and vegetables into bite-size pieces, toss with your favorite vinaigrette (a mustardy one would go well), and serve over lettuce or finely shredded cabbage.

* CHICKEN IN A POT *with Chervil-Chive-Parsley Butter*

SERVES 4, OR 2 WITH LEFTOVERS FOR SANDWICHES, CHICKEN POTPIE, ETC.

This is city mouse to the previous recipe's country mouse—a bit more refined, but by no means snooty. The quality of your chicken will out in a simple simmered dinner like this. It's a calming dish for grown-ups to enjoy—and to teach their children to appreciate. The world seems better with brothy chicken in your bowl.

For "Part 2," other vegetables, like parsnips, rutabaga, or turnip, can be substituted or added.

Part 1
1 (4-pound) chicken
2 medium (about 1½-inch diameter) leeks
4 quarts water
1 onion, quartered
1 carrot, scrubbed and chopped
1 large clove garlic, crushed
1 rib celery, chopped
3 sprigs fresh thyme
Parsley
2 whole cloves
10 black peppercorns

Part 2

4 small to medium red potatoes, halved

2 small onions, halved, retaining a bit of the root to hold
   layers together

2 carrots, peeled and halved lengthwise

½ medium celery root (about 6 ounces), peeled and quartered

½ head green cabbage, quartered

   Baguette slices or croutons

   Cornichons (p. 226)

   Chervil-Chive-Parsley Butter (p. 218)

Remove the leg quarters from the chicken and set aside. Cut out the backbone with poultry shears. Remove wings. Set the breast aside with the leg quarters. Trim and discard any dried-out or damaged parts of the leeks. Cut off the bottom 6 inches of the white part and set aside with the vegetables for Part 2. Rinse and coarsely chop the green leek tops. To a stockpot with 4 quarts of water add the chicken wings, backbone, and neck, if available, the chopped leeks, onion, carrot, garlic, celery, thyme, a handful chopped parsley stems, cloves, and peppercorns.

Bring to a boil and simmer, partly covered, for at least 1 hour (longer simmering will yield a more flavorful broth). Add the chicken leg quarters and cook for 10 minutes; then add the breast and simmer an additional 20 minutes. Turn off the heat, cover, and let stand 20 to 30 minutes. Remove the leg quarters and breast and set aside. Remove and discard the remaining solids. Strain the stock through cheesecloth into a large bowl, wash the pot, and return the stock to the pot.

About 40 minutes before serving, bring the stock to a simmer. Add a good pinch of salt. Separate thighs from drumsticks; remove the skin if you prefer. Remove the breast meat from the bone and set aside. Add the reserved whites of leek, potatoes, onions, carrots, and celery root to the stock and simmer for 15 minutes. Add the cabbage wedges and cook an additional 15 minutes. Add the chicken and simmer 10 minutes more. Remove the breasts from the stock and cut each into 4 slices.

Serve in wide soup bowls, a slice of breast and a leg portion, a selection of vegetables moistened to taste with broth. Bring a sliced baguette or croutons to the table, along with a bowl of chopped cornichons and Chervil-Chive-Parsley Butter.

CHICKEN *with Chestnuts and Cider*

SERVES 2 GENEROUSLY

In the last few years, chestnuts from midwestern growers have been available at co-ops and farmers markets for a few weeks in the fall. They are wonderful, much smaller and sweeter than the imported kind.

16 chestnuts
4 chicken thighs
Salt and freshly ground black pepper
2 teaspoons canola oil
1 medium onion, sliced
1 small carrot, sliced
1 cup dry hard apple cider or Hard Cider Sub (p. 231)
1 cup unsalted chicken stock or water
3 sprigs fresh thyme

First you need to get the chestnuts out of the shell. With good, fresh chestnuts, this task isn't difficult. Begin by cutting an X into the flat side of the shell, just barely penetrating the shell without cutting into the meat. I take a small paring knife and, CAREFULLY grasping nearly the entire blade in my fingers, draw the tip of the blade across the shell. Next, toast the nuts in a dry heavy skillet until the shell flaps start to peel back, or place them in a baking pan in a 400-degree oven for 10 to 15 minutes. Peel them as soon as they're cool enough to handle.

Season the chicken with salt and pepper. Heat the oil in a high-sided skillet or Dutch oven and brown the chicken well on both sides, about 15 minutes total. Remove the chicken from the pan and set aside.

Brown the chestnuts over medium-low heat, watching carefully and turning frequently to prevent burning. Remove nuts and set aside. Pour off excess fat, leaving about 2 teaspoons. Add the onions and carrot and cook, stirring, until the onions are wilted, about 5 minutes. Add the cider, scraping up the brown bits with a wooden spatula. Add the stock or water, thyme, and a pinch of salt. Return the chicken to the pan, bring to a simmer and cook, partly covered, for 30 minutes. Add the chestnuts and cook for 30 minutes more. The broth should now have the consistency of a light gravy; if it seems too thin, simmer uncovered for a few minutes more. Taste and adjust for salt and pepper. Remove thyme stem. Variation: finish the sauce with a couple tablespoons heavy cream, and you'll have something that would be quite at home in a Normandy farmhouse. ⌒

✳ SMOKE-GRILLED MA LA CHICKEN WINGS
SERVES 4

I first made this to add some spice to a cold winter evening, but it's a dish for all seasons. I never put my grill away. Why would you?

The fish sauce and Sichuan peppercorns are both available at Asian markets. You will need natural chunk charcoal and apple or other smoking wood for your grill. See Smoking Basics (p. 22).

¾ teaspoon salt

2 teaspoons fish sauce

1½ teaspoons sugar

Juice of ¼ lime (about 1½ teaspoons)

½ teaspoon crushed black peppercorns

1 teaspoon whole Sichuan peppercorns

2 large cloves garlic, sliced

2 green onions, chopped

2 small hot green or red chilies (serrano or cayenne), sliced

3 pounds chicken wings, separated at the joints (save wing tips for stock)

2 medium hot red chilies (jalapeño or Fresno), seeded and quartered lengthwise

2 small leeks, cleaned and sliced in half lengthwise, or 4 green onions

Chinese noodles tossed in sesame oil, toasted sesame seeds,
and a bit of salt
Sambal Carrot Slaw (p. 41)

In a large mixing bowl, combine the salt, fish sauce, sugar, lime juice, black and Sichuan pepper, garlic, green onions, and sliced hot chilies. Add the chicken wings and mix well. Refrigerate for several hours or overnight.

Light a fire of natural charcoal in your barbecue grill. When the coals are hot, distribute them under half of the grill grate, leaving half the grate with no coals beneath. Grill the chicken wings, turning often, until they are nicely browned; when they are brown and crisp, move them to the cool half of the grill. Grill the quartered chilies and leeks or green onions until tender crisp and a bit charred; keep these warm in a low oven.

With all the chicken wings on the coal-free side of the grill grate, add a few pieces of apple, oak, or hickory wood to the coals. Cover and smoke-roast for 30 to 45 minutes, until the wings are cooked through.

Before serving, chop most of the leeks for easier eating. Place a bed of noodles in a large shallow bowl; top with slaw and then wings. Drape a few leek shreds over top and chopped leeks and grilled chilies around edges. Serve with cold beer and paper towels to wipe your hands and greasy chin.

HAW JAM AND PAN-FRIED DUCK BREAST
with Celery Root Fries

The haw, or hawberry, is the fruit of the hawthorn tree. These gnarled, shrubby trees are a common feature of our northern landscape. The thorns are formidable: stout at the base, needle sharp at the tip. Shrikes, those peculiar carnivorous songbirds, sometimes impale their prey—smaller birds or rodents—on these spikes, the easier to dismember them; thus their nickname, "Butcher Bird."

    That grisly image aside, hawthorn trees are beautiful—splendid white flowers in early spring, brilliant red berries in late summer, graphic scrawls on the winter landscape—and their fruit can be delicious. I say can be, because not all are. Wild hawthorns hybridize freely, much like the apples to which they are related, so the quality of fruit from one tree to the next varies greatly. Start tasting haws in mid-September. Look for berries with some flesh on them—many will be all seed and skin. Taste around until you find some good ones. Ripe haws will be soft and a little sweet, with complex flavor—they remind me of apples, pears, quince, and rosehips. There's no hurry to pick them: they improve with a frost, and the fruits stay on the trees long after the leaves have fallen.

For a taste of haw cookery, pick a generous cup of flavorful berries. Rinse the haws and remove any stems. Place the berries in a saucepan, add 3 cups water, bring to a boil, and then reduce the heat and slowly simmer, covered, for 45 minutes. The haws may still look intact at this point, but if you press them they should yield, skin splitting, pulp emerging. Drain off most of the water but reserve some: it has quite a bit of flavor and will help as you sieve the pulp. Dump the berries and the reserved water into a wire mesh sieve set over a large bowl and press the fruit with the back of a spoon. The juicy stuff will come right out, and with a little more pushing, the pulpy stuff will follow. Soon you'll have nothing but dry seeds and skin in the sieve. Be sure to scrape the last of the pulp from the outside of the sieve.

Hawthorn trees in winter

Now, since you've been tramping through the blasted heath all afternoon and you have been industrious, you deserve a proper supper. Luckily you've had the foresight to procure a nice fat duck breast, *magret de canard,* and a celery root. There's a black iron skillet on the woodstove, hot enough but not too hot. Crosshatch the skin of the duck with a sharp knife—just cut a titch down into the fat, not reaching the meat—to release the fat as it cooks. Cook slowly, skin-side down most of the time. As the fat flows, add the celery root, peeled and cut into french fry shape (and also a handful of filet beans, if you have some). Everything sizzles away in duck fat. When the meat is cooked through (about 15 minutes for medium rare, turning twice), remove it to a plate and let it rest.

In a small saucepan combine ½ cup each chicken stock and dry red wine. Reduce by half. Stir in 3 tablespoons of the haw puree and 1 tablespoon maple syrup, a grind or two of pepper, a couple pinches of salt. Simmer very quietly as the duck rests. Pour into the sauce any juice the duck exudes while resting, and stir in 1 tablespoon butter. Slice the duck, fan the slices on a plate, and nap with sauce.

The magret is properly rosé. The haw sauce is something unique and delicious, an excellent partner to the rich, savory duck in all ways—in its mild sweetness, in its fragrance, and even in that lingering astringency. We are delighted to have made the acquaintance of the haw.

* DUCK BREAST *with Blackberry-Whisky Sauce*
SERVES 4

The Scotch-blackberry combination goes wonderfully with duck breast. The sauce may taste a bit intense on its own, but the rich, savory meat mellows it. Serve with Celery Root–Potato Puree (p. 197). A few leaves of kale or other greens cooked in a bit of the duck fat are excellent with this dish.

The breasts of ducks raised for foie gras are called magrets, *and they are huge, usually 12 to 14 ounces. Magrets are the best choice for this recipe, but regular duck breasts of 5 to 7 ounces each can be substituted.*

2 (12- to 14-ounce) duck magrets or 4 smaller (5- to 7-ounce) breasts (see headnote)
Salt and freshly ground black pepper

Preheat oven to 250 degrees. Lightly prick the duck skin all over with the tip of a sharp knife—don't go into the meat, just the skin and fat layer. Season well with salt and pepper. Heat an ovenproof skillet and add the duck breasts, skin-side down. Reduce the heat to medium-low and cook for 6 to 8 minutes, until the skin is very brown and a lot of fat has rendered. Turn the duck and cook for 3 minutes, and then place the pan in the oven for an additional 6 to 8 minutes. Remove from the oven and let the duck rest on a warm plate while you make the sauce. Slice the duck, arrange on plates, and spoon sauce over top.

BLACKBERRY-WHISKY SAUCE

This batch will coat four portions. The sauce would also be good with grilled lamb chops.

4 tablespoons (2 ounces) unsalted butter, divided
2 shallots, finely chopped (about ½ cup)
1 small carrot, peeled and cut into ¼-inch cubes
1½ cups dry red wine
2 cups unsalted chicken stock
3 sprigs fresh thyme
¼ cup good Scotch whisky
¼ cup blackberry jam (or Quick Wild Berry Sauce, p. 208)
Salt and freshly ground black pepper

In a small saucepan, melt 2 tablespoons of the butter. Add the shallots and carrot and cook over low heat until the shallots are soft and translucent but not browned, about 5 minutes. Add the wine, stock, and thyme. Bring to a boil and cook at a brisk simmer until reduced by half. Stir in the whisky and jam, a pinch of salt, a couple grinds of pepper. Continue cooking until reduced by half. Add any juices given off by the resting duck.

Swirl in the remaining 2 tablespoons butter, taste and adjust for salt, add another grind of pepper, and serve over the sliced duck breast.

Duck Confit

Confit was originally a method of preserving salted meat in fat; today we use the technique more for flavor than preservation, and, indeed, there's little more appetizing than a succulent leg of duck that's been spiced, salted, and then simmered slowly in duck fat to maximum tenderness.

Making confit is not difficult, but it can be a little messy. The first thing you need is a pot of duck fat. If you have access to a good butcher, you may be able to buy a pint or two of fat to get started. If that's not an option, you're going to have to get yourself a nice fatty duck or two and then proceed as follows.

Trim off all excess fat and fatty skin. Save the legs and breasts with the skin and take all the other skin off the carcass (the carcass can be used to make stock). Cut the skin and fat into roughly ½-by-3-inch strips and place them in a heavy saucepan with water to cover by an inch. Bring the pot to a boil and then simmer over medium heat. As the water boils off, the fat will render, and when the water is all gone, you'll be left with a pot of pure fat, with little cracklings of duck skin bobbing in it. Let the cracklings get nice and brown in the fat, and then remove them with a slotted spoon to drain on paper towels. They're delicious lightly salted as a cocktail nibble or sprinkled on a salad.

Now that you have a supply of fat, you can continue making your confit, as below. The hard part is over. Store the fat in a plastic container in the freezer and use it over and over. It gains character with each new confit. The fat is wonderful for frying or oven-roasting root vegetables, and it's the magic ingredient in Mary's Duck Fat Tortillas (p. 232).

* * *

If you have gizzards, hearts, wings, or necks, use those in the confit, too. The giblets and shreddy meat are great on a dinner salad. You need not absolutely submerge the meat in fat as it cooks; the legs do tend to float somewhat, and you can turn them a couple of times in the cooking.

    4 meaty duck legs, thigh and drumstick together
    ½ teaspoon quatre-épices (p. 20)
    Salt and freshly ground black pepper

8–10 cloves unpeeled garlic
2 bay leaves
3–4 sprigs fresh thyme
Duck fat to cover, about 4 cups

A day before you make the confit, dry the duck with paper towels, and sprinkle the spice blend and 1½ teaspoons salt evenly over both sides, along with a few grinds of pepper. Cover and refrigerate at least overnight and up to 3 days. Prior to cooking, drain off any accumulated juices and dry the duck with paper towels.

Preheat oven to 275 degrees. Arrange the duck in a single layer in a baking dish or heavy pot large enough to comfortably hold duck and fat. Spread the garlic, bay leaves, and thyme over the duck. Cover with melted fat. Cook, covered, for 2 to 3 hours, turning the duck once or twice. The fat will cloud as juices come off the duck; when it's done, the fat will be clear and bubbling. The juices will settle at the bottom of the pan, and you'll want to save them—they're a bit salty but absolutely delicious.

Let the duck cool in the fat. Use it the same day or store, refrigerated, in the fat for a couple of weeks. The salt plus the airtight seal formed by the fat helps preserve the meat. Prior to cooking, dig out the duck and let sit at room temperature to allow excess fat to melt off.

Here are a couple of simple confit presentations:

Brown the legs in a Dutch oven; set them aside and remove all but a tablespoon or two of fat. Add some chopped onion and garlic and then some homemade sauerkraut, rinsed, drained, and squeezed dry. A little of that delicious fond from the bottom of the confit pan and just a splash of water makes a savory sauce. Simmer everything very gently. Just before serving, add back the duck and some boiled fingerling potatoes to warm.

Boil together an assortment of root vegetables—carrot, parsnip, celery root, potato—peeled and cut in chunks. Cook until tender and drain, reserving a cup of the cooking liquid. Leave a bit of confit fat in the pan, add to it a chopped leek and a couple cloves of chopped garlic. Cook until the leek is

*Knife and Fork BOT
(Bacon, Onion, and
Tomato) (p. 133)*

Apple Blackberry Galettes (p. 205)

Watercress Bacon Salad (p. 46)

Chile Cheddar Spread (p. 28)

Stuffed Red Kale Leaves with Herb-Wine-Butter Sauce (p. 89)

Lacinato Kale Salad with Poached Egg on Toast (p. 41)

Smoke-Grilled Ma La
Chicken Wings (p. 144)

Meat tableau

Baked Pheasant with Wild Mushrooms and Cream (p. 157)

Roast Chicken with Wild Mushrooms (p. 76)

Brunch spread with cheese, pickles, smoked fish

Home-smoked Bacon (p. 138)

*Chanterelle,
trumpet, hedgehog
mushrooms*

Wild Mushroom Pizza (p. 106)

Prepared nettles and morels

Hen of the woods

Chanterelle Smoked Herring Bulgur Salad (p. 163)

*Oven Tomatoes
with Herbs (p. 229)*

*Pickled Red Cabbage
Wedges with Blue Cheese
Dressing (p. 49)*

Assorted beets, prepped for the Wine-Dark Beets (p. 48)

Farmers Market Confetti Vegetable Sauce for Pasta (p. 98)

*Summer Lake
Trout Chowder
(p. 69)*

*Fall Colors Soup
(p. 67)*

Crabs and Cukes (p. 225)

Trout Caviar
(p. 30)

Cornichons
(p. 226)

Blackberry-Mustard Grilled Carrots (p. 196)

Buckwheat Trout with Sorrel Sauce (p. 174)

wilted; then add the vegetables and some of their cooking liquid, and mash with a fork. Season to taste with salt and pepper, and serve browned duck on top of mash.

Make a batch of Mom's Hot Red Cabbage (p. 190). Brown confit and add it to cook with the cabbage for the final 10 minutes. Serve with boiled new potatoes.

In addition, see Sugar Bush Bean Pot (p. 85), Braised Sauerkraut (p. 189), Duck Confit Tacos (below), and Last Leg Duck Confit and Chickpea Soup (p. 73). ⌒

✳ DUCK CONFIT TACOS
SERVES 2

Shredded duck confit moistened with stock and wine, wrapped in a warm duck fat tortilla, a drizzle of cream, and something fresh and crunchy on top: could be the most luxurious taco ever.

   3 pieces Duck Leg Confit (p. 149), for example, 2 thighs and a
      drumstick
¼ cup dry red or white wine
¼ cup unsalted chicken stock or 2 tablespoons concentrated
      juices from confit
Freshly ground black pepper
   1 small red onion, sliced
¼ cup heavy cream mixed with ¼ cup sour cream or yogurt
      (goat milk yogurt would be excellent)
   1 recipe Mary's Duck Fat Tortillas (p. 149)
Snap Pea Salsa (p. 51) and/or Sambal Carrot Slaw (p. 41)
      and/or Sweet Corn Chile Relish (p. 167)

Remove the skin from the confit and set aside. Remove the meat from the bones, tear it into shreds, and place in a small saucepan along with the wine and stock or confit fond. Simmer until the meat is hot and the sauce is reduced to just coat the meat. Add a couple grinds of pepper.

Cook the duck skin in a small skillet over medium heat, turning often, until very crisp and brown. Drain skin on a paper towel and then slice it into strips. In the fat that has rendered from the skin, sear the onion slices until they take on some color but are still crisp.

Bring everything to the table on separate plates, and let the assembly begin. Put a smear of cream on the tortilla and top with duck meat, onion, fresh vegetable salsa, slaw, or relish, and some crispy skin. A roll of paper towels comes in handy. ⌒

Cooking Game Birds

Ruffed grouse, ring-necked pheasants, and the American woodcock are the main "upland game birds" of our region. While they differ greatly in flavor, they're all birds, just like the familiar chicken: to remove leg quarters or breast meat, treat them just the same way.

Game birds differ greatly from chicken, however, in their fat content. There's usually some fat under the skin, especially on migrating woodcock, but the meat is very lean and becomes tough, dry, and gamy if overcooked. That's why the game recipes here use tactics like quick cooking and steaming and rich ingredients like cream and bacon to complement the lean meat.

I like to pluck my birds, a tedious but necessary chore if you want to experience the glory of a whole roasted bird. Skinning the birds is a shortcut option for other types of recipes. A lot of hunters take the ultimate shortcut of "breasting out" their birds in the field—taking only the skinless breast meat and leaving the rest of the carcass for the foxes. This is a damn shame, in my opinion: the bones of wild game birds produce superb and distinctive stock, which, when reduced to make a sauce, becomes the kind of thing kings would dream of. ⌒

Grilled Woodcock with Apple-Bacon Relish

✳ GRILLED WOODCOCK *with Apple-Bacon Relish*

SERVES 2 AS AN APPETIZER

Woodcock, considered the choicest of game birds in much of Europe, aren't as well appreciated here. The breast meat is dense, dark, and savory; the plump legs are an absolute delicacy, the stuff of "last meal on earth" requests from knowing gourmands. In this preparation, the breast meat and legs are removed, quickly grilled, and then served with a tart and savory relish. I find a great simpatico between woodcock and bacon—maybe it's the scent of woodsmoke in the air on autumn hunt days. Sharing one woodcock between two people provides a few exquisite bites. If I'm fortunate in the field, I could eat a whole bird as a starter and not fill up.

1 slice thick-cut bacon, cut into ¼-inch cubes

1 shallot or ½ small onion, finely chopped

1 clove garlic, minced

1 small apple, peeled, cored, and cut into ¼-inch cubes

Salt and freshly ground black pepper

2 teaspoons maple syrup

1 tablespoon cider vinegar

Pinch cayenne or Espelette pepper, optional

½ teaspoon fresh thyme leaves or ⅛ teaspoon dried

1–2 woodcock, as the game gods permit

Olive oil

In a small saucepan, cook the bacon over medium-low heat. As fat starts to render, add the shallot and cook for 2 to 3 minutes, until the shallot is translucent and fragrant. Add the garlic, apple, a pinch of salt, and a few grinds of black pepper. Cook for 2 to 3 minutes, until the apple starts to break down but hasn't turned to mush. Add the maple syrup, vinegar, optional cayenne or Espelette, and thyme; simmer for 3 minutes, and remove from heat. The relish can be used right away but will improve if it sits, refrigerated, for a few hours and up to a few days.

Prepare a fire of natural wood charcoal. Remove the breast meat, with skin, from the woodcock. Remove the legs, keeping thigh and drumstick together. Brush lightly with olive oil on both sides, and season with salt and pepper. Grill over hot coals, 2 to 3 minutes per side, to medium rare. Serve with relish.

GROUSE *in Cider Cream*

SERVES 2

The ruffed grouse is the king of up-land game birds and pretty much un-matched in the world of game cook-ery as well. The lean meat benefits from some richness in the cooking. It must not be overcooked, lest the sub-lime become mediocre or worse. This recipe was developed to cook slowly on top of a woodstove, but if you're cooking in more civilized surround-ings, you can finish it in a gentle oven. This same method would elevate a pheasant (cut into quarters) or quail (left whole). I've made it successfully with Cornish hens, and a bone-in, skin-on breast of free-range chicken would come out of this creamy, cidery bath with a whole new outlook.

Grouse in
Cider Cream

> 1 ruffed grouse, cleaned and plucked
> Salt and freshly ground black pepper
> 1 slice thick-cut bacon, cut crosswise into ¼-inch pieces
> 1 apple, peeled, cored, and cut into eighths
> 1 tablespoon butter
> 1 small leek, chopped
> ¾ cup dry hard apple cider or Hard Cider Sub (p. 231)
> ¾ cup heavy cream
> 1 cup unsalted chicken or game bird stock
> 8 fingerling potatoes, cooked
> Sweet Buttered Cabbage (p. 190)

Halve the grouse (down the backbone, between the breasts) with poultry shears or a sharp heavy knife. Season with salt and pepper. In a large, oven-proof skillet, slowly cook the bacon until most of the fat has rendered. Add the apple and brown on both sides. Remove bacon and apples from the pan and set aside.

Add the butter to the pan. Brown the grouse on all sides. Add the leek and cook until wilted. Add the cider, scraping the pan to deglaze, and then add the cream and stock. Return the apples and bacon to the pan.

Cook very gently for 30 minutes on a stove top or in a 275-degree oven, turning and basting often. The sauce will slowly reduce. If it becomes too thick, add water or stock. Add the potatoes to pan to warm during the last 5 minutes of cooking. Serve with Sweet Buttered Cabbage.

✳ STEAMED GROUSE BREAST *with Black Trumpet Sauce*
SERVES 2

A rich and exotic sauce, an elegant presentation: it works with pheasant or chicken, too. You will need a wok and a bamboo steamer (or a steamer setup of your devising) for this recipe. If you have skin-on grouse breasts, leave the skin on while cooking and then remove and discard it before serving.

    12 fresh or dried black trumpet mushrooms
     4 teaspoons unsalted butter, divided
     1 small shallot, chopped
     1 tablespoon cognac or brandy
     ½ cup unsalted chicken stock
     ¼ cup heavy cream
       Salt and freshly ground black pepper
     2 boneless grouse breasts (see headnote)
     2 tablespoons dry vermouth, sherry, or rice wine
     2 tablespoons finely chopped carrot
     2 tablespoons finely chopped celery
     2 tablespoons finely chopped leek or green onion

If using dried mushrooms, cover them with water in a small bowl and let stand for at least 30 minutes. Strain the mushrooms, discarding the soaking liquid. Chop mushrooms into ½-inch pieces. Melt 2 teaspoons of the butter in a small saucepan. Add the shallot and cook very gently, without browning, until translucent and fragrant, 3 to 4 minutes. Add the mushrooms and cook for 1 minute. Remove the pan from the heat and add the cognac. If you are bold, flambé the cognac, tipping the pan toward the flame or lighting it with a match. Otherwise, return the pan to the heat and cook until the cognac has evaporated. Add the stock, cream, and a pinch of salt. Cook until reduced by two-thirds; remove from heat and set aside.

Lightly season the grouse with salt and pepper. Stir together the vermouth, carrot, celery, and leek or green onion. Spread half the vegetable mixture on a heat-proof plate that will fit in your steamer. Place the grouse on top, and spoon the remaining vegetables over top. Set aside to marinate for at least 30 minutes.

Add water to the wok to reach the bottom of the steamer and bring it to a boil. Place the plate holding the grouse in the steamer and the steamer in the wok. With the water at a brisk simmer, cook for 10 minutes. Turn off the heat, wait 2 minutes, and remove the steamer from the wok. Wait 5 minutes and then remove the grouse from the steamer, being careful to retain any accumulated juices.

Pour the juices into the sauce. Reduce gently until the sauce coats the back of a spoon. Swirl in the remaining 2 teaspoons butter. Slice the grouse and fan the slices out on serving plate. Nap a stripe of sauce down the center and serve.

✳ BAKED PHEASANT *with Wild Mushrooms and Cream*
SERVES 2

Any kind of fowl, from grouse to game hens, quail, or chicken, will shine in this easy treatment, which beats the canned cream-of-mushroom soup approach soundly. Serve with rice or buttered noodles.

> 1 pheasant, quartered
> Salt and freshly ground black pepper
> Flour
> 1½ cups chopped wild mushrooms (chanterelles, hedgehogs, hen of the woods, or an assortment)
> 1 medium onion, chopped

1 cup heavy cream
¼ cup dry white wine
   Rice or buttered noodles

Preheat oven to 425 degrees. Season the pheasant with salt and pepper, and toss it in flour to coat. Layer the mushrooms in the bottom of a baking dish. Place the pheasant on the mushrooms, and scatter the onions over the pheasant. Combine the cream and wine and pour over the pheasant. Bake for 15 minutes; baste pheasant with cream. Continue to bake, basting every 10 minutes, until the pheasant is brown and the cream well reduced, about 45 minutes total. Add a bit of water if the cream reduces too quickly. Serve with rice or buttered noodles. ⌒

November Cover

"When holy were the haunted forest boughs, holy the air, the water, and the fire," wrote the poet John Keats, describing a time when spirits animated the natural world. Sometimes, walking into the November woods, gun on my shoulder, behind a pair of ghost-gray griffons, I wonder if those boughs aren't haunted still. The autumnal pageantry of the October forest is moldering underfoot now. The palette is brown and black, gray and white. I start the hunt a little cold, not wanting to overdress because I know I'll be sweating by the time I'm deep in cover; that chill and the wind that knifes down my collar tell me the season is turning toward its inhospitable side. I'm out here after prey, to take life, violently; there's no point in pretending it's not so.

I came to this pursuit much later in life than most who hunt upland game birds—woodcock, ruffed grouse, and pheasant—over pointing dogs. I got a wirehaired pointing griffon because I'd come to love the breed, through one dog in particular, our Annabel's mother, Blam. Then to do my dog justice—let her fulfill her destiny, as it were—I had to get a gun and learn to hunt. To undertake such a thing at the age of forty involves a steep climb up the learning curve.

The beautiful thing about hunting, also true of fly-fishing, is that it leads you to splendid places you would not otherwise have seen. The view from one specific hill, down a long grassy sweep to the realm of those haunted boughs, ridgelines receding into the mist in every direction, compelled me to buy land in west-central Wisconsin. What you can see from the road is pretty enough, but when you leave the car behind and walk into the landscape, you really come to know and appreciate it: the welcoming island of white pines, an oasis in the tangle of prickly ash and dogwood; the curve of a creek where a spring trickles in and the dogs take the waters; a flooded patch of woods where pileated woodpeckers hammer at hulks of ancient oaks. These places and many more are now points on a map that would have remained blank had I not taken up hunting.

And yet it is hunting, not sightseeing. And it is a partnership, not a solitary opportunity for woolgathering. It's easy to take your dogs for granted—they do what they do so effortlessly, and they revel in it—but if you consider for a moment what they accomplish, you quickly see again that they are magnificent machines. They work their way through brambles and thickets, humpy marshes and alder labyrinths—and they do it with speed, and they do it with purpose, with awareness of where the hunter and the other dogs are. In the midst of a breakneck slalom through a dense dogwood patch, they will stop on a dime at the scent of a bird, freeze, and await your command. Then if you manage to drop a bird, they'll track it down in the thickest mess and bring it to you gently: here you are; I thought you might like this; I went to get it for you to save you the trouble. Dumb animals, indeed.

⁂ ⁂ ⁂

Now, about the killing: maybe it's because I'm coldhearted or because they're cold-blooded—I don't experience much emotion when I knock a trout on the head. I feel respect and a general thankfulness but am otherwise unmoved. It's different when you take in your hand something warm and feathered, with a big dark liquid eye, a woodcock still breathing, and you must twist its neck to dispatch it. Woodcock, grouse, and pheasant all are beautiful creatures, and I have mixed and complex feelings about hunting and killing them. But I do eat meat, and game birds are good and honorable meat. Any animal I kill has lived natural and free up to the moment it falls to the gun, has never seen a cage or a crowded pen. Given that the biggest threat to many kinds of wildlife is loss of habitat, the hunting population, by lobbying to protect wild lands, does much on behalf of these animals.

Ironically, no one cares more about a woodcock than someone who goes out to kill it.

*　*　*

A hunt takes on a rhythm, evolves character with each step, each flush, each shot, point and blown point. By the time it comes full circle back to the parking area, it is a story entire—the drama of getting turned around in the swamp and finding your way out; the close call with the porcupine; the dogs stopped still as statues (but for the quivering tails) with their noses two feet apart and a woodcock in between. A hunt is exhausting in the most complete and satisfying way—not just from bodily exertion, though it is by far the most physically demanding thing I do, but from the attention required to walk in dreadful terrain with a loaded firearm, to keep track of the dogs and your whereabouts, and to leave enough mind free so that you can remember how to shoot when the opportunity arises.

When I come out of the woods and start up the long grassy hill toward the parking area, the late afternoon sun is half hid at the horizon. There's still enough light to shoot, but I break open the gun and remove the shells. The old dog understands and keeps pace at my side. The young dog still has

Annabel with grouse

plenty of go: she races ahead and may put up a pheasant, but the shooting is over. The last few minutes are for taking it all in as the sun slips out of sight on a day slightly shorter than the last. The haunted boughs are behind us; I know that there are spirits there, but they are, for the most part, friendly ghosts. ⌒

8

FISH

*

HERRING CRUDO *with Cider Mustard Cream*

SERVES 2

While I doubt we're likely to see an explosion of sushi bars serving locally caught fish along the shores of Lake Superior, this raw fish dish is worth trying if you have access to the freshest herring. This discovery came about accidentally, really: I was brining some very fresh herring to pickle it, and it looked so nice and pearly coming out of the brine, I had to taste a sliver. It was exquisite in taste and texture, just barely salty, with a firm freshness to the bite that you rarely find even in really good sushi or sashimi. I created this "crudo" preparation to mark the occasion.

   Salt and freshly ground black pepper
1 cup hot water
4 ounces absolutely fresh herring, skin removed
½ cup heavy cream
½ teaspoon yellow mustard seeds

Herring Crudo with Cider Mustard Cream

3 tablespoons sweet apple cider

2 teaspoons cider vinegar

¼ teaspoon Dijon-style mustard

2 teaspoons oil

¼ cup thinly sliced leek, white only

Coarse sea salt

Dissolve 1 tablespoon salt in the hot water and let cool to room temperature. Immerse the herring, refrigerate, and leave it in the brine for 2 to 3 hours.

Combine the cream, mustard seeds, cider, vinegar, and mustard in a small saucepan. Add a generous pinch of salt and a grind of pepper. Bring to a boil and simmer briskly until reduced by half. Remove from heat, cover, and let cool. Just before serving, heat the oil in a small skillet and add the leek. When the leek shreds are brown and crisp—*frizzled,* I like to say—remove them from the pan.

Remove the herring from its brine (discard brine) and cut it crosswise into thin slices. Divide the sauce onto 2 small plates, top each with half the herring slices, and garnish with the frizzled leeks. Sprinkle a little sea salt over and around and serve.

CHANTERELLE SMOKED HERRING BULGUR SALAD

SERVES 4 AS A SIDE DISH, 2 AS A LUNCH MAIN COURSE

Summery, appetizing, very much of the place.

1 cup bulgur

1½ cups boiling water

1 tablespoon unsalted butter

8–10 chanterelles, 2½ to 3 inches across the cap, quartered (about 1½ cups)

Salt and freshly ground black pepper

1 shallot or small sweet onion, chopped

1 clove garlic, minced

2 tablespoons cider vinegar

¼ cup canola or sunflower oil

Half a smoked herring (or other hot-smoked fish), flaked
(a generous cup)

½ cup sugar snap peas, strings removed, coarsely chopped

½ cup cherry tomatoes, halved

⅓ cup shaved or thinly sliced fennel bulb

½ cup wood sorrel leaves, plus a few for garnish, optional
(or a few small leaves of garden sorrel, shredded)

2 pickled ramps (p. 224, or substitute 2 spring onions),
finely chopped

1 small red onion, sliced very thin

Rinse the bulgur in cold water and drain. Place the bulgur in a bowl, add boiling water, cover, and let sit at least 30 minutes. Drain thoroughly. Set aside 2 cups bulgur (use any leftovers for a tabbouleh lunch for one).

Heat a small skillet and melt the butter. Add the chanterelles and a couple pinches of salt and cook, stirring, over medium heat for 2 minutes. Add the shallot or onion, cook another minute, and then add the garlic and cook, stirring, 2 minutes more, until the mushrooms are just beginning to brown.

Either prepare the chanterelles immediately before mixing the salad or make ahead, set aside, and reheat just before mixing.

Combine the vinegar, oil, ⅛ teaspoon salt, and a few grinds of pepper in a small bowl. In a large salad bowl, mix the herring and reserved chanterelles into the reserved bulgur. Add the peas, tomatoes, fennel, sorrel, ramps, and onion. Pour on the dressing and gently mix with the vegetables. Taste and adjust for salt just before serving.

✳ DEVILED WHITEFISH *with Potato Chip Crust*
SERVES 2

Some dishes are inspired by travel, by what the market or nature provides, or by a memory of a treasured dish of one's childhood. This one was inspired by a packet of fast-food ketchup and a nearly empty bag of potato chips. Oh, and the martinis might have played a part. Nonetheless, I stand by it. Solid, old-

school camp fish cookery right here. *Any thick white fillet—walleye, northern, etc.—could stand in for the whitefish.*

- ½ cup milk
- ⅛ teaspoon cayenne pepper
- 2 teaspoons ketchup
- 1 teaspoon spicy brown mustard
- 2 teaspoons soy sauce
- 2 (6- to 8-ounce) whitefish fillets
- 2 cups crushed potato chips
- Canola or corn oil
- Wild Tartar sauce (p. 221)
- Apple Turnip Slaw with Buckwheat Honey Dressing (p. 38)

Mix the milk with the cayenne, ketchup, mustard, and soy sauce in a large bowl. Add the fish and soak for 1 hour in the refrigerator, turning halfway through.

Place the potato chip crumbs on a plate. Remove the fillets from the marinade (discard marinade) and press them into the crumbs, coating the fish well on both sides. Heat a heavy skillet and add oil to a depth of ¼ inch. Fry the fish for 3 to 4 minutes on one side, and then carefully flip and fry for 3 to 4 minutes more, until the crust is crisp and brown. Serve with Wild Tartar Sauce and Apple-Turnip Slaw with Buckwheat Honey Dressing.

❋ WALLEYE TACOS

SERVES 2

In spite of their sun-baked, beachy connotations—oh, wait, I meant because *of them—we tend to make fish tacos in the deepest stretch of winter. It's a little Mexican vacation on a plate. Any good-quality tortillas will do here, but make a batch of Mary's Duck Fat Tortillas (p. 232) if you really want to treat yourself.*

There will be extra batter, and the oil will already be hot, so if you have an onion lying around, and the inclination, seize the opportunity to make fantastic onion rings.

8–10 ounces walleye fillets (or another flaky white fish: pike, perch, cod)

Salt

3 tablespoons cornstarch, plus extra for coating the fish

Oil for frying (canola or peanut)

½ cup ice water

1 large egg white, beaten to stiff peaks

¼ cup all-purpose flour

Tortillas

Sour cream

Salsa (recipes follow, or use Sambal Carrot Slaw [p. 41] or Snap Pea Salsa [p. 51])

Greens

Cut the fish into fingers 3 to 4 inches long and about ¾ inch wide. Lightly season the fish with salt and toss with some cornstarch on a plate to coat. Heat 1½ to 2 inches of oil in a heavy saucepan or wok over medium-high heat.

Add the ice water to the beaten egg white along with a pinch of salt and then gently whisk in the flour and 3 tablespoons cornstarch. Don't over-mix—it's okay if there are a few lumps. The batter will be thin, much thinner than pancake batter, more like crêpe batter.

Dip the fish fingers in the batter, allow excess to drip off, and then place in the hot oil, 4 or 5 at a time. Fry for 2 to 3 minutes, carefully turning to cook evenly. When nicely brown, remove and drain on paper towels.

Serve wrapped in tortillas with sour cream and salsa of your liking and some green leaves—I like to tuck watercress in my fish tacos, seems to fit the theme.

BLACK RADISH AND BLOOD ORANGE SALSA

MAKES ABOUT ½ CUP

  1   black radish, a little smaller than a tennis ball (or use daikon),
       peeled and shredded or coarsely grated
  ⅛   teaspoon salt
  1   blood orange

Toss the radish with the salt and let sit 20 minutes. Rinse the radish thoroughly in a couple changes of water; then drain and squeeze out excess liquid by hand. Using a micro grater, grate the zest of the orange into the radish. With a sharp paring knife, remove the orange rind and outer membrane. Slice the orange flesh into ¼-inch rounds, then into thin strips, and add to the radish. Mix well and let sit 20 minutes before serving.

SWEET CORN CHILE RELISH

MAKES ABOUT 1 CUP

  1   tablespoon olive oil
  1   red Fresno or jalapeño chile, seeded and finely chopped
  1   fresh or pickled green Anaheim chile, seeded and
         finely chopped
  1–2   dried red chilies, broken in half
  ¼   cup chopped red onion
  ¾   cup corn kernels (if using frozen, thaw, rinse, and drain well)
  1   large clove garlic, chopped
         Salt and freshly ground black pepper
  2   teaspoons white wine or cider vinegar
  ½   teaspoon sugar
  ⅓   cup water

Heat a small skillet or saucepan over medium heat and add the olive oil. Add the chilies and onion, and cook for 2 minutes. Add the corn, garlic, and a good pinch of salt. Cook, stirring, for 2 to 3 minutes, until the corn is a little brown at the edges. Add the vinegar, sugar, and water. Simmer briskly until all the liquid has cooked away. Taste and adjust for salt, and add a few grinds of black pepper.

BROILED TROUT *with Ramp Watercress Pesto*

SERVES 4

The flavor of watercress can range from intriguingly peppery to sharply assertive depending on source and season. Here it's combined with pungent ramps, but both are tempered by the richness of cheese and toasted walnuts. Small, farm-raised rainbow trout are perfect for this preparation. Take a walk along the stream to gather the vegetables, and just wave hello to the fish.

3 tablespoons chopped walnuts

1 packed cup watercress, leaves and tender stems, chopped

2 tablespoons chopped ramps and their greens, or 2 tablespoons pickled ramps, chopped, rinsed, and drained

2 tablespoons olive oil, plus more for coating fish

Juice of ¼ lemon (about 2 teaspoons)

1 ounce Asiago or Parmesan cheese, grated (about ⅓ cup)

Salt and freshly ground black pepper

4 (6- to 8-ounce) boneless rainbow trout, butterflied

Heat a small skillet and add the walnuts. Cook over medium heat, stirring, until they are lightly browned and fragrant. Set aside. In the bowl of a small food processor, combine the watercress, ramps, olive oil, and lemon juice and process to a smooth paste. Add the cheese, walnuts, and 2 pinches of salt. Process for 5 seconds more.

Preheat a broiler. Lightly brush the fish on both sides with olive oil, season with salt and pepper, and place them flesh side up on a baking sheet. Spread each with cress-ramp paste, coating liberally; you may still have a bit left over. Broil for 6 to 8 minutes, until the coating is bubbling and starting to brown. Serve immediately.

From Northern Waters

Minnesota is the Land of Ten Thousand Lakes, and Wisconsin has extensive coastlines on two of the Great Lakes. Both states boast world-class trout streams, and fishing remains one of the most popular pastimes in our region. Yet when you think of representative midwestern food, fish is unlikely to top the list. The Great Lakes fish boil is a charming custom (I admit I have yet to partake) but more of a ceremonial vestige than an ongoing concern in the regional food culture. Friday night fish fries don't count—lord knows where that deep-fried stuff comes from.

It's a mystery to me why more people aren't aware of the splendid fish that are still being harvested from our northern waters, particularly Lake Superior. While the Great Lakes commercial fishing industry is much reduced from its height, you can still pick up some of the best "seafood" in the world along both Minnesota's well-appreciated North Shore and Wisconsin's more low-key South Shore.

My former favorite spot, mainly for smoked but also for fresh fish, was Mel's in Knife River (I eulogize it in the recipe on p. 68). Since the demise of Mel's, the best places I know of on the North Shore are Lou's in Two Harbors, Russ Kendall's in Knife River, and the Dockside Fish Market in Grand Marais. The Dockside has the best selection of fresh fish: indeed, the fishing boats pull right up to the market's back door. You can also eat a lunch of whitefish and chips there and pick up a little-known North Shore delicacy: herring roe, or "Superior Gold Caviar." Next door to the Dockside is the Angry Trout Cafe, open seasonally, featuring inventive treatments of that same fresh fish and other locally sourced products.

In recent years, my favorite place to get Lake Superior fish—indeed, one of my favorite places on earth, period—is the town of Cornucopia on Wisconsin's South Shore. Corny, as it's locally known, is a town with a place-out-of-time feeling and a lovely long sandy beach, almost always deserted, especially in the off-season. The three main points of interest in Corny are Ehlers General Store, where you can purchase anything from a pry bar to waders to fine wine and locally made goat cheese; the Village Inn, a swell supper club and tavern—fish chowder and whitefish livers among their specialties; and Halvorson Fisheries, on the Corny waterfront.

Halvorson's is a real commercial fishery with a small retail store attached. As you're purchasing your fish in the shop—lake trout, bluefin herring, whitefish, maybe smelt or even burbot, a freshwater cod—the fish is being unloaded from skiffs docked right outside and cleaned just through the door in the processing area. The shop's hours of operation can be a little iffy, but if you get there at the right time you can walk away with fish that was swimming in Superior's ice water mansions a few hours before—and at crazy bargain prices. We fill a cooler when we go and freeze what we can't eat within a few days; fish this fresh comes out of the freezer, even after a couple of months, in better shape than anything you can buy elsewhere.

Those Lake Superior fish and stream trout—brown and brook—make up most of the fish I eat. There's another excellent, sustainable, and even more readily available type of fresh fish in our area: farmed rainbow trout. In western Wisconsin, both the Star Prairie Trout Farm (www.starprairietrout.com) and Bulldog Fish Farm (www.eatmyfish.com) sell fresh and smoked trout that have earned excellent reviews from home cooks and restaurant chefs alike. I'd really like to play the elitist fly-fisherman and tell you that, while these

*Brown trout
on grill*

farmed fish are fine in a pinch, they really don't measure up to the taste of wild fish—but I can't. These plump, coddled rainbows make excellent eating. The websites can direct you to local retail sources; better yet, pack up your fishing gear, head for the farm, and catch your own from the spring-fed ponds where they are raised. Just like wild stream trout, these farmed fish also inhabit beautiful country.

While the various fishes of our region all have their distinctive tastes and textures, they are pretty much interchangeable in the recipes presented here. The sauces—sorrel, wild tartar, brown butter, cider mustard cream—can be served with any kind of grilled, baked, broiled, fried, or poached fish.

Grilling is my favorite way of preparing stream trout: their skin is fairly thick (but perfectly, deliciously edible, especially when nicely browned), and a 10- to 12-inch trout is very manageable on the average home grill. Lake fish like whitefish and lake trout tend to be more soft skinned and fleshed. They can be grilled successfully if you oil the skin generously and cook them on a clean, oiled grill grate. One of those fish-grilling cages can be handy in grilling whole fish. The broiler can provide some of the qualities of a grill without the potential trauma of seeing your dinner disintegrate and disappear through the grate.

For frying fish, a nonstick skillet is the way to go—or a very well-seasoned cast-iron pan that has earned your confidence. With nonstick, of course, you can use a minimum of fat and still avoid sticking.

While a rich sauce or more elaborate presentation of fish is wonderful from time to time, mostly I keep it simple: just grill the fish or lightly flour and fry it, and serve it straight up or perhaps with a very simple sauce like melted butter with a squeeze of lemon juice and some chopped chives or tarragon. Freshness is the best seasoning, and a good appetite the tastiest sauce. ◠

✳ HERRING MILKWEED *à la Meunière*
SERVES 2

La Meunière *is the miller's wife, and she is kind enough to spare some flour to give the fish fillets a light, crisp, golden crust. Herring is not traditional in this dish—sole and trout are the classics—but when our visits to Lake Superior give us beautiful fresh herring, this is a wonderful preparation.*

2 (6-ounce) bluefin (freshwater) herring fillets, skinned
   (or trout, or walleye—any small fillet will work)
Salt and freshly ground black pepper
All-purpose flour
2 tablespoons canola or grape seed oil
3 tablespoons unsalted butter
1 tablespoon chopped milkweed "capers" (p. 225; or use regular
   small capers, rinsed)
1 tablespoon milkweed pickling brine (or a splash of cider
   vinegar if using regular capers)
¼ cup chopped fresh parsley, divided
Juice of ¼ lemon (about 2 teaspoons)

Lightly season the fish with salt and pepper and then coat with flour. In a
large skillet, heat the oil. Knock excess flour from the fillets and fry for 2 to
3 minutes per side, until the crust is nicely browned. Transfer the fish to a
paper towel–lined plate and keep warm in a 200-degree oven.

In a small saucepan over medium heat, melt the butter and cook until it
starts to brown. When it takes on a hazelnut color (what the French call *noi-
sette*), remove it from the heat. Add the capers and brine or vinegar and half
the parsley.

Arrange the fish on plates and nap with the butter sauce. Give each fillet a
squeeze of lemon juice, a sprinkle of parsley, and a grind of pepper. Serve.

∗ "ESCABECHE" OF BROWN TROUT *with Ramps and Asparagus*

SERVES 2

*Crisp fried trout fillets sit on a bed of spring vegetables in a rich-tart sauce.
A couple of boiled new potatoes fill out the plate.*

6 thick spears asparagus
6–8 ramp bulbs and their greens
4 teaspoons canola oil, divided
3 tablespoons plus 2 teaspoons unsalted butter, divided

2 tablespoons cider or white wine vinegar

¼ cup dry white wine

¾ cup unsalted fish or chicken stock

¼ teaspoon sugar

Salt and freshly ground black pepper

4 brown or rainbow trout fillets (12–14 ounces total)

½ cup rye flour

With really good, fresh, springtime asparagus, nearly the entire stalk should be tender. Trim the bottom inch or so and take a nibble; if it is not tender, trim a bit more or peel the bottom couple of inches. Separate the tips, about 3 inches, and set aside. Thinly slice the rest of the asparagus on the diagonal and set aside. Thinly slice the ramp bulbs on the diagonal, to yield about ½ cup. Chop the ramp greens coarsely.

Heat a skillet or broad saucepan and add 2 teaspoons of the canola oil and 1 tablespoon of the butter. When it is very hot, add the sliced asparagus. Fry for a minute or so, to give it a little color. Remove from the pan with a slotted spoon, and add the sliced ramps. Fry at high heat for 1 minute or so, until

"Escabeche" of Brown Trout with Ramps and Asparagus

they begin to brown. Add the ramp greens and cook for 30 seconds to wilt. Stir in the vinegar, wine, stock, sugar, and a good pinch of salt. Cook at a fast simmer until reduced by half.

Meanwhile, cook the trout: season the fillets with salt and pepper and coat lightly with rye flour. Fry in a separate skillet in 2 teaspoons each oil and butter, 2 to 3 minutes per side, until nicely browned.

Add the asparagus tips to the sauce and cook for 1 minute. Return the sliced asparagus to the pan and add the remaining 2 tablespoons butter. Increase the heat to high, and boil furiously for 30 seconds to emulsify the sauce. Add a few grinds of pepper. Taste and adjust for salt—it will probably need a good pinch or two, to help balance the acidity. Don't be alarmed if it tastes quite tart—it will be offset by the rich fried fish.

Remove the asparagus tips from the sauce. Spoon the sauce into large bowls or plates, arrange the fish attractively on top, and surmount the whole with asparagus tips. Serve.

* BUCKWHEAT TROUT *with Sorrel Sauce*
SERVES 4

Sorrel is a relative of rhubarb and buckwheat. Its tart, lemony flavor is wonderful in this rich sauce for fried or grilled trout or salmon. Foragers: use a combination of sheep sorrel and wood sorrel in place of the garden sorrel.

- ¾ cup unsalted fish stock
- ¾ cup unsalted chicken stock
- 2 tablespoons dry white wine or dry vermouth
- 1 small onion, sliced
- ½ cup heavy cream, divided
- 1 small bunch sorrel, about a dozen good-size leaves
- Salt and freshly ground black pepper
- 2 tablespoons plus 2 teaspoons unsalted butter, divided
- 4–8 fillets rainbow or brown trout (1½ pounds total)
- ½ cup or more buckwheat flour
- 2 teaspoons canola oil

In a small saucepan combine the stocks, wine, onion, and ¼ cup of the cream. Bring to a boil, reduce the heat to maintain a quick simmer, and cook until reduced by half. Strain into a bowl to remove onion and then return the sauce to the pan. Discard onion.

Remove the thick stems from the sorrel. Chop ¾ of the sorrel leaves into rough confetti. Slice the remaining leaves into very fine ribbons—a chiffonade—and set aside.

Add the remaining ¼ cup cream and a pinch of salt to the sauce and simmer to reduce by one-third. Reduce heat to low and add the chopped sorrel. Cook for 1 minute and then whisk in 2 tablespoons of the butter. The sauce should now be thick enough to coat the back of a spoon; if not, simmer a bit longer. Taste and adjust for salt and add a few grinds of pepper. Keep warm.

Lightly season the trout with salt and pepper, and then coat in the buckwheat flour. Heat a large skillet over medium-high heat and add 2 teaspoons each butter and oil. Cook the fish 2 to 3 minutes per side, until brown. Remove the fish to serving plates and spoon the sauce over and around the fish. Garnish with sorrel chiffonade. Any extra sauce is fabulous on plain boiled new potatoes.

Of the Stream and the Season

I first picked up a fly rod and waded into a trout stream more than twenty years ago, and I've hardly wanted to put down the rod, or get out of the water, since. The annals of fishing literature, from Walton to Hemingway, Maclean, and McGuane, are replete with odes to manly romance, native grandeur, and the healing power of flowing waters. I'll second all those emotions and add that fly-fishing revealed to me a world I scarcely knew existed— a world within the world I've lived in all my life, but hidden. It also fundamentally changed the way I eat by putting fresh-caught fish back on my plate and leading me to discover wild-foraged foods like ramps, nettles, watercress, and wild mushrooms. While the term *foodshed* is trying to elbow its way into the modern lexicon to describe the natural and human catch basin in which we find sustenance, for much of the summer and fall I practice watershed eating, literally.

As much as I anticipate opening day of the stream trout season, I rarely fish it. Opening weekend on any well-known stream is a madhouse, a circus, amateur hour. I leave that seasonal rite to the once-a-year sports and give things a few days to calm down. Around the middle of the following week I load my gear and head for southeastern Minnesota down U.S. Highway 52.

I turn off the four-lane at Oronoco and roll east for twenty-five miles or so, through gently undulant farmland and pastureland. Just east of the tidy, pleasant town of Plainview, the road falls off a cliff. I take the car out of gear and sail down the long, winding hill as crenellated limestone bluffs rise higher and higher above, white pines and leafless birches at their tops.

Halfway down the hill is my turnoff, a washboard gravel lane not quite two cars wide. I cross a culvert where a spring pours out of the base of the hill into a little pool adjacent to the stream, and that pool is carpeted with brilliant green watercress. The road hugs the hill for a while, then turns to skirt a corn-field, just stubble now. Across the field I have a good view of the bluffs, with turkey vultures wheeling above them. I go all the way to the end of the road, two or three miles along. A gate blocks the way here—beyond it are hundreds of acres of state land, open to the public but closed to cars. In the middle of the sandy turnaround there's a fire pit filled with blackened beer cans. The yellow sign that spells out the fishing regulations on this stream is liberally perforated with bullet holes.

I don't know how many hundreds of times I've jointed and strung my rod, stepped into waders, and tied up wading boots; still, the first time I do it after the winter layoff, I always feel a bit awkward. The feeling persists as I walk to the stream—I stumble on roots, remember that I really need to pick up my feet with these studded soles—and when I step in the water it will take me a few minutes to find my footing. I play out line and imagine myself casting gracefully to a rising trout on my very first cast—the trout will take, of course—but more likely my backcast finds a tree branch or angelica stalk. It's all just part of the process.

Soon enough I recover some grace in wading and find my casting rhythm. At this time of year, there is very likely to be an emergence of small mayflies as the day warms. The flies bring up the trout—it's one of their first feasts of spring—and then the hours just vanish. All of a sudden the light is getting long, I'm sweaty and sunburned, and I've got an hour-and-a-half's drive ahead of me once I get back to the car.

Nothing is so urgent that I can't stop at that spring on the way out, bury my face in it, drink deeply. I'll gather a sack of cress to make a bed for the trout in my creel, with a dressing of sweet browned ramps on top, a ritual meal of the opening days. Back on the highway it's cruise control and anticipation of a shower, a cold beer, and a fine meal at the end of the drive. The sun is strong as it drops in the west; it roasts my left ear all the way home.

Come May, I return to my favorite Wisconsin waters; the season opens two weeks later there. The trees have yet to leaf out, but the forest floor is verdant and blooming, and the mayfly hatches of spring and early summer are in full swing. These are now evening hatches for the most part, so I can have a productive day and still fish to my heart's content. The drive to the stream involves rush hour traffic and freeways. When I reach the river, I'll open a beer (this used to be the time for a cigarette, too), walk to the bridge railing, and see what's happening on the stream.

It may be that the hatch is already on—mayfly nymphs rising from the bottom, shedding husks and unfurling wings, entering a whole new existence in the alien air. The trout are in their feeding lanes, the biggest fish in the best spots, of course, the smaller ones taking second best. The trout find a rhythm of rising, and if the hatch is strong the surface of the water can almost appear to be boiling. They won't stop eating until it's over—with bulging bellies they'll still try to cram more insects into their mouths. Above water, the birds—swallows, cedar waxwings, redstarts—are also taking advantage of this bounty, sweeping above the stream to pick off mayflies that have gained the air, dipping to the surface to snatch flies that haven't managed to take flight.

And then I wonder, *What am I doing here, spectating, when I could be fishing?* I tog up and get down to the water and fish it out until dark.

The most epic of the early summer hatches is the hex hatch: the coming out of the *Hexagenia limbata,* a mayfly that can exceed two inches in length. Its peculiar habit is that it only emerges as the light is fading on nights in late June—most often sweltering nights, in my memory. As mosquitoes start to swarm and bats to swirl, the nymphs of these largest of the mayflies emerge from silty beds (loon shit, in one local vernacular) and form a flotilla on the

Closing day on the upper Kinnickinnic River

surface before their wings are dry enough to fly. Even very large fish lose all caution; fisherfolk about lose their wits. You cast huge flies toward the sound of outrageous rises in the buggy dark. The tug of a trout bigger than any you've encountered—has to be a two-footer—in the instant before it breaks off, leaves you trembling. This delirium may go on until after midnight, and then you stumble out through the tall nettles down a mucky trail, finding your way with a faltering flashlight. The next morning, it hardly seems real.

Midsummer is for early-morning getaways or contemplative evening strolls in the water: not a lot of insect activity to bring out the fish, but plenty of beauty to be caught. The cool of the day, the hours of long light, that's when you want to be on the stream. There's much about fishing, an atavistic activity to start with, that encourages a sort of nostalgia.

In September, with the season on the wane, it gets serious again. As the month approaches the equinox, I hope for bad weather; I cross my fingers for the chance to fish a couple of days in pelting rain. Protected by my waders, my waxed-cotton wading jacket, my trusty old fishing hat, I don't mind the weather conditions at all. While the sportsman's adage says that the two best times to go fishing are when it's raining and when it ain't, the sports don't seem to heed it. On blustery wet days, I have the whole river to myself. With winter and spawning season approaching, these first storms of autumn raise a sense of urgency in the trout: they will strike aggressively at any reasonable presentation of a fly, and I can often take home a limit of three fat fish, perfect for the grill or smoker.

And then, the end. My final day of fishing is always like this, even if, technically, it is not: I close the year on a day of brilliant blue sky, cool, dry air, and sharp, clear light that can nearly make you cry—and not only because the angle of late-day sun is tough on the eyes. I take my old dog with me and fish the lower section of a famous west-central Wisconsin river, a stretch that travels through a canyon of towering limestone cliffs topped by tall white pines, springwater dripping from cracks in the rock and feeding moss and cress that cling to the cliff face. In that extraordinary September light, I see things with amazing detail—how the breeze ruffles the tips of Annabel's fur; how the sun catches every atom of water when she shakes after crossing the stream; threads of gossamer blowing by high overhead, caught and shining in that light, nearly as high as the tops of the pines. While I fish, Annabel stands in a shallow riffle, biting at a standing wave, a mini-grizzly faux-fishing, or muddles along the bank, sticking her nose into muskrat holes. I fish it out until the air starts to chill and the sun has dropped below the western hill and my dog is whining at me that she's cold, and it's time to go home.

I reel up, and we make our way through the cool, dusky, fragrant woods back to the car. Another season in the net; whether or not there are fish in the creel is entirely beside the point. ⌢

* OPENING DAYS GRILLED STREAM TROUT *with* Ramp Dressing on a Bed of Cress
SERVES 2

A ritual meal of the opening week of trout season.

 1 tablespoon unsalted butter
 1 cup sliced ramp bulbs plus their greens, chopped
 1 tablespoon cider vinegar

1 tablespoon water

2 tablespoons olive oil, plus more for coating fish

1 teaspoon maple syrup or honey

2 teaspoons Dijon-style mustard

Salt and freshly ground black pepper

2 (10- to 12-inch) brown, rainbow, or brook trout

Watercress or other wild salad greens—dandelion,
    lamb's-quarter, sheep sorrel

Prepare a hot fire of natural wood coals. In a medium skillet, melt the butter and add the sliced ramp bulbs. Cook over very low heat, stirring often, until they are very soft and brown and starting to caramelize. Add the ramp greens and cook for 2 minutes. Transfer the ramps to a mixing bowl. Deglaze the pan with the vinegar and water. Add the liquid to the ramps along with 2 tablespoons olive oil, the maple syrup or honey, mustard, and salt and pepper to taste.

Brush the fish on both sides with olive oil. Season with salt and pepper inside and out. Grill for 8 to 10 minutes, turning the fish as needed to keep the skin from charring too much. Serve the trout on a bed of cress or other greens; drizzle dressing over the top. ⌒

GRILLED TROUT, FIDDLEHEADS, AND RAMPS
in Nettles-Bacon Broth

Ideas about a dish, and the dish itself.

The idea was three key springtime ingredients—trout, ramps, and fiddleheads—prepared very simply and united by a sauce that shouldn't be too rich or saucy, more of a broth—a *nage*, in the fancy cooking world. With stinging nettles growing under the apple trees just down the path from the Bide-A-Wee cabin, I knew they would be part of it. Some ramp greens added to the broth would tie things together.

Nettles alone would make for thin soup. It needed something rich and maybe meaty: enter bacon—bacon rind, to be precise—which would add depth and savor. I pinched off the top six inches from about fifteen nettle plants, rinsed the leaves, chopped them coarsely, and added them to three cups of water. I added the chopped greens of three or four ramps and about a three-by-three-inch square of bacon rind, diced. I brought it to a boil and simmered it for around an hour, and then turned it off and let it sit while I made the other preparations.

The trout got salt and pepper and a little oil to keep it from sticking on the grill. The ramps and fiddleheads went naked to the grill, and halfway through I glazed them with a reduction of maple syrup, apple cider vinegar, and soy sauce flavored with more ramp greens.

While the fish and vegetables were grilling, I brought the broth up to heat again and strained it. It didn't taste like much at that point, but then I started to reduce it, and it really came together. When there was about a half to two-thirds of a cup left, I swirled in a couple teaspoons butter and added a pinch of salt and some pepper.

With a glass of cider fizzing companionably at my elbow, the dogs asleep on the floor, I sat down to dinner. It was just me that night. The trout was exquisite, and the broth was superb. It took up a little extra saltiness and sweetness as the glaze dissolved off the vegetables. The fiddleheads were perfectly tender crisp, the ramps more crisp than tender.

I really should have lingered over each bite, but it was so good, I was so hungry, and there was no one to talk to. I scarfed it down.

* BREAKFAST TROUT *with Bacon and Fried Apples*

Brook trout would be best, but brown trout are good, too. I've seen this sort of thing done with herring, as well.

> *Per person*
> 3 slices bacon
> 1 small (10-ounce) trout, filleted
> Salt and freshly ground black pepper
> Rye flour (or substitute cornmeal, buckwheat, or fine oatmeal)
> 1 small apple, peeled, cored, and quartered
> 1–2 slices good-quality bread, toasted

Brown trout fillets

In a skillet, cook the bacon gently over medium heat until the fat has rendered and the bacon is browned. Remove the bacon from the pan. Season the trout with salt and pepper and coat with flour. Fry the trout and apples in the bacon drippings until the trout is crisply brown and the apples have some color. Serve with bacon and toast.

✳ HOME-SMOKED TROUT

Be sure to read Smoking Basics (p. 22).

I usually smoke brown trout because that's mostly what I catch. If you're buying trout to smoke, it will probably be farmed rainbow trout, which have lived fat and happy lives up until their unfortunate end and will smoke up beautifully. I've also used this brine and method on lake trout and herring.

In a medium saucepan, heat 4 cups water and add ½ cup salt and ½ cup brown sugar, stirring to dissolve. Remove from heat and let cool. I have added cracked peppercorns and/or herbs to the brine; I'm not sure I could really taste them in the final product. Try different flavorings if you like.

A 12- to 14-inch fish is ideal for smoking, but smaller or larger ones can be smoked, too. Just brine and smoke for a longer or shorter time, depending on size. Given those ideal 14-inch trout, brine them, refrigerated, overnight. Fish smaller than 12 inches can take up sufficient brine in 4 to 6 hours. A couple of hours before you plan to smoke, remove the fish from the brine (discard brine), rinse in cold water, and set them on a wire rack set over a baking sheet. Using wooden picks—first break or snip off the sharp ends so they don't go right through the flesh—prop open the body cavity of the fish to allow them to cook evenly and take up a lot of smoke. Smoke at 200–220 degrees for 2 hours.

Use smoked stream trout in Frisée Salad with Smoked Trout (p. 40), Smoked Trout and Wild Rice Chowder (p. 68), or Potted Smoked Trout (p. 31).

*Smoking
herring*

✳ MAPLE-BASTED SMOKED LAKE TROUT FILLETS

See Smoking Basics (p. 22) for tips.

> 2 tablespoons salt
> 2 cups hot water
> 2 tablespoons maple syrup, plus more to brush on fish
> 1–3 (10- to 12-ounce) lake trout fillets

In a large bowl, dissolve the salt in the hot water and stir in 2 tablespoons maple syrup. Let this brine cool and then add the fish and set aside in the refrigerator for 4 to 6 hours. Remove the fish from the brine (discard brine) and dry on a wire rack for 1 hour. Just before smoking, brush the flesh side with 1 teaspoon maple syrup (per fillet) diluted with 1 teaspoon water. Smoke skin side down at 200–220 degrees for 1 to 1½ hours, until nicely colored and firm, brushing again with syrup-water halfway through.

Use to top cream-cheese schmeared crackers, in Frisée Salad with Smoked Trout (p. 40), or in Smoked Trout and Wild Rice Chowder (p. 183). ⌒

9

VEGETABLE

SIDES

*

GRILLED BUTTERNUT SQUASH *with Maple–Cider Vinegar Glaze*

SERVES 4

For the sake of ease, use only the solid top of the squash for this recipe. Save the bottom to roast or add to soup. Serve grilled squash alongside pork steaks or country-style ribs grilled and glazed with the same maple-vinegar reduction. You will need a hot fire of hardwood coals to prepare this recipe.

1 small butternut squash top (see headnote), peeled,
   cut into 4-by-1-by-½-inch planks
2 teaspoons olive oil
Salt and freshly ground pepper
1 teaspoon sambal oelek chili paste
Maple Syrup–Cider Vinegar Reduction (p. 217)

Toss the squash with the olive oil, a good pinch of salt, a few grinds of pepper, and the sambal oelek. Set aside for 30 minutes. Start the fire.

When the coals are ready, place the squash on a grate at a medium-hot spot. Check carefully in the first couple of minutes to make sure the squash isn't charring too quickly. Grill for about 10 minutes, turning often, until nicely colored and tender. Brush one side with maple-vinegar reduction and flip to brush the other side. Cook for 1 minute on each side, and serve hot. Add salt to taste and a fresh grind of black pepper at the table.

FIDDLEHEADS *in Brown Butter*

SERVES 4

Ostrich fern fiddleheads are our main midwestern edible fern. Easy to identify by the distinct groove that runs up the stem, they begin to appear in late April or early May, and they grow abundantly in moist woods as well as in shady backyards. They can be eaten as long as the leaf is still tightly coiled: when they start to unfurl, they are no longer edible. The stem below the coiled top—sometimes several inches long—is also edible and delicious. Take only two or three fiddleheads from each clump to preserve the resource. This preparation works well with asparagus, too.

2 cups ostrich fern fiddleheads

2 tablespoons unsalted butter

Juice of ¼ lemon (about 2 teaspoons)

Salt and freshly ground black pepper

Rinse the fiddleheads in several changes of water to remove their papery husks and any grit. Blanch the fiddleheads in salted water for 5 minutes. Refresh them in ice water and then drain well and set aside. In a medium saucepan, melt the butter and then cook over medium heat until it is hazelnut colored and fragrant. Remove from heat and add the lemon juice, fiddleheads, a good pinch of salt, and freshly ground black pepper. Return the pan to the heat for a minute to warm the fiddleheads, and serve. ⌁

SOY-SIMMERED BURDOCK ROOT

SERVES 2

If you spend any time in the northern fields and woods in the fall, you—or, more likely, your dog—will surely have encountered burdock. An abundant biennial, the second-year plants send up tall flower stalks that produce tenacious burrs.

Burdock has a nicer side, but it's kept hidden, way underground. The deep taproots, harvested in the plant's first year, are edible and tasty when properly prepared. Consult a foraging guide for harvesting tips. Sometimes sold under its Japanese name, gobo, burdock root is widely available in grocery stores, too.

For an Asian-themed supper, serve this dish with Smoke-Grilled Ma La Chicken Wings (p. 144) and Sichuan Stir-Fried Corn (p. 198).

1 burdock root the size of a large carrot, peeled, cut into 1½-by-½-inch batons (1½ cups)

1½ tablespoons soy sauce

2 tablespoons rice wine or dry sherry

1 tablespoon maple syrup

1 small fresh or dried red chile, seeded

1 green onion, chopped

1 cup water

1 teaspoon sesame oil
Toasted sesame seeds, optional

Place the burdock in a saucepan, cover with water, bring to a boil, and simmer for 10 minutes. Drain burdock and then add the soy sauce, rice wine or dry sherry, maple syrup, chile, green onion, and 1 cup water. Simmer, uncovered, for 20 minutes, or until the burdock is tender. Remove the burdock with a slotted spoon to a serving dish. Reduce the remaining sauce until it starts to look a bit syrupy. Pour it over the burdock. Before serving, add sesame oil and sprinkle on some toasted sesame seeds, if you like. ◡

✳ NETTLES RAMP CHAMP

SERVES 2

A wild iteration of the Irish standby, best in spring, when the nettles are young and tender and ramps abundant within their range.

4 ramp bulbs, fresh or pickled (p. 224)
1 packed cup young nettles (wood or stinging), leaves and tender stems
2 medium (5- to 6-ounce) Yukon gold potatoes, peeled and quartered, or 4 small (2-inch) red or yellow new potatoes, halved
2 tablespoons unsalted butter
2 tablespoons sour cream
Salt

If using fresh ramps, separate the leaves and bulbs; thinly slice the bulbs and coarsely chop the greens. If using pickled ramps, thinly slice the bulbs and rinse in two changes of water. Rinse the nettles in a couple changes of water and then blanch them in boiling water for 1 minute. Drain and chop.

Boil the potatoes until tender, about 15 minutes. Melt the butter in a medium skillet and add the sliced ramp bulbs. Cook gently without browning for 3 to 4 minutes. Add the potatoes to the skillet and crush them with a sturdy fork or potato masher. Add the nettles and ramp leaves, stirring to mix. Add the sour cream and 2 generous pinches of salt. Mix well and serve hot. ◡

BRAISED SAUERKRAUT

SERVES 4 TO 6

Humble kraut simmers to magnificence with wine, stock, bacon, and aromatic vegetables and herbs. This preparation is the basis of the famous Alsatian dish choucroute garnie, *in which sauerkraut (*choucroute*) is "garnished" with mounds of smoked meats and sausages. The classic's porcine extravagance will defeat most modern appetites, but braised sauerkraut still makes a delightful accompaniment to more modest portions of grilled sausages, smoked pork chops, or duck confit. Simply brown the meats well and add them to the sauerkraut to finish cooking/warming during the last 15 to 20 minutes of the braise. There are even fish versions of* choucroute garnie, *in which fresh fish is gently steamed, and smoked fish warmed, atop the kraut as it simmers.*

For any of these preparations, the sauerkraut can be made up to several days ahead and reheated.

> 2 packed cups sauerkraut, preferably home fermented (p. 222)
> 3 ounces slab or 3 slices thick-sliced bacon, cut into ½-inch cubes
> 1 small leek, sliced
> 1 onion, sliced
> 1 large carrot, sliced
> 1 cup unsalted chicken stock
> ½ cup dry white wine or dry vermouth
> 6 whole juniper berries
> 2 bay leaves
> 3 sprigs fresh thyme
> Salt and coarsely ground black pepper

Rinse the sauerkraut in two changes of water, drain it, and then squeeze out excess water. In a heavy Dutch oven or large saucepan, gently cook the bacon until the fat starts to render. Add the leek, onion, and carrot and cook over medium-low heat until the onions are translucent and wilted, about 5 minutes. Add the sauerkraut, stock, wine, juniper berries, bay leaves, thyme, a good pinch of salt, and a few coarse grinds of black pepper. Simmer, partly covered, stirring occasionally, for 45 to 60 minutes. Add water or additional stock if the kraut threatens to cook dry. Taste and adjust for salt. Discard the bay leaves, thyme stems, and juniper berries before serving. ⌒

❊ MOM'S HOT RED CABBAGE
SERVES 4

My mother, Grace Laidlaw, comes from German stock, which is reflected in this family heirloom cabbage recipe. Mom always serves it with braised spareribs; it would be good with any kind of pork or with Duck Confit (p. 149).

- ½ large head red cabbage (about 2 pounds), shredded ¼ inch thick
- 1 apple, peeled, cored, and chopped or coarsely grated
- 1 tablespoon canola or vegetable oil
- 1 cup water
- ⅓ cup cider or red wine vinegar
- 1½ tablespoons brown or maple sugar
- ¼ teaspoon salt

Combine all ingredients in a large saucepan. Bring to a boil and simmer, partly covered, for 30 to 40 minutes, until the cabbage is very tender. Check after 15 minutes and add water if necessary. Taste and adjust for salt. Serve. ⌒

❊ SWEET BUTTERED CABBAGE
SERVES 2

This dish can be made ahead and reheated just before serving. It's excellent with Grouse in Cider Cream (p. 155) or pork.

- ¼ medium head green cabbage, shredded ¼ inch thick
- 4 teaspoons butter
- 1 shallot, sliced
- 1 clove garlic, chopped
- ½ teaspoon sugar
- 2 tablespoons dry white wine

½ cup water

Salt and freshly ground black pepper

Bring a pot of water to a boil and add the cabbage. Once the water returns to a boil, blanch the cabbage for 1 minute, and then drain and set aside. In a sauté pan with a lid, melt the butter. Add the shallot and cook gently until wilted. Stir in cabbage, garlic, sugar, wine, water, a couple pinches of salt, and a few grinds of pepper. Cover and cook over low heat, stirring occasionally, for 15 to 20 minutes, until the liquid is absorbed and the thinner cabbage shreds are silken and the thicker ones retain a bit of bite. Taste and adjust for salt. Serve.

✳ ROOT VEGETABLE PANCAKES

SERVES 4

Equally good as a dinner side dish or at breakfast or brunch topped with poached or over-easy eggs.

- 1 large potato, peeled and coarsely grated
- 1 large parsnip, peeled and coarsely grated
- 1 carrot, peeled and coarsely grated
- ½ medium celery root (about 6 ounces), peeled and coarsely grated
- 1 small onion, coarsely grated
- 1 small leek, white and light green parts, thinly sliced
- 2 large eggs
- 2 tablespoons all-purpose flour
- 2 tablespoons cornmeal

Salt and freshly ground black pepper

Oil or duck fat for frying

In a large bowl, combine all the vegetables (potato through leek) and mix in the eggs, flour, cornmeal, ⅛ teaspoon salt, and a few grinds of pepper. Heat a large heavy skillet and add oil or duck fat to lightly cover the bottom. Add the vegetable mixture in ¼-cup portions. Flatten each scoop into pancakes, and cook until nicely brown on both sides, about 10 minutes total. Serve.

* OVEN-FRIED ROOTS

SERVES 2

Any of the vegetables listed here can be prepared in this way, alone or in combination. Cut into french fry shape, the vegetables present plenty of surface to brown and caramelize. I particularly like to use fat from Duck Leg Confit (p. 149) in this recipe; it really helps the vegetables brown and carries some of the confit spice aromas.

    1 parsnip
    1 large potato (russet, Yukon gold)
    1 large carrot
    ½ medium celery root (about 6 ounces)
    2 tablespoons fat (canola or olive oil, duck or chicken fat, lard)
       Salt and freshly ground black pepper

Preheat oven to 400 degrees. Peel vegetables and cut them into largish french fry shapes, 3 to 4 inches long by about ½ inch square. Rinse the potatoes, drain, and pat dry.

Place an ovenproof skillet or gratin dish in a preheated oven, empty, for 5 minutes. Remove from the oven and add the fat and then the vegetables, tossing well to coat. Roast vegetables for 20 minutes and then flip them. If the potatoes stick, don't rush it: give them another 5 minutes or so to brown up and release from the pan. Cook for an additional 20 to 30 minutes, until all the vegetables are tender and as brown and crisp as you like. If any seem to be getting overdone, remove them from the pan and return them for a couple of minutes at the end to reheat. Toss with salt and pepper. Serve plain or with aioli (p. 221).

* OVEN-ROASTED KALE

SERVES 2

Deceptively simple; truly delicious. Kale is good for you: eat all you want. Variations follow.

10–12 large kale leaves, stems removed, leaves rinsed and
  patted dry
1 tablespoon olive oil
Salt, optional

Preheat oven to 375 degrees. In a large mixing bowl, toss the kale with the olive oil and let stand for 15 minutes. Transfer the kale to a baking dish and bake for 20 to 25 minutes, until desired doneness. Stir with tongs every 5 minutes, or the leaves on top will cook and crisp too quickly.

Add salt only at the very end of cooking—there's a lot of natural savoriness in dark leafy greens like kale, and I often find they don't need any salt at all.

Some options:
* Add a few slices of onion or whole cloves of garlic at the beginning of cooking.
* Add sliced garlic about halfway through.
* Add a few sprigs of fresh thyme or rosemary.

If you continue roasting the kale in a single layer, you'll completely dry it out and, if you haven't burned it, you'll have kale chips, which are lovely.

* SWEET AND SOUR CHARD

SERVES 4

The sweet and sour combination works well with earthy chard. Young beets and their greens could get the same treatment: prepare the beet root as you would the chard stems, the greens as the leaves.

10 good-size chard leaves (to yield about 4 cups chopped)
3 tablespoons olive oil
1 medium onion, sliced

Salt and freshly ground black pepper
½ cup unsalted chicken stock
½ cup water
2 tablespoons cider vinegar, or to taste
3 teaspoons maple syrup, or to taste
Thyme, optional
Butter, optional

Cut the thick ribs from the chard leaves and slice the ribs diagonally into ½-inch pieces. Tear or cut each leaf into 4 or 5 pieces. Heat a 10-inch skillet and add the olive oil and then the onion and chard rib pieces. Stir in ⅛ teaspoon salt, the stock, and water. Cover and cook over medium heat for 6 to 8 minutes, until the chard stems begin to soften. Add the chard leaves, and as soon as they wilt into the liquid add the vinegar and maple syrup. Cook uncovered for 3 to 4 minutes, until the chard is tender and the liquid reduced. Taste and adjust for salt, sweet, and sour. Stir in a few grinds of black pepper, some thyme, and a knob of butter, if desired. Serve.

OVEN GREEN BEANS *with Bacon*
SERVES 2

This preparation is especially good with flat romano beans, which present a lot of surface for browning. For a meatless version, omit the bacon and add a tablespoon of olive oil and a good pinch of salt.

2 handfuls (5–6 ounces) green string or romano beans
1 thick slice bacon, cut into ½-inch pieces
4–6 cloves unpeeled garlic

Preheat oven to 375 degrees. Combine the beans, bacon, and garlic in a small baking pan or ovenproof skillet. Roast for 15 minutes; stir to distribute the fat given off by the bacon. Cook for 15 to 20 minutes more, until the beans are a bit wrinkled, brown, and tender. Serve.

Oven Green Beans with Bacon

✳ ROASTED BABY CARROTS *with Maple-Mustard Glaze*

SERVES 2

Use real baby carrots from your garden or farmers market, not the plastic bagged grocery store kind, which are really just big carrots whittled down.

2 cups baby carrots (about 8 ounces), scrubbed

1½ tablespoons maple syrup

1 teaspoon canola or grape seed oil

Salt and freshly ground black pepper

1 rounded teaspoon grainy mustard

⅛ teaspoon Espelette pepper, or a good pinch
    of cayenne, optional

1 teaspoon red wine vinegar

Preheat oven to 375 degrees. Combine the carrots, maple syrup, oil, a pinch of salt, and a grind of pepper in a gratin dish or small baking dish. Roast, uncovered, for 45 minutes, stirring every 15 minutes, until brown and glazy.

Remove from oven and stir in the mustard, optional Espelette or cayenne, vinegar, and another grind of pepper. Taste and adjust for salt. Serve warm or at room temperature. ⁓

❋ BLACKBERRY-MUSTARD GRILLED CARROTS

SERVES 4

Sweet young carrots gain a lot of character from a blackberry-mustard bath and a bit of char on the grill.

12–16 small (6- to 7-inch) carrots
1 tablespoon blackberry jam (or Quick Wild Berry Sauce, p. 208)
1 tablespoon grainy mustard
1 tablespoon unsalted butter, melted
Salt and freshly ground black pepper
⅛ teaspoon Espelette or cayenne pepper, optional

Prepare a fire of natural wood charcoal. Trim the carrots, leaving a half inch or so of the leaf stems, and scrub them well. Blanch the carrots in boiling water for 3 minutes and then refresh in cold water and drain. Combine the jam, mustard, butter, salt and pepper to taste, and the Espelette or cayenne if desired. Toss the carrots in this mixture.

Grill the carrots, turning often, until they are nicely charred, even a bit black in spots, and as tender as you like, 5 to 8 minutes. ⁓

❋ MIXED MASH

SERVES 4

Mashed potatoes with attitude. Grate in a little horseradish for even more. Also: you can use the leftover cooking liquid as the basis for a vegetable stock.

2 medium (5- to 6-ounce) potatoes, peeled, quartered
1 carrot, peeled, cut into 1-inch pieces
1 parsnip, peeled, cut into 1-inch pieces
½ medium celery root (about 6 ounces), peeled, cut
   into 1-inch pieces

Mixed Mash

2 tablespoons unsalted butter
Salt and freshly ground black pepper

Bring a pot of water to a boil, add the potatoes, carrot, parsnip, and celery root, and simmer briskly until very tender, about 20 to 25 minutes. Drain, reserving 1 cup cooking liquid. Mash the vegetables with a fork or potato masher. Stir in the butter, salt to taste, and a few grinds of pepper. Add cooking liquid until the puree is as smooth as you like. Serve.

✳ CELERY ROOT—POTATO PUREE

SERVES 4

Excellent with Duck Breast with Blackberry-Whisky Sauce (p. 147) or any savory sauced meat dish. I find it's easiest to peel celery root if I cut it in half, place a flat side on the cutting board, work around it with a paring knife to remove most of the peel, and then finish up with a vegetable peeler.

1 medium (10-ounce) celery root, trimmed, peeled, and cut
   into 2-inch pieces
2 large Yukon gold or russet potatoes, peeled, quartered
2 cloves garlic, crushed
Salt
3 tablespoons unsalted butter
½ cup heavy cream

Place the celery root, potatoes, garlic, and ¼ teaspoon salt in a saucepan with water to cover generously. Cook until very soft, 25 to 30 minutes. Drain the vegetables, retaining ½ cup cooking liquid. Using a food mill, puree the vegetables and then stir in the reserved cooking liquid (or, using a food processor, puree vegetables and cooking liquid). Return the mixture to the saucepan, and over low heat stir in the butter and cream. Taste and adjust for salt. Serve.

SICHUAN STIR-FRIED CORN *with Chilies*

SERVES 4

Corn is fairly common in southwestern China, and I ate this simple stir-fry often in the year I taught English in Chengdu, the capital of Sichuan Province. While I usually serve this dish as part of a Chinese meal, it's also very good as a side to a grilled steak or trout. Summer, when fresh sweet corn is in the markets, is the best time for it, but it works with frozen corn, too. Omit or cut back on the dried red chile if you prefer less heat.

2 tablespoons canola or peanut oil
2 dried red chilies, broken in three or four pieces
2 fresh green Anaheim chilies, stems, seeds, and veins removed,
   cut into ½-inch squares
4 cloves garlic, cut into ⅓-inch chunks
2 cups corn kernels (about 3 ears fresh, or use frozen, thawed,
   rinsed, and drained)
¼ teaspoon salt
½ teaspoon sugar, optional (a good idea with frozen corn)

2 green onions, cut into ½-inch pieces

½ teaspoon sesame oil

½ teaspoon ground roasted Sichuan pepper

Heat a wok or skillet and add the canola or peanut oil. When the oil is very hot, add the dried chilies and stir-fry until they just begin to darken. Add the fresh chilies and stir-fry for 30 seconds. Add the garlic and stir-fry for 30 seconds. Add the corn, salt, and sugar if using, and stir-fry for 3 minutes, until the corn is beginning to brown. Add the green onions and stir-fry 1 minute more. Add the sesame oil and mix well. Remove from heat. Place the corn on a serving plate, sprinkle with Sichuan pepper, and serve.

10

DESSERTS

and

DRINKS

＊

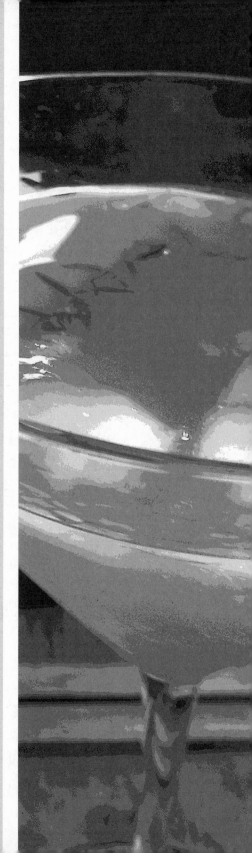

✳ GOOSEBERRY AND RASPBERRY FOOL

SERVES 2 GENEROUSLY

A simple, delicious summer dessert with a striking color contrast—the brilliant raspberry red, the cool, muted gooseberry green.

    1 cup gooseberries, rinsed
    Sugar
    1 cup raspberries, black or red or both—or blackberries,
        mulberries, etc., plus more for garnish
    1 cup heavy cream
    Sprig fresh mint

Place the gooseberries in a small saucepan with ¼ cup sugar and a splash of water. Bring to a boil, reduce the heat, and simmer, covered, until the berries are very soft, 8 to 10 minutes. Remove from heat. Place the raspberries in a small saucepan with 2 tablespoons sugar and a splash of water. Bring to a boil, reduce the heat, and simmer, covered, until the berries are very soft, 4 to 5 minutes. Remove from heat. Strain the berries separately through a sieve or food mill to remove the seeds. The resulting purees can be made several days in advance and stored in the refrigerator.

Whip the cream with 1 teaspoon sugar, if desired, until quite stiff. Divide the whipped cream into two bowls and fold the gooseberry puree into one, the raspberry puree into the other. Garnish with a sprig of mint or a few whole raspberries. Serve with Buckwheat Sablés (p. 202) or another type of cookie, if you like. ⌒

✳ MAPLE FLAN *with Maple-Calvados Sauce*

SERVES 4

The custard is rich and light at the same time, just barely sweet. The caramel and syrup are intensely mapley, quite sweet; the Calvados and vinegar cut the sweetness and complement the maple flavor beautifully.

    ¾ cup plus 6 tablespoons maple syrup, divided
    1 teaspoon cider vinegar

Maple Flan with Maple-Calvados Sauce

3 tablespoons Calvados or applejack (or, in a pinch, brandy or rum), divided

Salt

3 large egg yolks

1 large egg

1 cup whole milk

½ cup heavy cream

2 teaspoons unsalted butter

Preheat oven to 300 degrees. For the sauce, reduce ¾ cup maple syrup by half in a small saucepan over medium heat, taking care that it does not boil over. When it is very thick and dark, spoon 1 tablespoon into each of 4 half-cup ramekins, turning and tipping the ramekins to distribute the syrup partway up the sides. To the remaining reduced syrup add the vinegar, 1½ tablespoons Calvados, and a pinch of salt, stirring to mix. Set aside.

For the custard, whisk together the egg yolks and whole egg. In a small saucepan, heat the milk and cream to a boil. Remove from the heat and let sit 2 minutes. Starting with a couple tablespoons, slowly whisk the milk-cream mixture into the eggs. When half the milk and cream have been added, pour the rest in a steady stream, continuing to whisk. Stir in 6 tablespoons maple syrup, 1½ tablespoons Calvados, and a pinch of salt. Strain the custard into a large measuring cup and then pour it into the ramekins.

Place the ramekins in a cake pan and add hot water to halfway up the ramekins. Loosely cover the pan with aluminum foil and bake for 45 to 50 minutes, until the custard is mostly firm, with just a wee wiggle in the center. Let cool to room temperature and then refrigerate until ready to serve.

Just before serving, reheat the sauce. Stir in the butter and bring to a boil. It should have a syrupy consistency; if you want it thicker, reduce it a bit more. Run a paring knife around the edges of the ramekins, and invert each onto a plate. Spoon a bit of sauce over the custards, and bring the rest to the table. ⌒

CORNMEAL MAPLE BAKED PUDDING *with Dried Apples*
SERVES 4

A comforting, old-fashioned sweet corn mush, often called Indian Pudding.

   3 cups whole milk, divided
   ½ cup cornmeal
   ½ cup chopped dried apples
   ⅓ cup plus 2 tablespoons maple syrup, divided, plus extra
       for serving
   Salt
   2 tablespoons unsalted butter, plus more to grease baking dish
   1 large egg, lightly beaten
   Cream, whipped cream, or ice cream

Preheat oven to 300 degrees. Heat 2½ cups of the milk in a heavy-bottomed saucepan over medium heat. Gradually add the cornmeal, whisking briskly to avoid lumps. When the mixture starts to bubble, turn the heat to low and cook, stirring frequently, until thick, 6 to 10 minutes. Stir in the apples, ⅓ cup of the maple syrup, a good pinch of salt, and 2 tablespoons butter. Let cool, and then whisk in the egg.

Butter a 4-cup baking dish and pour in the cornmeal mixture. Bake for 45 minutes. Mix the remaining ½ cup milk with remaining 2 tablespoons maple syrup, and spoon it over the pudding. Bake for another 45 to 60 minutes, until the top is brown and the pudding is set—a toothpick will come out clean.

Serve warm with cream, whipped cream, or ice cream. Bring a small pitcher of maple syrup to the table for those who like it sweeter.

APPLE BLACKBERRY GALETTES

SERVES 2 TO 4

These rustic tarts will each satisfy two moderate appetites, especially if accompanied by a scoop of whipped cream or ice cream. If you're dealing with hungry lumberjacks or teenage hockey players, serve one galette per person. I use homemade preserves made from wild blackberries harvested on our land. Good store-bought blackberry or raspberry preserves will work fine.

> 1 cup plus 1 teaspoon flour, divided
> Salt
> 4 tablespoons (2 ounces) cold unsalted butter, cut into ½-inch cubes, plus 2 tablespoons unsalted butter
> 3–4 tablespoons ice water
> 2 medium apples (7–8 ounces), peeled, cored, and cut into ¼-inch-thick slices (2 cups)
> 1 tablespoon sugar, plus more to glaze the dough
> 2 pinches quatre-épices (p. 20), or 1 pinch each ground cinnamon and cloves
> ¼ cup blackberry jam (or Quick Wild Berry Sauce, p. 208)
> Milk
> Whipped cream, crème fraîche, or ice cream

Combine 1 cup flour and ¼ teaspoon salt in the bowl of a food processor fitted with the metal cutting blade. Pulse a few times to mix. Add the cubed butter and pulse a few times to blend. Add 3 tablespoons ice water and pulse a few times; then blend 10 seconds. If the dough hasn't started to come together, add another tablespoon of water, and pulse until the dough starts to gather. Don't expect a uniform dough at this point: it will look a bit crumbly. Dump the dough onto a lightly floured counter, gently bring it together into a ball, and divide it in half. Make a ball of each half, gently pat each into a disk, wrap in plastic wrap, and refrigerate at least 1 hour. Bring the dough out of the fridge 15 minutes before rolling.

Preheat oven to 400 degrees. Toss the apple slices with the sugar, 1 teaspoon flour, the spices, and a pinch of salt. Roll the dough into roughly 8-inch circles, leaving the center a bit thicker than the edges. Heap half the apple mixture into the center of one circle, leaving about 1½ inches of the edge uncovered. Repeat with remaining dough and apples. Spoon 2 tablespoons jam over each pile of apples. Dot 1 tablespoon butter evenly over the fruit in each galette.

Carefully gather the edges of the dough up toward the center, making loose pleats: the dough will not cover the fruit. With a pastry brush, moisten the dough with milk and sprinkle with sugar. Place galettes on a parchment-lined baking sheet with a lip on the edge. Bake for 25 minutes, reduce heat to 350 degrees, and bake an additional 10 to 15 minutes, until the crust is very nicely browned and the fruit is soft. Remove to a wire rack to cool. Serve with whipped cream, crème fraîche, or ice cream.

✳ BUCKWHEAT SABLÉS

MAKES ABOUT 6 DOZEN

My favorite cookie. A buttery, light, and elegant shortbread—not exactly what you'd expect from rustic buckwheat. These cookies are great on their own or to accompany Gooseberry and Raspberry Fool (p. 202).

8 ounces (2 sticks) unsalted butter, at room temperature
⅔ cup sugar
1 cup buckwheat flour
1 cup unbleached all-purpose flour
½ teaspoon baking powder
¼ teaspoon salt
2 large egg yolks

*Buckwheat
Sablés*

Preheat oven to 325 degrees. In a large mixing bowl, thoroughly mix the butter and sugar. In a separate bowl, combine the flours, baking powder, and salt. Add the flour mixture to the sugar and butter, mixing with your hands to make a uniform texture. Form a well in the center and add the egg yolks. Mix with a fork until the texture is uniform, a bit like wet sand. Test the dough to see if it will come together by squeezing a little ball in your hand. If it's crumbly, mix in cold water a tablespoon at a time until the dough coheres.

Two ways to proceed: roll out the dough ¼ inch thick and cut out cookies with a small fluted cutter (or another shape of your choice). Or, divide the dough into four pieces, roll each into a 1-inch diameter log, wrap in plastic wrap, and refrigerate for at least 45 minutes. Then cut into ⅓-inch slices. Place on nonstick or parchment-lined baking sheets, leaving a good inch between cookies.

Bake 18 to 20 minutes, until lightly browned: it can be hard to tell because of the color of the buckwheat. Remove from the oven and let cool on the baking sheets for 2 to 3 minutes; transfer to wire racks and allow to cool completely.

QUICK WILD BERRY SAUCE

MAKES 1 CUP

If there's a berry patch near your campsite, you can prepare this sauce—a very runny jam, really—while the coffee perks and the pancakes fry. It's also good on ice cream. Cultivated or frozen berries work just fine, too.

    2 cups blackberries, raspberries, or black cap raspberries—
      or a combination
    ½ cup water
    Sugar

Combine the berries and water in a saucepan, bring to a boil, and simmer for 10 minutes, until the berries have collapsed. Push the mixture through a sieve with a spatula or the back of a spoon, or run it through a food mill. Discard the seeds and return the puree to the saucepan. Add a couple tablespoons sugar and taste. Berries vary greatly in natural sweetness, so add sugar to taste and then simmer until the sauce reaches desired thickness.

MAPLE ICE CREAM TOPPING

MAKES 1 CUP

This recipe is so simple, I hesitate to write it down—but one shouldn't overlook the obvious, or the obviously delicious.

Marking the initial level of the maple syrup on a bamboo chopstick or skewer will help you judge when the reduction is complete.

    1½ cups maple syrup
    Salted pecans or walnuts, chopped
    Coarse sea salt

In a small saucepan, bring the syrup to a boil over medium heat. Turn the heat to low and reduce by one-third, watching the syrup carefully to be sure it doesn't boil over. Transfer to a half-pint canning jar.

Spoon the topping on ice cream. Sprinkle chopped salted nuts over top or, for a salted caramel sensation, add a few grains of coarse sea salt. The topping will keep indefinitely in the refrigerator.

The Cheeses of Our Climate

I really love French cheese, but I hardly eat it anymore. It's not a political thing: *freedom fries* never entered my vocabulary. In fact, I love France, the French, and their *fromage,* but I find myself in a "So many cheeses, so little time," situation, and with so much good cheese being produced in our region, there's not room on my plate for foreign guests (though I will always make space for a nice ripe Époisses).

There has always been good cheese produced in Minnesota and Wisconsin, but it hasn't always been easy to find, and the last few years surely have seen a renaissance in artisanal and farmstead cheesemaking. Today if I draw a circle around our Bide-A-Wee cabin to describe an hour's drive in any direction, I lasso three or four prizewinning cheesemakers, from LoveTree Farmstead's superb sheep cheese, to Holland's Family Farm's remarkable Goudas, to Black River Blue and Castle Rock Dairy's fine raw-milk cheddars. Take in the whole state of Wisconsin, and you'd be a long time tasting fabulous local cheeses before you started to crave a rubbery slice of under-ripe industrial grocery store Brie.

Like many people, I've become a much more conscious, intentional eater in recent years. I want to cook and eat on purpose, not out of habit. I used to always keep a piece of Italian Parmigianino in the fridge, but more recently I've been reaching for an aged Wisconsin Gouda or sharp white cheddar to grate on my pasta, and it's been revelatory. You can also pick up homegrown versions of "parmesan" and "asiago," and while I wonder a bit about the wisdom of using those proprietary European labels, I see its sense as a marketing shorthand, perhaps an homage. The fact that the name is a bit ersatz doesn't mean the cheese is bad; many of them are very, very good.

Having grown up in that time when Colby and Monterey Jack were exotic cheeses, I'm amazed to find fresh local chèvre at all the co-ops and most grocery stores. From southern Wisconsin comes a Gruyère-type cheese, the Pleasant Ridge Reserve, that's won every prize possible and which truly is as good as the best mountain cheeses I've tasted in France.

And then there are cheese curds, not the deep-fried state fair abominations, but the squeaky, salty, just-made kind, minutes away from their former life as milk. There's nothing upscale about them, but I'll take a good fresh sack of white curds over bland imported fresh mozzarella any day. I'll even serve them on a plate of tomatoes and basil—take that *insalata caprese* (I mean, I would love that salad were I dining in Campania, but generally I'm not).

Traveling through the Wisconsin countryside, you often come upon small cheese shops or dairy cooperative outlet stores, and you can find some wonderful cheeses there (you can also find weird flavored cheeses, processed "cheese food" spreads, and even chocolate cheese; there's no accounting for taste). Often these small shops offer a line of cheddars from one to twelve years old. These aged cheddars may not even carry the name of the cheese-maker, and their prices are absurdly low, but they are utterly delicious, full of character. It's just one of those humble Wisconsin traditions to make excellent cheese available to the people at a fair price.

The cheese course is my idea of a fine way to end a meal—and to finish a bottle of wine, too. It can be as easy as apple pie.

* Pair sharp cheddar with slices of crisp, sweet-tart apple. Homemade blackberry preserves and cheddar is another great combination.
* Aged Gouda, with its caramel notes, goes really well with Quick Blackberry-Apple Compote (p. 217).
* Try fresh chèvre with a drizzle of honey and a sprinkling of thyme leaves or a grind of black pepper.
* Turn dessert into salad, or vice versa: dollop some chèvre or crumble feta or blue cheese over the Wine-Dark Beets (p. 48).
* Blue and pear, with perhaps a few walnuts, is a classic combination.
* Put together a tasting plate of various blues—a sheep, goat, and cow; or Goudas of various ages, starting young; compare washed-rind cheeses.

But let's not forget that simplicity often shines brightest: a fine artisanal cheese doesn't really need anything to prop it up—perhaps a piece of bread and some butter, no more. It's often true that the cheese really can stand alone.

✳ RAMP-A-TINI

If you're a martini fancier, it's worth making pickled ramps (p. 224) just for this drink. Think, Gibson on steroids.

> *Per drink*
> 2 ounces (¼ cup) gin or vodka
> 1 capful dry vermouth, or to taste
> ½ pickled ramp bulb, halved lengthwise
> 1 teaspoon ramp pickling brine
> Twist lemon

Combine the gin or vodka and vermouth in a cocktail shaker over cracked ice. Resolve the perennial quandary, "Shaken or stirred?" Strain into a chilled martini glass and add the ramp half and brine and lemon twist. ⌒

✳ HIGHWAY 64 REVISITED

Wisconsin State Highway 64 crosses the state west to east from the Minnesota border to Lake Michigan, passing through the town of New Richmond, where 45th Parallel vodka is made, and skirting just south of our Bide-A-Wee cabin in northern Dunn County.

Eager to start the apple harvest, I'll sometimes puree green apples, squeeze out a bit of juice with cheesecloth, and use it to flavor these drinks.

> *Per drink*
> 2 ounces (¼ cup) 45th Parallel vodka
> 2 tablespoons unfiltered fresh apple cider
> 1 teaspoon pure maple syrup
> 1 capful dry vermouth
> 1 sprig fresh thyme, optional

Put cracked ice in a martini shaker. Add vodka, cider, maple syrup, and vermouth. Shake or stir. Strain into a martini glass. Garnish with a sprig of thyme, if you like. I do. ⌒

Highway 64
Revisited

⁎ BIDE-A-WEE KIR

Northwestern France is apple country: the rest of France drinks wine; the Normans and Bretons drink cider. Bide-A-Wee is apple country, too. This aperitif cocktail is inspired by one tasted in Brittany.

> *Per drink*
> 1 ounce (2 tablespoons) Calvados or applejack
> 2 ounces (¼ cup) hard dry apple cider, chilled
> 2 ounces (¼ cup) sweet apple cider, chilled
> ½ teaspoon maple syrup
> 1 small sprig thyme, optional

Combine all. Serve in a small wine or lowball glass. Potted Pork Pâté (p. 31) and slices of baguette are ideal companions. ⌒

✳ MAPLE SPRITZER/CALVA COCKTAIL

As a spritzer, it's a refreshing nonalcoholic aperitif; add the Calvados for grown-up apple juice with a kick.

Per drink
2 tablespoons maple syrup
6 ounces sparkling water
Lemon juice
Calvados or applejack, optional

Combine the maple syrup and sparkling water in a glass. Add fresh squeezed lemon juice to taste. Optional: add 1 tablespoon to 1 shot Calvados. Drop in a couple of ice cubes, and imbibe. ⌒

And . . .

CONDIMENTS

✳

CRANBERRY MAPLE CHUTNEY

MAKES ABOUT ¾ CUP

This chutney is a bright, sweet-tart, slightly spicy ode to the Badger State. Wisconsin is one of the nation's largest cranberry producers, and I use local apples and maple syrup, too. For less heat, omit or reduce the chile.

Serve with Hazelnut-Crusted Goat Cheese (p. 26) as a first course or alongside a chunk of aged cheddar at the end of the meal. Or spread some on a turkey sandwich, or serve a dollop alongside grilled or roasted pork.

    2 teaspoons butter
    1 small shallot, minced
    ½ cup fresh cranberries, halved
    ¼ cup chopped dried apples
    ½ small dried red chile, crumbled, optional
    2 tablespoons maple syrup
    ½ cup water
    Pinch salt

In a small saucepan, melt the butter and add the shallots, allowing them to gently sweat without browning for 4 or 5 minutes. Add the cranberries, apples, chile, maple syrup, water, and salt. Bring to a boil, and simmer, partly covered, until the mixture is thick and most of the water has evaporated, 10 to 15 minutes.

PICKLED CRAB AND RAMP CHUTNEY

MAKES ½ CUP

Treasure from the larder, excellent with a wedge of blue cheese at meal's end, as consort to a grilled cheese sandwich, or alongside pork any way.

    1 tablespoon canola or sunflower oil
    5–6 pickled ramp bulbs (p. 224), rinsed, halved lengthwise,
        sliced ¼-inch thick (¼ cup)
    4–5 Pickled Crab Apples (p. 227), cored and chopped (½ cup)
    2 tablespoons pickled crab apple liquid

2 teaspoons pickled ramp liquid
Pinch salt

In a small sauté pan, heat the oil and add the ramps; cook very gently, without browning, until they start to soften, 4 to 5 minutes. Add the crab apples, the pickling liquids, and a pinch of salt. Simmer gently, uncovered, stirring frequently, until the chutney thickens, 3 to 5 minutes. Transfer to a small bowl, cool, cover, and refrigerate. Let sit a few hours before serving. ⤳

❋ QUICK BLACKBERRY-APPLE COMPOTE

MAKES ¾ CUP

This compote was originally concocted to accompany the caramel notes and sharp saltiness of aged Gouda.

> 1 tablespoon butter
> 2 small apples, peeled and chopped
> 3 tablespoons blackberry jam (or Quick Wild Berry Sauce, p. 208)
> Salt and freshly ground black pepper

In a small skillet or saucepan, melt the butter and add the apples. Cook over medium heat until the apples begin to brown and caramelize. Add the jam, a good pinch of salt, and a grind of pepper. Cook for 1 minute. Transfer to a small bowl and serve at room temperature. ⤳

❋ MAPLE SYRUP–CIDER VINEGAR REDUCTION

MAKES ½ CUP

My goal was a sort of rustic condiment with balsamic vinegar qualities, and while this concoction misses that mark, the result is a wickedly flavorful reduction with many uses, from glazing grilled meats and vegetables to pepping up a vinaigrette, from spooning over vanilla ice cream to spicing up a baked apple.

Combine ½ cup maple syrup and ½ cup cider vinegar in a small saucepan. Bring to a boil over medium heat—watch the pot constantly as it comes to a boil, adjusting heat to avoid boilovers. Cook over medium-low heat until reduced by half. Remove from heat and let cool and then store, refrigerated, in a small glass jar. It will keep indefinitely.

✳ HONEY MUSTARD

    1 tablespoon honey
    1 tablespoon Dijon-style mustard
    2 teaspoons olive oil
    Coarsely ground black pepper to taste

Stir together all the ingredients. This mixture will keep indefinitely in the refrigerator. Good on ham sandwiches and with Maple-Spice Gravlax (p. 28).

✳ CHERVIL-CHIVE-PARSLEY BUTTER

MAKES ABOUT ¼ CUP

If you don't have chervil, use tarragon or tender fennel greens instead, or a bit of basil in a pinch—they'll all give a hint of anise flavor.

    4 tablespoons (2 ounces) unsalted butter, at room temperature
    2 teaspoons each chopped chives, parsley, and chervil (see headnote)
    ¼ teaspoon coarse sea salt

Mash the butter together with the herbs and salt until you have a homogeneous blend. Serve on steamed or roasted vegetables or grilled meats, or add a pat to brothy soups.

✳ CIDERED SHALLOTS

MAKES ABOUT ⅔ CUP

This concoction is excellent with charcuterie or a cheese plate or on a turkey sandwich. The creamy version is great with smoked fish.

    2 tablespoons unsalted butter
    8 ounces shallots, sliced ¼ inch thick

¼ teaspoon salt

1 large clove garlic, sliced

Freshly ground black pepper

½ cup sweet apple cider

¼ cup cider vinegar

¼ cup water

3 sprigs fresh thyme

½ cup heavy cream, optional

In a heavy-bottomed saucepan, melt the butter over medium heat. Add the shallots and salt. Cook gently, stirring frequently, until the shallots are much reduced in volume and start to look and smell a bit caramelized, 5 to 6 minutes. Stir in the garlic and a few grinds of black pepper. Cook for 2 minutes. Add the cider, vinegar, water, and thyme; simmer until almost all the liquid is gone. Taste and adjust for salt. Remove thyme stems.

Variations: add heavy cream in the last minute of cooking. Or, go half and half: remove half the shallots to a small bowl and add ¼ cup cream to what remains in the pan.

MAYONNAISE *and Its Variations*

MAKES ABOUT 1 CUP

Making mayonnaise is a milestone for any home cook, I think. To the uninitiated, the notion that one can take an egg yolk and a cup of oil and produce, by simple whisk work, a delicious, creamy emulsion, seems like magic—and you know, it kind of is.

I don't use homemade mayonnaise for everything. I make my own mayo when I really want to taste it—in an aioli to serve with summer crudités, for dabbing on roasted beets, or as a dip for roasted root fries.

Homemade mayonnaise involves raw egg. You can buy pasteurized eggs, though I've never used them. I won't discount anybody's health concerns, but I will say that making mayonnaise with locally raised, very fresh eggs, I have never, in decades of mayo-making, ever had a problem.

½ cup canola oil
¼ cup extra-virgin olive oil
1 fresh large egg yolk
1 teaspoon Dijon-style mustard
Juice of ¼ lemon (about 2 teaspoons)
Salt

Combine the oils in a measuring cup with a pouring spout. Use a 4-quart or larger mixing bowl to keep the oil from splattering all over the kitchen and the mayonnaise whisker. Twist a kitchen towel into a snake, form the snake into a circle on the countertop, and place the bowl within the circle to hold it steady while you whisk.

Add the egg yolk to the bowl along with the mustard, and whisk for 30 seconds. Start adding the oil: it's crucial to add the oil *very slowly* at the beginning. Rather than trying to pour tiny drops, I dip a spoon into the oil and lift it out vertically and then simply let the oil that coats the spoon drip into the egg yolk as I whisk. Do this several times, until you start to see an emulsion forming. Then you can start to pour very slowly from the measuring cup. The first ¼ cup goes painfully slow. After that, you should have a good emulsion formed—it will look like a homogeneous, creamy mayo, not separate oil and egg—and you can pour a little faster. Having a partner helps: one can whisk and one add oil; then switch off.

When the mayonnaise starts to thicken, add a bit of lemon juice to lighten it. If after using all the juice it's still too thick, add a few drops of water. Add a couple pinches of salt at the end, stirring well. Let the mayo rest for a few minutes and then stir again and taste for salt: it can take a little while for the salt to become integrated. Go easy with the salt, as you'll likely be serving the mayo with salty dishes.

This base can accept any number of flavorings, herbs, spices, pickles, you name it. Some of my favorite variations follow.

AIOLI

The sunshine of Provence, this intensely garlicky mayonnaise is wonderful with summer vegetables—raw, blanched, or grilled—and equally good on Oven-Fried Roots (p. 192). Chop *at least* 2 large cloves garlic to a puree by first peeling the garlic and crushing it with the side of a large chef's knife. Then start chopping. When garlic is fairly well minced, add a good pinch of salt and keep chopping. When garlic is nearly a puree, scrape it across the cutting board with the edge of your knife. Chop and scrape; chop and scrape. Add to 1 cup mayonnaise and mix well. Refrigerate at least 30 minutes before using.

PICKLED RAMP MAYONNAISE

To 1 cup mayonnaise, add 2 finely chopped pickled ramp bulbs (p. 224) and 1 tablespoon pickled ramp brine; mix well. You can use the mixture right away, but the ramps' flavor will continue to infiltrate the mayo for a couple of days, becoming ever more pungent—a ticket back to springtime foraging grounds even in the heart of winter. This mayonnaise is lovely with fried fish, in tuna salad, alongside fresh or oven-fried vegetables, or on a hot dog (pile on some Sambal Carrot Slaw, p. 41, too).

A WILD TARTAR

To ⅓ cup mayonnaise, add 1 finely chopped pickled ramp bulb (p. 224) and 1 tablespoon chopped pickled milkweed pods (p. 224); mix well. Serve with "Deviled" Whitefish with Potato Chip Crust (p. 164).

Making your own home-fermented sauerkraut is right up there with home-made mayonnaise in terms of a home cook's adventures in cooking arcana. Making mayonnaise becomes simple once you've done it a few times; making sauerkraut is simple from the get-go. Here, nature does all the work—or most of it.

Many good books on the topic of fermenting vegetables, fruits, and other food products are available. I often refer to Wild Fermentation *by Sandor Katz,* The Joy of Pickling *by Linda Ziedrich, and* Preserving Food without Freezing or Canning, *a compilation from the Terre Vivante collective in France. Given these abundant resources, I'll keep my fermentation dissertation brief.*

Every year I ferment cabbage (sauerkraut) and beets. Recently I made fermented kale for the first time, and it will surely be put into the regular rotation. Though I prepared it without any additional flavors, it reminds me strongly of kimchi, *Korean fermented vegetables.*

The method of fermentation is exactly the same for cabbage, beets, and kale. With the cabbage, you can do green or red or a mix. To any of these you could also add some carrot, turnip, chile, garlic, or ginger.

For each 2 pounds of vegetables, add 4 teaspoons salt (I use sea salt; canning salt is often recommended). Two pounds of vegetables fill a quart jar, with perhaps some left over. I am a big proponent of small-batch fermenting and canning. Too often these sorts of things involve a big production, which I think scares off a lot of people from trying them—I know it did me, for a long time.

For cabbage: remove and discard outer dirty or damaged leaves. Quarter, core, and shred, either by hand, on a mandoline or kraut cutter, or with the slicing blade on a food processor.

For beets: peel and grate medium to coarse.

For kale: roll up a stack of leaves and slice into thin shreds.

In a large mixing bowl, toss the vegetables with the salt. Get in there with your hands and kind of scrub the shreds against each other—doing so will help get the juices flowing and promote prompt fermentation (the beets, with all their sugar, will need less encouragement).

Pack the vegetables into quart canning jars with two-part lids. Fill the jars right to the top and then press down firmly to create a little space, which should fill with liquid expressed by the vegetables. If there's not enough liquid to cover, top off the jars with a bit of brine made by mixing 1 teaspoon salt into ½ cup warm water. Screw on the lids, not too tight.

Place the jars on a platter or baking sheet to catch any overflow. Place in a coolish spot, around 60 degrees, perhaps the basement. In just a day or two you'll notice bubbling, and there will be juice running over the tops of the jars. If you're tempted to unscrew the lid to see how things are going, be careful: juice can shoot out like soda from a shook-up can.

Let the jars ferment at cool room temperature for 7 to 10 days. The bubbling will have died down and no more liquid will be coming out of the jar. Tighten lids, rinse jars, and refrigerate. Protected by the natural preservatives created in the fermentation, the vegetables will now keep indefinitely, but I encourage you to use them up within a few months. By that time, you'll be getting fresh vegetables from your market and the garden anyway.

My Russian friend Tata says that cabbage for sauerkraut is best after a couple of frosts, and I agree. Late-season cabbage tend to be firm, sweet, and mild.

I've never had any of my fermented vegetables go "off," but I've heard it can happen. If anything you ferment comes out looking or smelling horrible, by all means do not eat it. ⌐

WILD AND PICKLED: BASIC BRINES

MAKES 2 PINTS

The season for wild plants in the north country is extremely limited, but we keep wild flavors on the table throughout the year with various methods of preservation. Pickling is a favorite.

Pickled ramps and milkweed pickles and "capers" are good keepers. The pickled crab apples and cucumbers should be eaten promptly. It's a wonderfully refreshing pickle to put out on a summer buffet.

- 2 cups water
- 1 cup cider vinegar
- ¾ cup sugar
- Scant 2 tablespoons salt
- 2 small dried red chilies, seeds removed (or retained for more heat)
- 1 teaspoon black peppercorns

Mix all ingredients in a saucepan over medium heat, stirring to dissolve the sugar. Remove from heat and let cool.

For the pickled ramps (2 pints):
Clean 1½ pounds ramp bulbs, leaves removed. Keep a couple inches of stem. Combine the ramps and brine in a nonreactive saucepan. Bring to a boil and simmer for 3 minutes. Let the ramps cool in the brine and then remove them with tongs and line them up prettily in 2 pint jars. Divide the chilies and peppercorns between the jars. Pour brine over the ramps to cover. Seal with sterilized two-part lids and process in a hot-water bath for 10 minutes. Or skip the processing and refrigerate; they will keep indefinitely.

For the milkweed pickles (2 half pints):
Make half the brine recipe. Rinse 2 cups milkweed pods, about 1 inch long. Bring a pot of water to a boil and add 1 teaspoon salt. Blanch the pods for 2 minutes and then drain. Place the pods in half-pint jars and add brine to cover. Seal with sterilized two-part lids and process in a hot-water bath for 10 minutes. Or skip the processing and refrigerate; they will keep indefi-

nitely. These have a really interesting texture, a nice sort of popping crunch, and the flavor is very like green beans.

For crabs and cukes (2 pints):
Quarter and core, but do not peel, 8 to 10 crab apples or other small, firm, tart apples (about 2 cups). Cut pickling cucumbers into 1½- to 2-inch lengths, and quarter those (about 2 cups); if they're very seedy, trim some of the seeds. Combine the apple and cucumber pieces and divide between 2 pint canning jars. Add brine to cover. Do not process. Refrigerate for a day before eating, and consume within a week.

For the milkweed "capers" (1 half pint):
Pick 1 cup of the tiniest milkweed pods you can find, no more than ½ inch long. Rinse, drain, and toss with ½ teaspoon salt. Let sit overnight. Rinse and drain the pods and then place in a half-pint canning jar along with a few black peppercorns, a sprig of tarragon, a clove of garlic, and 3 whole cloves. Add cider vinegar to cover; then pour off the vinegar into a small saucepan and bring to a boil. Pour the vinegar back into the jar. Refrigerate and wait at least 3 days before using. Use as you would capers. See Herring Milkweed à la Meunière (p. 171).

Milkweed pods for pickling

CORNICHONS (*French Sour Gherkins*)

MAKES 2 CUPS

Serve these with Potted Pork Pâté (p. 31), Confit of Fresh Ham on Sauerkraut (p. 128), or any terrine or charcuterie.

- 1 pint (2 cups) fresh gherkin-size cucumbers, 1½ to 2½ inches long, rinsed, stems trimmed
- 1 teaspoon salt
- 2 cloves garlic, halved lengthwise
- 4 pearl onions, peeled
- Few sprigs fresh tarragon
- 3 whole cloves
- 1 cup good cider vinegar (or ⅔ cup white vinegar and ⅓ cup white wine or champagne vinegar)

Place the cucumbers in a glass or ceramic bowl and toss with the salt. Refrigerate overnight; stir occasionally if you think of it.

Rinse and drain the cucumbers and place them in a pint jar, alternating with garlic, onions, tarragon, and cloves. Add vinegar to cover; then pour off the vinegar into a small saucepan and bring it to a boil. Pour the vinegar back into the jar. Refrigerate and wait at least 3 days before using. Kept refrigerated, they will last indefinitely.

SWEET AND SPICY APPLE SLICES

MAKES ½ CUP

A fresh, intriguing quick pickle to serve with grilled pork or alongside a BLT or BOT (p. 133).

- 1 large, firm, tart-sweet apple (like a Haralson), peeled, quartered, and cored
- ⅛ teaspoon salt
- ½ teaspoon sambal oelek chili paste
- 1½ tablespoons Maple Syrup–Cider Vinegar Reduction (p. 217)

Sweet and Spicy Apple Slices

Cut each apple quarter into 6 slices. Mix with the salt, sambal oelek, and maple-vinegar reduction. Refrigerate for an hour or two before serving. Use within 2 days. ⌒

✳ PICKLED CRAB APPLES

MAKES 4 CUPS

These beautiful and fragrant pickled crabs are lovely on a cheese plate or with grilled or roasted pork or duck. Chop with some pickled ramps to make a unique quick chutney (p. 216).

  ¾ cup water

  1 cup sugar

  1 cup cider vinegar

  1 (2-inch) stick cinnamon

  1 teaspoon allspice berries

Pickled
Crab Apples

½ teaspoon whole cloves
1 whole star anise
6 (⅛-inch-thick) slices fresh ginger
½ teaspoon black peppercorns
1 small dried red chile, optional
1½ pounds whole crab apples, stems on

In a large stainless or enameled saucepan, combine the water, sugar, vinegar, and spices (cinnamon through optional red chile). Bring to a boil, stirring to dissolve the sugar. Remove from heat and let cool.

Pierce each apple in a couple spots with a metal or bamboo skewer—this is to keep the apples from exploding, though many will probably crack anyway. Add the apples to the syrup and bring to a simmer over medium-low heat. Cook until translucent, 15 to 20 minutes.

With a slotted spoon, transfer the apples to sterilized canning jars—1 quart jar or 2 pint jars. Strain the syrup to remove the spices; discard solids. Boil the syrup and then pour it over the apples to cover. Seal with sterilized two-part lids and process in a hot-water bath for 10 minutes—or simply refrigerate; they will keep indefinitely.

Save any extra syrup in a jar in the fridge. The leftovers—and any liquid from the canned apples—are great in a dressing for beet or cabbage salads.

✳ OVEN TOMATOES WITH HERBS

MAKES ABOUT 6 CUPS

This is my favorite technique for dealing with the late-summer glut of tomatoes and of putting up tomatoes for winter. After trying various ways, I've decided it's best if the tomatoes are peeled and seeded. But see the "sauce option," below.

> 5 pounds ripe tomatoes, a mix of colors is nice
> Olive oil
> Garlic, optional
> Fresh thyme, basil, and parsley, optional
> Sea salt
> Freshly ground black pepper

Bring a large pot of water to the boil, and have a large bowl of ice water at the ready. Cut an X in the bottom of each tomato. Working in batches, blanch the tomatoes for 15 seconds and then transfer them to the ice water. Peel the tomatoes and cut out the stem end; then halve and seed. Tear the tomatoes into large pieces and drop them into a big, wide baking dish or ovenproof Dutch oven.

Preheat oven to 325 degrees. Drizzle the tomatoes with a couple tablespoons olive oil, slice a couple big cloves of garlic over top, if you like, and add some herbs, also optional; I usually include a good bit of basil, thyme, and parsley. Sprinkle on ½ teaspoon salt, and give it a few grinds of pepper.

Bake for 20 minutes and then stir: the herbs will float to the top, so you need to push them back in, lest they burn. Now bake, stirring occasionally, until reduced by half, about 3 hours.

Remove the thyme twigs and basil stems. Now you can use the mixture as is or freeze it in pint containers, pop out the frozen bricks, and store them in plastic freezer bags. The tomatoes can be used as the basis for pasta or pizza sauce or to add bright tang and color to stews and soups. Or, just smear it on some good bread, top with a little grated cheese, and run it under the broiler.

The sauce option: don't bother peeling or seeding the tomatoes. Instead, prepare just as above and pass through a food mill when done.

✳ FRESH TOMATO SAUCE
MAKES ABOUT 2 CUPS

Serve over pasta with a grating of cheese or with Wild Mushroom Lasagna (p. 101; this quantity will sauce four portions), Stuffed Delicata Squash (p. 87), or Buckwheat Crêpes with Creamed Leeks (p. 84).

> 1½ tablespoons olive oil
> 1 small onion, chopped
> 2 large cloves garlic, chopped
> 1½ pounds fresh ripe tomatoes, seeded and chopped,
>   or 2 cups Oven Tomatoes (p. 229)
> ¼ cup dry red wine
> ½ teaspoon red wine vinegar
> Salt and freshly ground black pepper to taste
> Fresh herbs to taste (basil, thyme, parsley)

Heat the oil in a skillet and add the onion. Cook over medium heat for 2 minutes; add the garlic and cook for 30 seconds. Stir in the tomatoes, wine, vinegar, and a bit of salt and simmer for 10 minutes. Taste and adjust for seasoning; add herbs if you like.

*Hard apple
cider*

✳ HARD CIDER SUB (*and a drink called Shrub*)

MAKES ABOUT 1 CUP

*There's no real substitute for good hard (alcoholic) cider, at least not for
drinking. For cooking purposes, though, this ersatz will work quite well. And,
with minor tweaking, it produces an old-fashioned beverage called* shrub,
*which you might enjoy on a hot summer's afternoon when you're relaxing un-
der your apple tree, planning to make your own hard cider come fall.*

> ½ cup sweet cider, preferably the cloudy "farmers market" kind
> 2 tablespoons unpasteurized cider vinegar
> 6 tablespoons water

Combine all ingredients and use in recipes calling for hard dry cider.

For shrub: use sparkling water instead of tap water. Mix sweet cider, sparkling water, and 1 tablespoon vinegar or to taste. Try also stirring in a spoonful of good blackberry or raspberry jam. Serve over ice.

MARY'S DUCK FAT TORTILLAS

Probably the most common fat in traditional tortillas is lard, but using spice-scented confit fat turns ordinary tortillas into something remarkable.

- 1 cup all-purpose flour, plus more for kneading and rolling
- ¼ teaspoon salt
- ¼ teaspoon baking powder
- 2 tablespoons fat from Duck Leg Confit (p. 149), melted
- ⅓ cup hot water

Combine the flour, salt, and baking powder in a mixing bowl. Add the melted duck fat and mix with your fingers until well distributed. Add hot water, and mix to form a soft dough. Knead for 1 minute and then let rest for 15 minutes.

On a lightly floured work surface, divide the dough into 8 equal pieces and roll into balls. Flatten the balls into disks, cover with a towel, and let rest 15 minutes. Roll each disk into a tortilla 5 to 6 inches across. Heat a skillet over medium-high heat. Cook the tortillas for 30 to 45 seconds per side, until they are blistered and brown in spots.

A Wild Food Year

Watercress is usually our first wild harvest of the year. Because cress grows in springs that bubble up from the earth at a fairly constant temperature year-round, the plants are protected in a microclimate created by the forty-degree water. The fine white roots dangle over the sandy bottom—it's Great Nature's hydroponic salad garden. If winter temperatures stay above zero, cress may be available throughout the year. I like cress best as a salad green, alone or with other wild greens or garden lettuce. It can also be added to soups or made into a pesto.

Nettles emerge in very early spring. There are two kinds in our woods: stinging nettles and wood nettles. They both sting; in fact, I think wood nettles' sting is worse than that of stinging nettles. Young specimens of both kinds are good just steamed. As they get older they're best blanched, chopped, and added to soups or stews. Wood nettles are the superior vegetable for eating plain, but stinging nettles produce a beautiful broth or tea, vegetal and deeply savory.

NETTLE TEA

SERVES 1

Carefully rinse 1 packed cup nettle leaves. Bring 1½ cups water to a boil and add the nettles. Simmer for 1 minute, cover, and let steep for 5 minutes. Strain into a mug. Add a teaspoon or so of maple syrup or honey, if you like.

* * *

We also encounter the wild leeks known as ramps in those early spring woods, and fiddleheads, and wild asparagus. Ramps can be used anywhere you'd use an onion or leek, though their wildly pungent aroma and flavor are distinctive. Ramps can be harvested throughout the summer and into fall—they just become much harder to find when their broad green leaves die back and the forest floor grows up around them. If you know how to identify the flowers and then the seed stalks, you can enjoy them well past the spring.

Fiddleheads of ostrich ferns are like asparagus in texture, though not in flavor, which is an acquired taste, I think: deep and earthy, reminiscent of both moss and iron. They benefit from pairing with something sharp, like lemon juice or goat cheese. Fiddleheads can be prepared as you would asparagus.

As for wild asparagus, it's just asparagus that happens to be growing in the wild. Use it as you would . . . asparagus.

I doubt that most people think of maple syrup as a wild food, but it is derived, for the most past, from trees growing wild in the woods. It's a simple process: you drill a hole, insert a spigot (a length of plastic pipe will do), and wait for the freeze-thaw cycle of late winter/early spring to start the sap flowing. From there, it's a matter of patience and quite an expense of firewood to reduce the sap to concentrate the sugar. The process is tedious with the primitive equipment I use, but the first time I served homemade maple syrup on our own apples, sautéed in local butter, served over toasted homemade sourdough, with fresh yogurt on top, I'm pretty sure I heard angels, singing on high.

The spring brings mushrooms, too: oysters grow on aspen logs, and I usually find a few specimens of a little-known shelflike mushroom fancifully called a dryad's saddle or, more descriptively, a pheasant back. The latter

Clockwise from top: wild asparagus, ostrich fern fiddleheads, yellow morels, bracken fern, wood nettles

doesn't have a pronounced flavor of its own, but it does have a pleasantly firm texture, a lot like the vaunted porcini or cèpe, and it takes up flavors splendidly. In a stir-fry with garlic, ginger, scallion, and a splash of rice wine and soy sauce, it's excellent.

The most sought-after mushroom of the spring—of any season, for many people—is the morel. I've had pretty spotty luck finding morels; those with the knowledge or the knack can harvest buckets full. Volumes have been written about morels, and recipes galore. Since my acquaintance with them is somewhat slim, I'll defer to my betters.

The call of the wild is less pressing in full summer, when the domestic products are so attractive. What shall we have for dinner: heirloom tomatoes warm from the sunny garden and sweet corn from the market still damp with morning dew? Or some weeds from the sweltering, itchy, bug-ridden woods? Civilization does have its rewards.

Wild fruit catches our interest in midsummer, though. We gather red and black raspberries, and then blackberries, black currants, gooseberries, and plums. The apples we pick from the several dozen trees we inherited with our land are more like foraged fruit than a domestic crop.

Two kinds of sorrel, linked only by name, find their way into soups and salads throughout the summer: sheep sorrel is related to garden sorrel and grows widely, though unobtrusively, in our region; the low rosettes can be hard to find in taller growth. Wood sorrel, which looks like a delicate clover plant with sweet yellow flowers, is easy to find and makes a pretty garnish.

Midsummer brings another prime mushroom, my favorite: the golden chanterelle. Their fragrance is far more subtle and transporting than the usual cliché that they "smell like apricots." If they were completely inedible, if all I could take from them was their sight and the smell, I think I'd seek them out just the same. Black trumpets, nearly as fragrant as chanterelles, fruit at about the same time. These gray to black, thin-fleshed cornets that disguise themselves amazingly in fallen oak leaves are perhaps the most exotic fungus I gather. Their French name, *trompettes des morts,* "trumpets of the dead," makes them seem all the more so.

Sulfur shelf, or chicken of the woods, is a beautiful yellow orange fungus with highly variable eating qualities. They may be exquisitely tender and flavorful or fibrous and insipid. Unfortunately, you can't tell which it will be

*Bide-A-Wee
annex*

until you cook them—so make a little sample first before committing to a meal of them.

It's usually September when I find my first hen of the woods, one of my favorite mushrooms. These beautiful, many-branched mushrooms grow at the base of white oak trees. Their mottled brown, gray, and cream coloring mimics the plumage of a ruffed grouse, of the autumn woods as a whole. Their woodsy flavor is distinctive but not overpowering, so they match equally well with trout, grouse, or roast chicken.

Then there is the hedgehog mushroom, another fragrant beauty, blushed pink, with spiky spore-producing structures under the cap instead of the common gills. Giant puffballs are those weird, ghostly white orbs that can grow to practically basketball size seemingly overnight. They're nearly as versatile as hen of the woods, though their soft texture is less interesting.

As the leaves drop from the trees, the brilliant red berries of the hawthorn remain. They can be made into jam or a distinctive sauce for duck (p. 145). Nannyberries, or wild raisins, have darkened and sweetened, and their dense sticky flesh tastes intriguingly like a combination of bananas and dates. I haven't found a cooking use for them; I just snack on them when I'm out on a walk or a hunt.

And now there have been a few frosts, and the watercress that turned so sharp and hot in the warm months is tender and mild again.

'Round and 'round. ⌒

Where to Forage for Wild Food
Resources and Considerations

The first consideration: forage where it's safe. Right behind that: where it's legal.

Where it's safe is in a setting where chemicals aren't being used on lawns, parklands, highway shoulders, or railroad rights-of-way.

Learn about hazardous plants—poison ivy, poison oak, etc.—and if you live where there are poisonous snakes or insects, know what you're dealing with there, too. The Upper Midwest, thankfully, is relatively free of fauna dangerous to the forager. The big exception here is an extremely tiny pest: the deer tick, which carries Lyme disease, which can be very nasty, indeed. Educate yourself about this menace. Wood ticks, which are much larger and generally more common than deer ticks, are creepy and annoying but generally harmless. A post-foraging tick check (strip naked, look closely, have your dear one scan the parts that you can't see) is de rigueur.

Having taken good precautions and perhaps conquered a few qualms, we get on to the fun—and the good news: while some natural areas are so heavily used and/or sensitive that the "take nothing but photographs" ethic makes good sense, in our region there are vast areas of public land where harvest of wild foods, from nuts and berries to fish and game, is not only legal but actively encouraged. "Public" means these lands are our lands, and where it doesn't harm the resource, respectful harvest is a very good thing. I have a real affection for and feeling of stewardship toward the public lands where I forage wild foods, which is not something I tend to feel about "stay on the trail, don't touch a thing" sorts of nature preserves.

Both Minnesota and Wisconsin have public hunting and fishing grounds—*wildlife management areas* is a common name for them—where you can hunt and fish in season and gather the edible parts of wild plants.

State, county, and national forests are also generally open to this kind of harvest. Limited foraging is permitted in some state parks as well. Always check on what's allowed and what's not. Nothing—save, perhaps, an unintentional encounter with poison ivy during a sylvan potty break—will ruin a pleasant day in the woods like getting busted for poaching.

Foraging on private lands is another option. By knocking on a few doors in a rural area, you may secure your own private foraging grounds and meet some nice people along the way. Large expanses of privately owned forest remain in our region, and other than the spring morel hunt and maybe a nostalgic interest in elderberry wine, I don't think edible wild plants are much appreciated by rural folk. It's a great resource to tap into if you're outgoing and eager.

You needn't necessarily travel far to forage: from my own yard in St. Paul I have harvested dandelion greens, lamb's-quarters, fiddleheads, and morels. Within the limits of the Twin Cities I've also found ramps and watercress, nettles galore, wild raspberries, and a variety of mushrooms—sulfur shelf, hen of the woods, oysters, tooth mushrooms, pheasant back. Great Nature does not recognize municipal boundaries.

Good maps and a compass are useful foraging tools. These days a lot of cell phones have GPS apps and built-in compasses, making it a lot harder to get lost (even if you want to). The DeLorme gazetteers have good, detailed maps of roadways and general topography, and the All-Outdoors Atlas and Field Guides from Sportman's Connection are even more detailed. They publish guides covering Minnesota, Wisconsin, Michigan, Pennsylvania, and New York.

Along the way, you'll come up with your own list of dos and don'ts, discover when the mosquitoes will be most ravenous, the nettles at their stinging height, the burrs most tenacious (sorry, Rover, you stay home this time). Overcoming a few obstacles is part of the journey, but in the end you may find, as I have, that foraging for wild food provides far, far more joys than troubles.

* * *

A few books, organizations, and websites of interest to wild foods enthusiasts:

Tops on my list are Samuel Thayer's books—*The Forager's Harvest, Nature's Garden*—and website, www.foragersharvest.com. The books include detailed descriptions and excellent photos of most of the important wild foods in our region—except mushrooms. The website features articles on select wild edibles and a section of book reviews that amounts to a detailed bibliography of wild food literature. Thayer has recently established a wild food interpretive trail in north-central Wisconsin (details on the website).

Another excellent book, this one by a Minnesota author (and a friend of mine), is *Abundantly Wild* by Teresa Marrone. She writes in the introduction that it's not a field guide, but it reads like one to me. While the photos don't match the quality of the Thayer books, the descriptions are meticulous—and she includes hundreds of mouth-watering recipes. Teresa has also written field guides to wild fruits, among other books. Information on all of them can be found at www.northerntrailspress.com/teresa_marrone.

The definitive work on North American mushrooms, edible and otherwise, is David Arora's *Mushrooms Demystified*. His website is www.david arora.com.

David Fischer's *Edible Wild Mushrooms of North America: A Field-to-Kitchen Guide* has been extremely useful to me. His website, www.american mushrooms.com, is another stellar resource, with scads of photos, articles, and links to dozens of other sites.

Mycological societies are an excellent, safe way to gain entrée to the world of foraging for fungi. Both Minnesota (www.minnesotamushrooms. org) and Wisconsin (www.wisconsinmycologicalsociety.org) have them. The websites offer lots of useful information, and each group's organized, regular forays are the ideal way to acquaint yourself with your region's wild mushrooms.

Acknowledgments

I'm grateful to

My wife, Mary Eckmeier, Pastry Goddess, Plate Licker, Bread Sniffer, Soup Smiler; this book is dedicated to her, but she deserves acknowledgment, too, and all possible plaudits.

My extremely encouraging and supportive family: my mother Grace Laidlaw and stepfather Roy Gomm; brother and sister-in-law Bill and Sue Laidlaw; enviable in-laws Willie and Don Piccard.

Friends who've shared meals, walks, and wood ticks at Bide-A-Wee and elsewhere: Nina and Jean-Louis LeSaout; Mary Stoyke and Will Agar; I-ming Shih and Arnold Chu; Diane Hellekson; Fred and Kim Petters; Kathleen Stoddart; Marsha Macey; Martha Garcés and Tom Nehil; Peter Galindo; our "daughter" Melinda (Lulu, the Tsarina) Macey and Tim (Starbuck) Voigts; and my number-one hunting and fishing buddy, Lynn Ann Sauby.

Teresa Marrone, who showed us how to tap a maple tree and whose writing opened new realms of wild food to me well before I met her.

The friends of Real Bread, our former home-based farmers market bakery, who stuck with us from St. Luke's to the winter market, Kingfield, Midtown, Mary's mom's backyard, and on into cyberspace via the Trout Caviar blog— and those who read and comment on the blog and inspire me with their experiences and insights. We were privileged to share a parking lot with many wonderful fellow vendors in the Real Bread years, but I must mention one in particular: master crêpe-maker, co-commiserator, and the snotty little sister I never had, Mala Vujnovich.

Our "country friends," who have made us see that life can be very bright indeed, even far from the city lights: Don Roberts and Joni Cash, Renee and Mark Bartz and family, Tina Blomer, Ramon and Darlene Ramos (and all the lovely ladies of her Corner Cupboard café in Boyceville).

And my editor, Shannon Pennefeather, who plucked *Trout Caviar* from the blogosphere and worked very hard to turn an enthusiastic mess into something a good deal less messy, while leaving all the enthusiasm in.

To Annabel and Lily, a couple of sweet griffons. They can't read, but they are great pals, worthy of acknowledgment.

Finally: memories of my father, A. W. "Bill" Laidlaw, are often with me in the kitchen, as he savors a smoked Lake Winnipeg goldeye warmed in foil, mixes English mustard to a paste with a toothpick in a shot glass to dab on a roast beef sandwich, or tastes slivers of extra-sharp Canadian Black Diamond cheddar.

We didn't eat fancy, but we ate good.

Index

Page numbers in *italic* refer to illustrations.

A

Abundantly Wild (Marrone), 239
Aioli, 221
    companion dishes, 192
    Roasted Beet Salad with Aioli and Walnuts, 47
alcoholic drinks, 211–13. *See also* apple cider, hard;
        wine
    Bide-A-Wee Kir, 212
    Calvados
        Bide-A-Wee Kir, 212
        Maple Flan with Maple-Calvados Sauce,
            202–3, *203*
        Maple Spritzer/Calva Cocktail, 213
    Highway 64 Revisited, 211, *212*
    Maple Spritzer/Calva Cocktail, 213
    Ramp-A-Tini, 211
    Scotch
        Blackberry-Whisky Sauce, 148
alliums (onion family), substitutions within, 18
Angry Trout Cafe (Grand Marais, MN), 169
appetizers. *See* starters
apple
    Apple-Blackberry Galettes, 205–6
    Apple Turnip Slaw with Buckwheat Honey
        Dressing, 38
        companion dishes, 164–65
    Buttermilk, Apple, and Cucumber Gazpacho, *71*,
        71–72
    Carrot Apple Soup, 64–65
        companion dishes, 134
    cheese with, 210
    dried
        Cornmeal Maple Baked Pudding with, 204–5,
            206–7
        Kale, Apple, Blue Cheese Pizza, 104
        making and uses of, 18
    Fried, Breakfast Trout with Bacon and, 181–82
    Grilled Woodcock with Apple-Bacon Relish, *153*,
        153–54

    pickled, 225
    Pickled Crab and Ramp Chutney, 216–17
    Pickled Crab Apples, 227–29, *228*
    Quick Blackberry-Apple Compote, 217
    Sweet and Spicy Apple Slices, 226–27, *227*
    trees, around Bide-A-Wee cabin, 12–13
    uses of, 13
    wild, gathering of, 235
apple cider
    hard
        Bide-A-Wee Kir, 212
        buying of, 17
        Chicken with Chestnuts and Cider, 143–44
        Grouse in Cider Cream, *155*, 155–56
        making of, 13, 17
        substitutes for, 17
    sweet
        Bide-A-Wee Kir, 212
        buying of, 17
        Cidered Shallots, 218–19
        Herring Crudo with Cider Mustard Cream, *162*,
            162–63
        production of, at Bide-A-Wee cabin, 13
apple cider vinegar
    Cidered Shallots, 218–19
    Hard Cider Sub, 231
    Herring Crudo with Cider Mustard Cream, *162*,
        162–63
    making of, 17
    Maple Syrup–Cider Vinegar Reduction, 217–18
    in pickling, 224–25
    substitutes for, 17
applejack
    Maple Flan with Maple-Calvados Sauce, 202–3,
        203
    Maple Spritzer/Calva Cocktail, 213
Arora, David, 239
Asian-themed dishes
    Sichuan Stir-Fried Corn with Chilies, 198–99
    Smoke-Grilled Ma La Chicken Wings, 144–45
    Soy-Simmered Burdock Root, 187–88

asparagus
    in Brown Butter, 186–87
    "Escabache" of Brown Trout with Ramps and
        Asparagus, 172–74, *173*
asparagus, wild
    gathering of, 233
    preparation of, 234
authentic, natural foods, as inspiration, 4
Autumn Vegetable, Chicken, and Sausage Hot Pot,
    140–41

B

bacon
    Bacon Fougasse, 112
    Bacon Onion Tart, 108–9
    Breakfast Trout with Bacon and Fried Apples,
        181–82
    culinary importance of, 135–36
    Grilled Woodcock with Apple-Bacon Relish, *153,*
        153–54
    Hens and Eggs and Bacon, 131–33, *132*
    home smoking of, 136–38
    judicious use of, 7, 136
    Knife and Fork BOT (Bacon, Onion, and Tomato),
        133–34
        companion dishes, 226
    Oven Green Beans with Bacon, 194, *195*
    smoking of, 136–38
    Tartiflette, 82–83
    versatility of, 136
    Watercress Bacon Salad, 46–47
Bacon Onion Tart (*Tarte Flambée; Flammekueche*),
    108–9
Baked Pheasant with Wild Mushrooms and Cream,
    157–58
beans
    Oven Green Beans with Bacon, 194, *195*
    Sugar Bush Bean Pot, 85–86
    Warm Salad of Wax Beans with Caramelized Shal-
        lots and Blackberry Vinaigrette, 45–46, *46*
beef
    Burger, 120–23
    Oxtails, Wine-Braised, with Shallots and Carrots,
        Cumin and Cocoa, 124–25

    Steak Stroganoff, Chanterelle and, *118,* 118–19
    Steak Tartare Maison, 119–20
beet
    Big Borscht, 60
    home fermenting of, 222–23
    Roasted, Salad with Aioli and Walnuts, 47, *48*
    salad, dressing for, 229
    Sweet and Sour, 193–94
    Wine-Dark, 48–49
Berg, Nathan, 52
beverages. *See also* alcoholic drinks; Hard Cider Sub
    Maple Spritzer, 213
    Nettle Tea, 233
    Shrub, 231
Bide-A-Wee cabin, 9–16, *11*
    amenities in, 11
    artisanal cheesemakers near, 209
    cabin construction, 10–11
    cooking in, 7, 15, *15,* 140
    evening entertainment at, 14–15
    naming of, 11
    property, described, 12–14
    purchase of property, 9–10
    wild foods on, 12–13, 113
Bide-A-Wee Kir, 212
Big Borscht, 60
Black and Gold Mushroom "Caviar," 34–35
blackberries, wild
    at Bide-a-Wee cabin, 13
    boyhood experiences of picking, 3
    gathering of, 235
    uses of, 13
blackberry jam
    Apple-Blackberry Galettes, 205–6
    Blackberry-Mustard Grilled Carrots, 196
    Blackberry-Whisky Sauce, 148
    cheese with, 210
    Quick Blackberry-Apple Compote, 217
    Warm Salad of Wax Beans with Caramelized
        Shallots and Blackberry Vinaigrette, 45–46, *46*
Blackberry-Mustard Grilled Carrots, 196
Blackberry Vinaigrette dressing, 45–46, *46*
Blackberry-Whisky Sauce, 148
black currents, gathering of, 235

Black Radish and Blood Orange Salsa, 167
blueberry pie, grandmother's, excellence of, 3
Blue Cheese Dressing, 49–50
books and websites on foraging, 238–39
Braised Pork Belly with Fennel, 130–31
Braised Sauerkraut, 189–90
breads
    Cornmeal Honey Butter Bun, 120–22
    focaccia, 110–11
    fougasse (Provençal hearth bread), 109–12
        Bacon Fougasse, 112
        dough, mixing and shaping, 109–10, 110
        Ramp Fougasse, 111
        Wild Mushroom Fougasse, 111
    stale
        croutons from, 72, 74
        Winter Tomato Soup with Fried Bread, 72–73
    toast
        Breakfast Trout with Bacon and Fried Apples
            with, 181–82
Broiled Trout with Ramp Watercress Pesto, 168
buckwheat
    Buckwheat Crêpes with Creamed Leeks and
        Gruyère, 84–85
    companion dishes, 230
    Buckwheat Honey Dressing, 38
    Buckwheat Sablés, 206–7, 207
    companion dishes, 202
    Buckwheat Trout with Sorrel Sauce, 174–75
bulgur
    Chanterelle Smoked Herring Bulgur Salad, 163–64
Bulldog Fish Farm, 170
burdock root
    gathering of, 187
    Soy-Simmered, 187–88
burgers
    Burger, 122–23
    Cornmeal Honey Butter Bun, 120–22
buttermilk
    Buttermilk, Apple, and Cucumber Gazpacho, 71,
        71–72
    Buttermilk Cucumbers with Chervil and Garlic
        Chive Shoots, 38–39, 39
    Easy Creamy Dressing, 51–52

C
cabbage
    cabbage salad, dressing for, 229
    green
        Sweet Buttered, 190–91
    home fermenting of, 222–23
    red
        Mom's Hot, 190
        Pickled Wedges with Blue Cheese Dressing,
            49–50
Calvados
    Bide-A-Wee Kir, 212
    Maple Flan with Maple-Calvados Sauce, 202–3, 203
    Maple Spritzer/Calva Cocktail, 213
capers. See also Milkweed Capers
    Herring Milkweed à la Meunière, 171–72
carrot
    Blackberry-Mustard Grilled, 196
    Carrot Apple Soup, 64–65
        companion dishes, 134
    Chickpea, Pickled Ramp, and Carrot Frittata, 81–82
    Mixed Mashed Potatoes, 196–97, 197
    Oven-Fried Roots, 192
    Roasted Baby Carrots with Maple-Mustard Glaze,
        195
    Root Vegetable Pancakes, 191
    Sambal Carrot Slaw, 41–42
        companion dishes, 50, 144–45
    Wine-Braised Oxtails with Shallots and Carrots,
        Cumin and Cocoa, 124–25
Castle Rock Dairy, 209
celery root
    Celery Root–Potato Puree, 197–98
        companion dishes, 125, 145–47, 197
    Celery Root Watercress Remoulade, 50–51
    Fries, Haw Jam and Pan-Fried Duck Breast with,
        145–47
    Mixed Mashed Potatoes, 196–97, 197
    Oven-Fried Roots, 192
    Root Vegetable Pancakes, 191
Chang, David, 134
Chanterelle and Steak Stroganoff, 118, 118–19
Chanterelle Smoked Herring Bulgur Salad, 163–64
Chard, Sweet and Sour, 193–94

cheese
  blue
    Black River Blue, 209
    Blue Cheese Dressing, 49–50
      in Grilled Pork Steaks and Greens with Easy
        Creamy Dressing, 134–35
    Kale, Apple, Blue Cheese Pizza, 104
    pear with walnuts and, 210
    Pickled Red Cabbage Wedges, with Blue Cheese
      Dressing, 49–50
    Red Wine–Blue Cheese Butter, 124
  cheddar
    Chile Cheddar Spread, 28
    Linguine with Guanciale, Potatoes, Kale and
      Cheddar, 100–101
  cream cheese
    Pickled Ramp Cream Cheese, 27
  curds
    fresh, delights of, 209–10
  goat (chèvre)
    availability of, 209
    Hazelnut-Crusted Goat Cheese, *25*, 26–27
    honey and thyme on, 210
    Shallot-Scented, 27–28
    Squash, Leek, Goat Cheese Pizza, 105, *105*
  Gouda
    companion dishes, 217
  Gouda, smoked
    Fettuccine with Hen of the Woods, Gouda, and
      Red Onion, *99*, 99–100
  Gruyère
    Buckwheat Crêpes with Creamed Leeks and,
      84–85
    Gruyère, Garlic, Rosemary Pizza, 106
  of Minnesota and Wisconsin, 209–10
  Pleasant Ridge Reserve, 209
  Reblochon
    Tartiflette, 82–83
  serving ideas for, 210
  shopping for, 209–10
chervil
  Buttermilk Cucumbers with, and Garlic Chive
    Shoots, 38–39, *39*

Chervil-Chive-Parsley Butter, 218
    companion dishes, 141–43
chestnuts
  Chestnut Butternut Soup, 61
  Chicken with Cider and, 143–44
  removing from shell, 143
chèvre (goat cheese)
  availability of, 209
  Hazelnut-Crusted Goat Cheese, *25*, 26–27
  honey and thyme on, 210
  Shallot-Scented, 27–28
  Squash, Leek, Goat Cheese Pizza, 105, *105*
chicken
  Autumn Vegetable, Chicken, and Sausage Hot Pot,
    140–41
  with Chestnuts and Cider, 143–44
  "Iron on the Fire" Grill-Roasting technique for, 128
  in a Pot with Chervil-Chive-Parsley Butter, 141–43
  Roast, with Wild Mushrooms, 76
  Smoke-Grilled Ma La Wings, 144–45
chicken stock
  buying of, 21
  soft-scrambled eggs, with sautéed wild
    mushrooms, 75
chickpea
  Chickpea, Pickled Ramp, and Carrot Frittata, 81–82
  Last Leg Duck Confit and Chickpea Soup, 73–74
Chile Cheddar Spread, 28
chile peppers. *See also* cayenne pepper
  Chile Cheddar Spread, 28
  dried red
    in pickling, 224
  Espelette (*piment d'espelette*), 21
  Sichuan Stir-Fried Corn with Chilies, 198–99
  Sweet Corn Chile Relish, 167
chives
  Chervil-Chive-Parsley Butter, 218
  Chive-Dill Dressing, 44–45
  Spring Lamb's-Quarters and Dandelion Salad with
    Chive-Dill Dressing, 44–45
choucroute garnie, 189
chutneys
  Cranberry Maple Chutney, 216

Pickled Crab and Ramp Chutney, 216–17

pickled ramps and crab apples, 227

cider. *See* apple cider

Cidered Shallots, 218–19

cochonnailles, 31

cocoa

Wine-Braised Oxtails with Shallots and Carrots, Cumin and, 124–25

collard greens, stuffing of, 89

condiments, 215–21. *See also* sauces and relishes

Aioli, 221

Chervil-Chive-Parsley Butter, 218

companion dishes, 141–43

Cidered Shallots, 218–19

Cranberry Maple Chutney, 216

Honey Mustard, 218

companion dishes, 28–29

Maple Syrup–Cider Vinegar Reduction, 217–18

Mayonnaise, and variants, 219–21

Pickled Crab and Ramp Chutney, 216–17

Pickled Ramp Mayonnaise, 221

Quick Blackberry-Apple Compote, 217

Tartar Sauce, 221

Confit of Fresh Ham on Sauerkraut, 128–30, *129*

companion dishes, 226

cookies

Buckwheat Sablés, 206–7, *207*

corn

Cream of Chanterelle and Sweet Corn Soup, *62*, 62–63

Sichuan Stir-Fried Corn with Chilies, 198–99

Sweet Corn Chile Relish, 167

Cornichons (French sour gherkins), 226

companion dishes, 31–32, 119, 134, 140–41, 141–43

as ingredient, 50

Cornmeal Honey Butter Bun, 120–22

Cornmeal Maple Baked Pudding with Dried Apples, 204–5, 206–7

Cornucopia, Wisconsin, 169

Cranberry Maple Chutney, 216

companion dishes for, 26

cream

Bacon Onion Tart, 108–9

Buckwheat Crêpes with Creamed Leeks and Gruyère, 84–85

Chanterelle and Steak Stroganoff, *118*, 118–19

Cream of Chanterelle and Sweet Corn Soup, *62*, 62–63

Easy Creamy Dressing, 51–52

Grouse in Cider Cream, *155*, 155–56

Herring Crudo with Cider Mustard Cream, *162*, 162–63

judicious use of, 7

soft-scrambled eggs, with sautéed wild mushrooms, 75

Tartiflette, 82–83

Wild Mushroom and Ramp Cream Toasts, 33

Cream Cheese, Pickled Ramp, 27

Cream of Chanterelle and Sweet Corn Soup, *62*, 62–63

Creamy Herby Dressing, 52

crème fraîche, Apple-Blackberry Galettes with, 205–6

Crêpes, Buckwheat, with Creamed Leeks and Gruyère, 84–85

cucumbers

Buttermilk, Apple, and Cucumber Gazpacho, *71*, 71–72

Buttermilk, with Chervil and Garlic Chive Shoots, 38–39, *39*

Cornichons (French sour gherkins), 226

pickled, 225

cumin

Wine-Braised Oxtails with Shallots and Carrots, Cumin and Cocoa, 124–25

custards and puddings

Cornmeal Maple Baked Pudding with Dried Apples, 204–5, 206–7

Maple Flan with Maple-Calvados Sauce, 202–3, *203*

D

dandelion

gathering, 238

Spring Lamb's-Quarters and Dandelion Salad with Chive-Dill Dressing, 44–45

Dave's BrewFarm, 16

desserts, 202–10

Apple-Blackberry Galettes, 205–6

Buckwheat Sablés, 206–7, *207*
    companion dishes, 202
Cornmeal Maple Baked Pudding with Dried Apples, 204–5, 206–7
Gooseberry and Raspberry Fool, 202
    companion dishes, 206–7
Maple Flan with Maple-Calvados Sauce, 202–3, *203*
Maple Ice Cream Topping, 208
Quick Wild Berry Sauce, 208
Deviled Whitefish with Potato Chip Crust, 164–65
    condiments for, 221
dill
    Chive-Dill Dressing, 44–45
    Spring Lamb's-Quarters and Dandelion Salad with Chive-Dill Dressing, 44–45
Dockside Fish Market (Grand Marais, MN), 169
dressings
    Blackberry Vinaigrette, 45–46, *46*
    Blue Cheese, 49–50
    Buckwheat Honey, 38
    Chive-Dill, 44–45
    Creamy Herby, 52
    Easy Creamy, 51–52
    Horseradish, 40
    Mustard Vinaigrette, 141
    Pickled Ramp, 52
    Ramp, 179–80
drying, of apples, 18
duck
    breast (*magret de canard*)
        with Blackberry-Whisky Sauce, 147–48, 197
        Pan-Fried, Haw Jam and, with Celery Root Fries, 145–47
    Duck Confit, 149–51
        companion dishes, 189
        in Duck Confit Tacos, 151–52
        in Last Leg Duck Confit and Chickpea Soup, 73–74
    duck fat
        rendering of, 149
        uses of, 32, 85, 147, 191, 192, 232
    giblets, 149
    skin, deep-fried, 149

E
Easy Creamy Dressing, 51–52
    Grilled Pork Steaks and Greens with, 134–35
Eckmeier, Mary, 4, 9, 21, 91
Eden Prairie, Minnesota, author's boyhood in, 1–2
egg
    Bacon Onion Tart, 108–9
    Chickpea, Pickled Ramp, and Carrot Frittata, 81–82
    Hen of the Woods and Potato Frittata, 80–81
    Hens and Eggs and Bacon, 131–33, *132*
    Lacinato Kale Salad with Poached Egg on Toast, 41
    omelet with sautéed wild mushrooms, 75
    soft-scrambled, stir-fried with garlic chives, 38
    soft-scrambled, with sautéed wild mushrooms, 75
eggplant
    Grilled Ratatouille, *86*, 86–87
Ehlers General Store (Cornucopia, WI), 169
endive, curly (frisée)
    Frisée Salad with Smoked Trout and Horseradish Dressing, 40
"Escabeche" of Brown Trout with Ramps and Asparagus, 172–74, *173*

F
Fall Colors Soup, 67
Farmers Market Confetti Vegetable Sauce for Pasta, 98–99
farmers markets
    author's farmers market bakery business, 4, 92–93
    bond between shoppers and vendors, 5
    connection to seasonal changes through, 94–96
    Marché des Lices market (Rennes, France), 91–92
    passion of shoppers and vendors, 92–93
    surprises at, 93–94
fennel
    Braised Pork Belly with, 130–31
    Fennel-Chive-Parsley Butter, 218
fermentation
    home preservation with, 222–23
    Sauerkraut, Home Fermented, 189, 222–23
    vegetables, home-fermented, in Big Borscht, 60
Fettuccine with Hen of the Woods, Gouda, and Red Onion, *99*, 99–100

fiddleheads
    in Brown Butter, 186–87
    gathering of, 233, 238
    Grilled Trout and Ramps with, 180–81
    identification of, 186
    preparation of, 234
    Ramp and Fiddleheads Tart, 107–8
    season for, 114
    substitution for, 19
    taste of, 233–34
Fischer, David, 239
fish, 161–84
    fresh, smell of, 2
    fried
        boyhood experiences of, 3
        condiments for, 221
        frying of, 171
    herring
        Chanterelle Smoked Herring Bulgur Salad,
            163–64
        Herring Crudo with Cider Mustard Cream, *162*,
            162–63
        Herring Milkweed à la Meunière, 171–72
        home smoking of, 182–84, *183*
        roe, shopping for, 169
    interchangeability of, 171
    shopping/foraging for, 5–6, 169–71
    storage of, 170
    trout, *182*
        Breakfast, with Bacon and Fried Apples, 181–82
        Broiled, with Ramp Watercress Pesto, 168
        Buckwheat, with Sorrel Sauce, 174–75
        "Escabache" of, with Ramps and Asparagus,
            172–74, *173*
        farm-raised, 170–71
        fishing for, 175–79
        Grilled, with Fiddleheads and Ramps, 180–81
        grilling of, 171, 198
        Lake Trout Maple-Spice Gravlax, 28–29, *29*, 218
        Opening Days Grilled, with Ramp Dressing on a
            Bed of Cress, 179–80
        Summer Lake Trout Chowder, 69–70
        Trout Caviar, 6, 30, 114
        trout milts, 30

trout, smoked
    Frisée Salad with, and Horseradish Dressing, 40
    home-smoked, 182–84
    Maple-Basted Fillets, 184
    Potted, 31
    Summer Lake Trout Chowder, 69–70
    and Wild Rice Chowder, 68–69
trout skin, crispy, as garnish, 70
Walleye Tacos, 165–67
whitefish
    Deviled, with Potato Chip Crust, 164–65
    grilling of, 171
    Summer Lake Trout Chowder, 69–70
whitefish, smoked
    Summer Lake Trout Chowder, 69–70
fishing
    author's adult experiences of, 3, 175–79
    author's boyhood experiences of, 1, 2–3
Flammekueche (*Tarte Flambée;* Bacon Onion Tart),
    108–9
focaccia, 110–11
foodshed, as term, 175–76
The Forager's Harvest (Thayer), 238
foraging. *See also* shopping/foraging for ingredients
    benefits of, 5, 112–15
    expanded definition of, 4–5
    hazardous flora and fauna, learning about,
        8, 237
    information sources on, 238–39
    as lifestyle, pleasures of, 8
    locations for, 237–38
    seasons for specific plants, 233–37
    stern caution, 8–9
    tools for, 238
fougasse (Provençal hearth bread), 109–12
    Bacon Fougasse, 112
    dough, mixing and shaping, 109–10, *110*
    Ramp Fougasse, 111
    Wild Mushroom Fougasse, 111
Fresh Tomato Sauce, 230
    companion dishes, 84, 87, 101
frisée (curly endive)
    Frisée Salad with Smoked Trout and Horseradish
        Dressing, 40

Frittata
    Chickpea, Pickled Ramp, and Carrot,
        81–82
    Hen of the Woods and Potato, 80–81
fruit, wild
    gathering of, 235

G

game birds, 152–60
    Baked Pheasant with Wild Mushrooms and Cream,
        157–58
    cooking of, 152
    Grilled Woodcock with Apple-Bacon Relish, *153*,
        153–54
    Grouse in Cider Cream, *155*, 155–56
    hunting of, 158–60
    interchangeability of, 155
    Steamed Grouse Breast with Black Trumpet Sauce,
        156–57
game bird stock, 152
gardening
    childhood experiences with, 54–55
    lazy-man's technique for, 55–58
    permaculture, 114
    pleasures of, 53–54, 57–58
garlic
    Aioli, 221
    Gruyère, Garlic, Rosemary Pizza, 106
    in mushroom dishes, 75
garlic chives
    Buttermilk Cucumbers with Chervil and Garlic
        Chive Shoots, 38–39, *39*
    gathering, 38
    stir-fried, with soft-scrambled eggs, 38
    uses of, 38
gobo. *See* burdock root
Goetze, Becky, 55
gooseberry
    gathering of, 235
    Gooseberry and Raspberry Fool, 202
        companion dishes, 206–7
Great Lakes, fish of, 169
Greg's Meats (MN), 43

grilling
    Blackberry-Mustard Grilled Carrots, 196
    of fish, 171, 198
    Grilled Butternut Squash with Maple–Cider
        Vinegar Glaze, 186
    Grilled Pork Steaks and Greens with Easy Creamy
        Dressing, 134–35
    Grilled Ratatouille, *86*, 86–87
    Grilled Trout, Fiddleheads, and Ramps, 180–81
    Grilled Venison with Red Wine–Blue Cheese But-
        ter, 123–24
    Grilled Woodcock with Apple-Bacon Relish, *153*,
        153–54
    "Iron on the Fire" Grill-Roasted Lamb and Veg-
        etables, 126–28, *127*
    Opening Days Grilled Stream Trout with Ramp
        Dressing on a Bed of Cress, 179–80
    of pork, companion dishes, 226–27
    Smoke-Grilled Ma La Chicken Wings, 144–45
Grouse in Cider Cream, *155*, 155–56
Gruyère, Garlic, Rosemary Pizza, 106
guanciale (cured pork jowl)
    Linguine with Guanciale, Potatoes, Kale and
        Cheddar, 100–101
    substitutions for, 100

H

Halvorson Fisheries (Cornucopia, WI), 5–6, 169–70
hamburger
    Burger, 122–23
    Cornmeal Honey Butter Bun, 120–22
Hard Cider Sub, 231
haw (hawberry)
    gathering, 145–46, *146*, 236
    Haw Jam and Pan-Fried Duck Breast with Celery
        Root Fries, 145–47
hazelnuts
    chopping, 26
    Hazelnut-Crusted Goat Cheese, *25*, 26–27
        companion dishes, 216
    wild, picking, 26
Hen of the Woods and Potato Frittata, 80–81
Hens and Eggs and Bacon, 131–33, *132*

herring
    Chanterelle Smoked Herring Bulgur Salad, 163–64
    Herring Crudo with Cider Mustard Cream, *162,* 162–63
    Herring Milkweed à la Meunière, 171–72
    home smoking of, 182–84, *183*
    roe, shopping for, 169
high-fat ingredients, judicious use of, 7
Highway 64 Revisited, 211, *212*
Holland Family Farm, 209
honey
    Apple Turnip Slaw with Buckwheat Honey Dressing, 38
    Cornmeal Honey Butter Bun, 120–22
    Honey Mustard, 218
horseradish
    Frisée Salad with Smoked Trout and Horseradish Dressing, 40
    Horseradish Dressing, 40
hunting, of game birds, 158–60

I

ice cream, toppings
    Maple Ice Cream Topping, 208
    Quick Wild Berry Sauce, 208
ingredients. *See* foraging; shopping/foraging for ingredients; substitutions
"Iron on the Fire" Grill-Roasted Lamb and Vegetables, 126–28, *127*

J

The Joy of Pickling (Ziedrich), 222

K

kale
    cooked in duck fat, 147
    home fermenting of, 222–23
    Kale, Apple, Blue Cheese Pizza, 104
    Lacinato Kale Salad with Poached Egg on Toast, 41
    Oven Roasted, 193
    Stuffed Red Leaves of, with Herb-Wine-Butter Sauce, 89–91
Katz, Sandor, 222

Keats, John, 112, 158
Knife and Fork BOT (Bacon, Onion, and Tomato), 133–34
    companion dishes, 226

L

Lac Courte Oreilles Ojibwe reservation, 14
Lacinato Kale Salad with Poached Egg on Toast, 41
Lake Trout Maple-Spice Gravlax, 28–29, *29*
lamb
    chops, Blackberry-Whisky Sauce for, 148
    "Iron on the Fire" Grill-Roasted, and Vegetables, 126–28, *127*
    Pan-Fried Leg Cutlets, 125–26
lamb's quarters
    and Dandelion Salad with Chive-Dill Dressing, 44–45
    gathering, 238
Last Leg Duck Confit and Chickpea Soup, 73–74
leek
    Creamed, Buckwheat Crêpes with, and Gruyère, 84–85
    Squash, Leek, Goat Cheese Pizza, 105, *105*
    substitution for, 18
Lévi-Strauss, Claude, 6
Linguine with Guanciale, Potatoes, Kale and Cheddar, 100–101
local food. *See also* shopping/foraging for ingredients
    cheeses, 209–10
    high quality of, 6–7
Lou's (Two Harbors, MN), 169
LoveTree Farmstead, 209

M

magret de canard
    with Blackberry-Whisky Sauce, 147–48
    defined, 147
    Pan-Fried, Haw Jam and, with Celery Root Fries, 145–47
main dishes, fish, 161–84
    Breakfast Trout with Bacon and Fried Apples, 181–82
    Broiled Trout with Ramp Watercress Pesto, 168

Buckwheat Trout with Sorrel Sauce, 174–75
Chanterelle Smoked Herring Bulgur Salad, 163–64
Deviled Whitefish with Potato Chip Crust, 164–65
"Escabache" of Brown Trout, with Ramps and As-
    paragus, 172–74, *173*
Grilled Trout with Fiddleheads and Ramps, 180–81
Herring Crudo with Cider Mustard Cream, *162,*
    162–63
Herring Milkweed à la Meunière, 171–72
interchangeability of species, 171
Maple-Basted Smoked Lake Trout Fillets, 184
Opening Days Grilled Stream Trout with Ramp
    Dressing on a Bed of Cress, 179–80
Walleye Tacos, 165–67
main dishes, meat
beef
    Burger, 120–23
    Chanterelle and Steak Stroganoff, *118,* 118–19
    Steak Tartare Maison, 119–20
    Wine-Braised Oxtails with Shallots and Carrots,
        Cumin and Cocoa, 124–25
chicken
    Autumn Vegetable, Chicken, and Sausage Hot
        Pot, 140–41
    with Chestnuts and Cider, 143–44
    "Iron on the Fire" Grill-Roasting technique for,
        128
    in a Pot with Chervil-Chive-Parsley Butter, 141–43
    Roast, with Wild Mushrooms, 76
    Smoke-Grilled Ma La Wings, 144–45
duck
    breast (*magret de canard*)
        with Blackberry-Whisky Sauce, 147–48, 197
        Pan-Fried, Haw Jam and, with Celery Root
        Fries, 145–47
    Duck Confit, 149–51
        companion dishes, 189
    Duck Confit Tacos, 151–52
game birds, 152–60
    Baked Pheasant with Wild Mushrooms and
        Cream, 157–58
    cooking of, 152
    Grilled Woodcock with Apple-Bacon Relish, *153,*
        153–54

Grouse in Cider Cream, *155,* 155–56
    hunting of, 158–60
    interchangeability of species, 155
    Steamed Grouse Breast with Black Trumpet
        Sauce, 156–57
lamb
    "Iron on the Fire" Grill-Roasted, and Vegetables,
        126–28, *127*
    Pan-Fried Leg Cutlets, 125–26
pork
    Braised Pork Belly with Fennel, 130–31
    Confit of Fresh Ham on Sauerkraut, 128–30, *129*
        companion dishes, 226
    Grilled Pork Steaks and Greens with Easy
        Creamy Dressing, 134–35
    Hens and Eggs and Bacon, 131–33, *132*
    Knife and Fork BOT (Bacon, Onion, and
        Tomato), 133–34
        companion dishes, 226
venison
    Grilled, with Red Wine–Blue Cheese Butter,
        123–24
main dishes, vegetable, 79–91
    Buckwheat Crêpes with Creamed Leeks and Gru-
        yère, 84–85
        companion dishes, 230
    Chickpea, Pickled Ramp, and Carrot Frittata, 81–82
    Hen of the Woods and Potato Frittata, 80–81
    Ratatouille, Grilled, *86,* 86–87
    Stuffed Delicata Squash, 87–89, *88*
    Stuffed Red Kale Leaves with Herb-Wine-Butter
        Sauce, 89–91
    Sugar Bush Bean Pot, 85–86
    Tartiflette, 82–83
Maple-Basted Smoked Lake Trout Fillets, 68, 184
Maple Flan with Maple-Calvados Sauce, 202–3, *203*
maple syrup
    Bide-A-Wee Kir, 212
    buying, 16
    Cornmeal Maple Baked Pudding with Dried
        Apples, 204–5
    Cranberry Maple Chutney, 216
    Lake Trout Maple-Spice Gravlax, 28–29, *29*
    making of, 234

Maple-Basted Smoked Lake Trout Fillets, 184
Maple Flan with Maple-Calvados Sauce, 202–3, *203*
Maple Ice Cream Topping, 208
Maple Syrup–Cider Vinegar Reduction, 217–18
real, importance of using, 16
Roasted Baby Carrots with Maple-Mustard Glaze,
    195
uses of, 16
Maple Syrup–Cider Vinegar Reduction, 217–18
maps for foraging, 238
Marché des Lices market (Rennes, France), 91–92
Marrone, Teresa, 239
Mary's Duck Fat Tortillas, 232
Mayonnaise, and variants, 219–21
meat. *See* main dishes, meat; *specific meats*
Mel's Smokehouse (Knife River, MN), 68, 169
midwestern food
    cheeses, 209–10
    high quality of, 6–7
Milkweed Capers, 225, *225*
milkweed pickles, 224–25
Mills, Mike, 23
Minne'sconsin Margherita Pizza, 106
Minnesota
    author's boyhood in, 1–2
    fishing in, 169–70
    foraging areas in, 237–38
    mycological society of, 239
Mixed Mashed Potatoes, 125, 196–97, *197*
Momofuku Ssäm Bar (New York City), 134
Mom's Hot Red Cabbage, 151, 190
Morin, Timmy, 55
mushrooms
    dried, in Big Borscht, 60
    washing of, 75
mushrooms, wild
    Baked Pheasant with Wild Mushrooms and Cream,
        157–58
    black trumpet, *34*
        Black and Gold Mushroom "Caviar," 34–35
        gathering of, 235
        Steamed Grouse Breast with Black Trumpet
            Sauce, 156–57
    chanterelles, *113*

Black and Gold Mushroom "Caviar," 34–35
Chanterelle and Steak Stroganoff, *118,* 118–19
Chanterelle Smoked Herring Bulgur Salad, 163–64
cooking of, 75
Cream of Chanterelle and Sweet Corn Soup, *62,*
    62–63
gathering of, 235
preservation of, 77
chicken of the woods (sulfur shelf)
    gathering of, 235–36
cooking basics, 75
dryad's saddle (pheasant back)
    cooking of, 234–35
    gathering of, 234
gathering of, 113–14, 234–35, 238
giant puffballs
    cooking of, 75
    gathering of, 236
hedgehog
    gathering of, 236
hen of the woods
    Fettuccine with Hen of the Woods, Gouda, and
        Red Onion, *99,* 99–100
    gathering of, 236
    Hen of the Woods and Potato Frittata, 80–81
    Hens and Eggs and Bacon, 131–33, *132*
    preservation of, 76
    Roast Chicken with Wild Mushrooms, 76
    substitution for, 89
information resources on, 239
"Iron on the Fire" Grill-Roasted chicken and, 128
morels
    cooking of, 75
    gathering of, 235
    preservation of, 76
oyster
    cooking of, 75
    gathering of, 234
preservation of, 76–77
as purifiers of forest, 113
Roast Chicken with Wild Mushrooms, 76
substitution for, 19–20
sulfur shelf (chicken of the woods)
    gathering of, 235–36

Wild Mushroom and Ramp Cream Toasts, 33

Wild Mushroom Fougasse, 111

Wild Mushroom Lasagna, 101–2

Wild Mushroom Pizza, 106–7

Mushrooms Demystified (Arora), 239

mustard

    Dijon-style

        Herring Crudo with Cider Mustard Cream, *162,*
            162–63

        Honey Mustard, 28–29, 218

        mayonnaise, and variants, 219–21

    grainy

        Blackberry-Mustard Grilled Carrots, 196

        Roasted Baby Carrots with Maple-Mustard
            Glaze, 195

    Honey Mustard, 218

        companion dishes, 28–29

    Mustard Vinaigrette, 141

mustard greens

    stuffing of, 89

Mustard Vinaigrette, 141

mycological societies, 239

N

nannyberries (wild raisins), gathering, 236

Native Bay Restaurant (Chippewa Falls, WI), 52

Native Bay Tomato Clock, *52,* 52–53

natural, authentic foods, as inspiration, 4

nature deficit disorder, 115

Nature's Garden (Thayer), 238

nettles, wild

    gathering of, 233

    Grilled Trout, Fiddleheads, and Ramps,
        180–81

    Nettles Ramp Champ, 188

    Nettles and Wild Rice Soup, 63–64

    Nettle Tea, 233

    substitution for, 19

    types of, 233

nuts

    chestnuts

        Chestnut Butternut Soup, 61

        Chicken with Cider and, 143–44

        removing from shell, 143

hazelnuts

    chopping, 26

    Hazelnut-Crusted Goat Cheese, *25,*
        26–27

        companion dishes, 216

    wild, picking, 26

walnuts

    Maple Ice Cream Topping, 208

    pear with blue cheese and, 210

    Roasted Beet Salad with Aioli and, *47, 48*

O

oeufs en meurette, 131

onion

    Bacon Onion Tart, 108–9

    Chicken in a Pot with Chervil-Chive-Parsley But-
        ter, 141–43

    green

        "Iron on the Fire" Grill-Roasted Lamb and Veg-
            etables, 126–28, *127*

        Knife and Fork BOT (Bacon, Onion, and Tomato),
            133–34

    red

        Fettuccine with Hen of the Woods, Gouda, and
            Red Onion, *99,* 99–100

    sweet, in mushroom dishes, 75

    Wine-Braised Oxtails with Shallots and Carrots,
        Cumin and Cocoa, 124–25

onion family (alliums), substitutions within, 18

Opening Days Grilled Stream Trout with
    Ramp Dressing on a Bed of Cress,
    179–80

orange, blood

    Black Radish and Blood Orange Salsa, 167

outdoor life, pleasures of, 114–15

Oven-Fried Roots, 192, 221

    companion dishes, 119

Oven Green Beans with Bacon, 194, *195*

Oven Roasted Kale, 193

Oven Tomatoes with Herbs, 229–30

Oxtails, Wine-Braised, with Shallots and Carrots,
    Cumin and Cocoa, 124–25

P

Pancakes, Root Vegetable, 191

pancetta

Linguine with Guanciale, Potatoes, Kale and Cheddar, 100–101

Pan-Fried Lamb Leg Cutlets, 125–26

parsley

Chervil-Chive-Parsley Butter, 218

Chicken in a Pot with Chervil-Chive-Parsley Butter, 141–43

parsnips

Mixed Mashed Potatoes, 196–97, *197*

Oven-Fried Roots, 192

Root Vegetable Pancakes, 191

pasta

Farmers Market Confetti Vegetable Sauce for Pasta, 98–99

Fettuccine with Hen of the Woods, Gouda, and Red Onion, *99*, 99–100

Linguine with Guanciale, Potatoes, Kale and Cheddar, 100–101

noodles, Chinese

Smoke-Grilled Ma La Chicken Wings, 144–45

Wild Mushroom Lasagna, 101–2

Peace, Love, and Barbecue (Mills), 23

pear, with blue cheese and walnuts, 210

peas, sugar snap

Snap Pea Salsa, 51

Pépin, Jacques, 75

pepper. *See also* chile peppers

red bell

Grilled Ratatouille, *86*, 86–87

peppercorns, Sichuan, 144–45

permaculture, 114

Pickled Crab and Ramp Chutney, 216–17

Pickled Crab Apples, 227–29, *228*

pickled ramps, 224

Broiled Trout with Ramp Watercress Pesto, 168

Chickpea, Pickled Ramp, and Carrot Frittata, 81–82

Nettles Ramp Champ, 188

Pickled Ramp Cream Cheese, 27

Pickled Ramp Dressing, 52

Pickled Ramp Mayonnaise, 221

Ramp-A-Tini, 211

Wild Tartar Sauce, 221

Pickled Red Cabbage Wedges (Reconstructed Coleslaw) with Blue Cheese Dressing, 49–50

pickling

basic brines for, 224–25

Cornichons (French sour gherkins), 226

companion dishes, 31–32, 119, 134, 140–41, 141–43

as ingredient, 50

Pickled Crab and Ramp Chutney, 216–17

Pickled Crab Apples, 227–29, *228*

Pickled Red Cabbage Wedges (Reconstructed Coleslaw) with Blue Cheese Dressing, 49–50

Sweet and Spicy Apple Slices, 226–27, *227*

pizza. *See also* fougasse (Provençal hearth bread)

Bacon Onion Tart (*Tarte Flambée; Flammekueche*), 108–9

dough, 103–4

Gruyère, Garlic, Rosemary Topping, 106

Kale, Apple, Blue Cheese Topping, 104

Minne'sconsin Margherita, 106

Ramp and Fiddleheads Tart, 107–8

Squash, Leek, Goat Cheese Topping, 105, *105*

Wild Mushroom Topping, 106–7

Plash, Cindy, 43

plums, wild, gathering of, 235

polenta, Braised Pork Belly with Fennel over, 130–31

Popcorn Salad, *42*, 43

pork. *See also* bacon

chops, companion dishes, 189

grilled, companion dishes, 226–27

guanciale (cured pork jowl)

Linguine with Potatoes, Kale Cheddar and, 100–101

substitution for, 100

Ham, Fresh, Confit of, on Sauerkraut, 128–30, *129*

pork belly

Braised, with Fennel, 130–31

shopping for, 136

Potted Pork Pâté (*Rillettes*), 31–32

companion dishes, 226

revival of interest in, 31

Shoulder, Fresh, Confit of, on Sauerkraut, 128–30, *129*

Steaks, Grilled, and Greens with Easy Creamy
  Dressing, 134–35
potato
  Celery Root–Potato Puree, 197–98
  Chickpea, Pickled Ramp, and Carrot Frittata, 81–82
  Hen of the Woods and Potato Frittata, 80–81
  Linguine with Guanciale, Potatoes, Kale and
    Cheddar, 100–101
  Mixed Mash, 196–97, *197*
  Nettles Ramp Champ, 188
  Root Vegetable Pancakes, 191
  Root Vegetables, Oven-Fried, 192
  Smoked Trout and Wild Rice Chowder, 68–69
  Sorrel Shallot Potato Soup, *66*, 66–67
  Summer Lake Trout Chowder, 69–70
  Tartiflette, 82–83
Potato Chip Crust, Deviled Whitefish with, 164–65
Potted Pork Pâté (*Rillettes*), 31–32
  companion dishes, 226
Potted Smoked Trout, 31
poultry, 139–58
  chicken
    Autumn Vegetable, Chicken, and Sausage Hot
      Pot, 140–41
    with Chestnuts and Cider, 143–44
    "Iron on the Fire" Grill-Roasting technique for, 128
    in a Pot with Chervil-Chive-Parsley Butter, 141–43
    Roast, with Wild Mushrooms, 76
    Smoke-Grilled Ma La Wings, 144–45
  duck
    breast (*magret de canard*)
      with Blackberry-Whisky Sauce, 147–48, 197
      Pan-Fried, Haw Jam and, with Celery Root
        Fries, 145–47
    Duck Confit, 149–51
      companion dishes, 189
      in Duck Confit Tacos, 151–52
      in Last Leg Duck Confit and Chickpea
        Soup, 73–74
    duck fat
      rendering of, 149
      uses of, 32, 85, 147, 191, 192, 232
    giblets, 149
    skin, deep-fried, 149

game birds, 152–60
  Baked Pheasant with Wild Mushrooms and
    Cream, 157–58
  cooking of, 152
  Grilled Woodcock with Apple-Bacon Relish, *153*,
    153–54
  Grouse in Cider Cream, *155*, 155–56
  hunting of, 158–60
  interchangeability of, 155
  Steamed Grouse Breast with Black Trumpet
    Sauce, 156–57
preparation methods, traditional, renaissance of, 6
preservation methods, traditional. *See also* fermenta-
    tion; pickling
  drying, of apples, 18
  renaissance of, 6
Preserving Food without Freezing or Canning (Terre
    Vivante Collective), 222

Q

quatre-épices, 20
Quick Blackberry-Apple Compote, 210, 217
Quick Wild Berry Sauce, 208

R

radio, in rural Wisconsin, 14
radish
  Black Radish and Blood Orange Salsa, 167
ramps
  Broiled Trout with Ramp Watercress Pesto, 168
  Dressing, Opening Days Grilled Stream Trout with,
    on Bed of Cress, 179–80
  "Escabache" of Brown Trout with, and Asparagus,
    172–74, *173*
  gathering of, 114, 177, 233, 238
  Grilled Trout, Fiddleheads, and, 180–81
  Nettles Ramp Champ, 188
  Pickled Crab and Ramp Chutney, 216–17
  Ramp and Fiddleheads Tart, 107–8
  Ramp-A-Tini, 211
  Ramp Fougasse, 111
  substitution for, 19
  uses of, 233
  Wild Mushroom and Ramp Cream Toasts, 33

ramps, pickled, 224
    Broiled Trout with Ramp Watercress Pesto, 168
    Chickpea, Pickled Ramp, and Carrot Frittata, 81–82
    Nettles Ramp Champ, 188
    Pickled Ramp Cream Cheese, 27
    Pickled Ramp Dressing, 52
    Pickled Ramp Mayonnaise, 221
    Ramp-A-Tini, 211
    Wild Tartar Sauce, 221
raspberry
    gathering of, 235
    Gooseberry and Raspberry Fool, 202
        companion dishes, 206–7
Ratatouille, Grilled, *86*, 86–87
Real Bread bakery, 4, 92–93
Red Wine–Blue Cheese Butter, 124
relish. *See* sauces and relishes
rhubarb, raw, with sugar, 54
rice, wild
        best varieties of, 68
        Nettles and Wild Rice Soup, 63–64
        Smoked Trout and Wild Rice Chowder, 68–69
Rillettes (Potted Pork Pâté), 31–32
    companion dishes, 226
Roast Chicken with Wild Mushrooms, 76
Roasted Baby Carrots with Maple-Mustard Glaze, 195
Roasted Beet Salad with Aioli and Walnuts, 47, *48*
    companion dishes, 50
roasting
    "Iron on the Fire" Grill-Roasted Lamb and
        Vegetables, 126–28, *127*
    Kale, Oven Roasted, 193
    Roast Chicken with Wild Mushrooms, 76
    Roasted Baby Carrots with Maple-Mustard Glaze,
        195
    Roasted Beet Salad with Aioli and Walnuts, 47, *48*
        companion dishes, 50
root vegetables
    Oven-Fried, 192
    Pancakes, 191
rosemary
    Gruyère, Garlic, Rosemary Pizza, 106
    in mushroom dishes, 75
Russ Kendall's (Knife River, MN), 169

S
sage, in mushroom dishes, 75
salads, 37–53
    Apple Turnip Slaw with Buckwheat Honey Dress-
        ing, 38
        companion dishes, 164–65
    Buttermilk Cucumbers with Chervil and Garlic
        Chive Shoots, 38–39, *39*
    Celery Root Watercress Remoulade, 50–51
    Chanterelle Smoked Herring Bulgur, 163–64
    Frisée, with Smoked Trout and Horseradish Dress-
        ing, 40
    Lacinato Kale, with Poached Egg on Toast, 41
    Native Bay Tomato Clock, *52*, 52–53
    Pickled Red Cabbage Wedges (Reconstructed
        Coleslaw) with Blue Cheese Dressing, 49–50
    Popcorn Salad, *42*, 43
    Roasted Beet, with Aioli and Walnuts, 47, *48*
        companion dishes, 50
    Sambal Carrot Slaw, 41–42
    Snap Pea Salsa, 51
    Spring Lamb's-Quarters and Dandelion, with
        Chive-Dill Dressing, 44–45
    Warm, of Wax Beans with Caramelized Shallots
        and Blackberry Vinaigrette, 45–46, *46*
    Watercress Bacon, 46–47
    "weeds" as ingredients in, 43–45
    Wine-Dark Beets, 48–49
salsa
    Black Radish and Blood Orange, 167
    Snap Pea, 51
salt, adding of, 21
Sambal Carrot Slaw, 41–42
    companion dishes, 50, 144–45
sambal oelek (ground fresh chili paste), 20
    Sambal Carrot Slaw, 41–42
    substitution for, 20
sauces and relishes
    Apple-Bacon Relish, 153–54
    Blackberry-Whisky Sauce, 148
    Fresh Tomato Sauce, 230
        companion dishes, 84, 87, 101
    Maple-Calvados Sauce, 202–3, *203*
    Maple Ice Cream Topping, 208

Quick Wild Berry Sauce, 208
Red Wine–Blue Cheese Butter, 124
Sweet Corn Chile Relish, 167
Tartar Sauce, 221
sauerkraut
    Braised, 189–90
        in Confit of Fresh Ham on Sauerkraut, 128–30
    Home-Fermented, 222–23
    naturally-fermented, small-batch, 128
sausage
    Autumn Vegetable, Chicken, and Sausage Hot Pot,
        140–41
    grilled, companion dishes, 189
    Sugar Bush Bean Pot, 85–86
Schrock, Ivan, 10–11
seasonal change, and availability of wild food, 233–37
seasonal change, remaining connected to
    through farmers markets, 94–96
    through foraging, 114
shallot
    Cidered Shallots, 218–19
    in mushroom dishes, 75
    Shallot-Scented Chèvre, 27–28
    Sorrel Shallot Potato Soup, *66*, 66–67
    substitution for, 18
    Warm Salad of Wax Beans with Caramelized Shal-
        lots and Blackberry Vinaigrette, 45–46, *46*
    Wine-Braised Oxtails with Shallots and Carrots,
        Cumin and Cocoa, 124–25
sherry
    soft-scrambled eggs, with sautéed wild
        mushrooms, 75
shopping/foraging for ingredients. *See also* foraging
    apple cider, 17
    at Bide-A-Wee cabin, 16
    burdock, 187
    cheeses, 209–10
    chicken stock, 21
    fiddleheads, identification of, 186
    fish, 5–6, 169–71
    hawberries, gathering of, 145–46
    hazards of, 8
    hazelnuts, wild, 26
    importance of, for good cooking, 5

maple syrup, 16
pleasures of, 5–6
pork belly, 136
sambal oelek (ground fresh chili paste), 20
wild mushrooms, picking of, 113–14
Shrub, 231
Sichuan Stir-Fried Corn with Chilies, 187–88, 198–99
slaw
    Apple Turnip, with Buckwheat Honey Dressing, 38,
        164–65
    Reconstructed (Pickled Red Cabbage Wedges)
        with Blue Cheese Dressing, 49–50
    Sambal Carrot, 41–42
        companion dishes, 50, 144–45
    from Wine-Dark Beet dressing, 49
smoked trout
    Frisée Salad with, and Horseradish Dressing, 40
    home-smoked, 182–84
    Maple-Basted Fillets, 184
    Potted, 31
    Summer Lake Trout Chowder, 69–70
    and Wild Rice Chowder, 68–69
smoked whitefish
    Nettles and Wild Rice Soup, 63–64
    Summer Lake Trout Chowder, 69–70
Smoke-Grilled Ma La Chicken Wings, 144–45, 187–88
smoking
    of bacon, 136–38
    of fish, 182–84
    process, 22–24
    storage of smoked foods, 24
Snap Pea Salsa, 51
sorrel, wild
    Buckwheat Trout with Sorrel Sauce, 174–75
    characteristics of, 174
    gathering of, 235
    Sorrel Shallot Potato Soup, *66*, 66–67
    substitution for, 19
    types of, 235
Sorrel Shallot Potato Soup, *66*, 66–67
soup, 59–74
    Big Borscht, 60
    Buttermilk, Apple, and Cucumber Gazpacho, *71*,
        71–72

Carrot Apple, 64–65
    companion dishes, 134
Chestnut Butternut, 61
Cream of Chanterelle and Sweet Corn, *62,*
    62–63
Fall Colors, 67
Last Leg Duck Confit and Chickpea, 73–74
Nettles and Wild Rice, 63–64
Smoked Trout and Wild Rice Chowder, 68–69
Sorrel Shallot Potato, *66,* 66–67
Summer Lake Trout Chowder, 69–70
Winter Tomato, with Fried Bread, 72–73
sour cream
    Chanterelle and Steak Stroganoff, *118,* 118–19
    Wild Mushroom and Ramp Cream Toasts, 33
soy sauce
    Soy-Simmered Burdock Root, 187–88
spreads and dips
    Black and Gold Mushroom "Caviar," 34–35
    Black Radish and Blood Orange Salsa, 167
    Celery Root Watercress Remoulade, 50–51
    Chile Cheddar Spread, 28
    Mayonnaise, and variants, 219–21
    Pickled Ramp Cream Cheese, 28
    Potted Pork Pâté (*Rillettes*), 31–32
    Snap Pea Salsa, 51
    Steak Tartare Maison, 119–20
Spring Lamb's-Quarters and Dandelion Salad with
    Chive-Dill Dressing, 44–45
squash
    butternut
        Chestnut Butternut Soup, 61
        Grilled, with Maple–Cider Vinegar Glaze, 186
        Squash, Leek, Goat Cheese Pizza, 105, *105*
    delicata
        Stuffed, 87–89, *88*
    zucchini
        Grilled Ratatouille, *86,* 86–87
Squash, Leek, Goat Cheese Pizza, 105, *105*
Sriracha chile sauce, 20
Star Prairie Trout Farm, 170
starters, 25–35
    Black and Gold Mushroom "Caviar," 34–35
    Chile Cheddar Spread, 28

Hazelnut-Crusted Goat Cheese, *25,* 26–27
Lake Trout Maple-Spice Gravlax, 28–29, *29*
Pickled Ramp Cream Cheese, 27
Potted Pork Pâté (*Rillettes*), 31–32
Potted Smoked Trout, 31
Shallot-Scented Chèvre, 27–28
Trout Caviar, 30
    preparation of, 6
    as symbol of fine local food, 6
Wild Mushroom and Ramp Cream Toasts, 33
Steak Tartare Maison, 119–20
Steamed Grouse Breast with Black Trumpet Sauce,
    156–57
Stuffed Delicata Squash, 87–89, *88,* 230
Stuffed Red Kale Leaves with Herb-Wine-Butter Sauce,
    89–91
substitutions
    for espelette pepper (*piment d'espelette*), 21
    for fiddlehead ferns, 19
    for guanciale (cured pork jowl), 100
    for hen of the woods mushrooms, 89
    for leeks, 18
    for mushrooms, wild, 19–20
    for nettles, 19
    for onion family, 18
    for ramps, 19
    for sambal oelek (ground fresh chili paste), 20
    for shallots, 18
    for sorrel, wild, 19
    for wheat berries, sprouted, 89–90
    for wild foods, 18–19
Sugar Bush Bean Pot, 85–86
Summer Lake Trout Chowder, 69–70
Sweet and Sour Chard, 193–94
Sweet and Spicy Apple Slices, 134, 226–27, *227*
Sweet Buttered Cabbage, 119, 155–56, 190–91
Sweet Corn Chile Relish, 151–52, 165–67

T
tacos
    Duck Confit Tacos, 151–52
    Walleye Tacos, 165–67
tarragon
    Tarragon-Chive-Parsley Butter, 218

Tartar Sauce, 164–65, 221
Tarte Flambée (Bacon Onion Tart; *Flammekueche*), 108–9
Tartiflette, 82–83
tarts
Apple-Blackberry Galettes, 205–6
Bacon Onion, 108–9
Ramp and Fiddleheads, 107–8
Thayer, Sam, 113, 238–39
thyme
and honey, on chèvre, 210
in mushroom dishes, 75
tomato
Fresh Sauce, 230
companion dishes, 84, 87, 101
Grilled Ratatouille, *86*, 86–87
Knife and Fork BOT (Bacon, Onion, and Tomato), 133–34
Native Bay Tomato Clock, *52*, 52–53
Oven Tomatoes with Herbs, 229–30
Winter Tomato Soup with Fried Bread, 72–73
trout, *182*
Breakfast, with Bacon and Fried Apples, 181–82
Broiled, with Ramp Watercress Pesto, 168
Buckwheat, with Sorrel Sauce, 174–75
"Escabache" of, with Ramps and Asparagus, 172–74, *173*
farm-raised, 170–71
fishing for, 175–79
Gravlax, Lake Trout Maple-Spice, 28–29, *29*, 218
Grilled, with Fiddleheads and Ramps, 180–81
grilling of, 171, 198
Opening Days Grilled, with Ramp Dressing on a Bed of Cress, 179–80
Summer Lake Trout Chowder, 69–70
trout, smoked
Frisée Salad with, and Horseradish Dressing, 40
home-smoking of, 182–84
Maple-Basted Fillets, 184
Potted, 31
Summer Lake Trout Chowder, 69–70
and Wild Rice Chowder, 68–69
Trout Caviar, 30
preparation of, 6

season for, 114
as symbol of fine local food, 6
Trout Caviar Manifesto, 6
trout milts, 30
turnip
Apple Turnip Slaw with Buckwheat Honey Dressing, 38

V
vegetable main dishes, 79–91
Buckwheat Crêpes with Creamed Leeks and Gruyère, 84–85
companion dishes, 230
Chickpea, Pickled Ramp, and Carrot Frittata, 81–82
Hen of the Woods and Potato Frittata, 80–81
Ratatouille, Grilled, *86*, 86–87
Stuffed Delicata Squash, 87–89, *88*
Stuffed Red Kale Leaves with Herb-Wine-Butter Sauce, 89–91
Sugar Bush Bean Pot, 85–86
Tartiflette, 82–83
vegetables, home-fermented, in Big Borscht, 60
vegetable side dishes, 185–99
Blackberry-Mustard Grilled Carrots, 196
Braised Sauerkraut, 189–90
Celery Root–Potato Puree, 197–98
companion dishes, 125, 145–47, 197
Fiddleheads in Brown Butter, 186–87
Grilled Butternut Squash with Maple–Cider Vinegar Glaze, 186
Mixed Mashed Potatoes, 196–97, *197*
Nettles Ramp Champ, 188
Oven-Fried Roots, 192
Oven Green Beans with Bacon, 194, *195*
Oven Roasted Kale, 193
Roasted Baby Carrots with Maple-Mustard Glaze, 195
Root Vegetable Pancakes, 191
Sichuan Stir-Fried Corn with Chilies, 198–99
Soy-Simmered Burdock Root, 187–88
Sweet and Sour Chard, 193–94
Sweet Buttered Cabbage, 190–91
Venison, Grilled, with Red Wine–Blue Cheese Butter, 123–24

vermouth
    Stuffed Red Kale Leaves with Herb-Wine-Butter
        Sauce, 89–91
Village Inn (Cornucopia, WI), 169
vinegar. *See also* apple cider vinegar
    blackberry
        Warm Salad of Wax Beans with Caramelized
            Shallots and Blackberry Vinaigrette, 45–46,
            46

W

Walleye Tacos, 51, 165–67
walnuts
    pear with blue cheese and, 210
    Roasted Beet Salad with Aioli and, 47, *48*
Warm Salad of Wax Beans with Caramelized Shallots
        and Blackberry Vinaigrette, 45–46, *46*
watercress
    Broiled Trout with Ramp Watercress Pesto, 168
    Celery Root Watercress Remoulade, 50–51
    flavor variation in, 168
    gathering of, 177, 233, 238
    Opening Days Grilled Stream Trout with Ramp
        Dressing on a Bed of, 179–80
    uses of, 233
Watercress Bacon Salad, 46–47
weeds, as salad ingredient, 43–45
wheat berries, sprouted
    Stuffed Red Kale Leaves with Herb-Wine-Butter
        Sauce, 89–91
    substitutions for, 89–90
whitefish
    Deviled, with Potato Chip Crust, 164–65
    grilling of, 171
    smoked
        Nettles and Wild Rice Soup, 63–64
        Summer Lake Trout Chowder, 69–70
    Summer Lake Trout Chowder, 69–70, 171
Whole Grain Milling Co., 81
Wild Fermentation (Katz), 222
wild foods. *See also* fishing; foraging; hunting
    boyhood experiences of, 2
    edible plants, great range of, 113
    substitution for, 18–19

Wild Mushroom and Ramp Cream Toasts, 33
Wild Mushroom Lasagna, 101–2, 230
Wild Mushroom Pizza, 106–7
Wild Mushrooms of North America (Fischer), 239
Wild Tartar Sauce, 164–65, 221
wine
    red
        Red Wine–Blue Cheese Butter, 124
        Wine-Braised Oxtails with Shallots and Carrots,
            Cumin and Cocoa, 124–25
        Wine-Dark Beets, 48–49
    sherry
        soft-scrambled eggs, with sautéed wild
            mushrooms, 75
    white
        soft-scrambled eggs, with sautéed wild
            mushrooms, 75
        Stuffed Red Kale Leaves with Herb-Wine-Butter
            Sauce, 89–91
Wine-Braised Oxtails with Shallots and Carrots,
        Cumin and Cocoa, 124–25
Wine-Dark Beets, 48–49
    with cheese, 210
Wisconsin
    fishing and fish markets in, 169–71
    foraging areas in, 237–38
    mycological society of, 239
    rural (*See also* Bide-A-Wee cabin)
        attractions of, 9
        radio in, 14
woodcocks, at Bide-a-Wee cabin, 13–14

Y

yogurt
    Easy Creamy Dressing, 51–52

Z

Ziedrich, Linda, 222
zucchini
    Grilled Ratatouille, *86,* 86–87

Trout Caviar was designed by Cathy Spengler and set in type by Judy Gilats. The text face is Archer. Printed by Friesens, Manitoba, Canada.